D0712412

MEMORIES OF A LIFETIME
IN THE
PIKE'S PEAK REGION

PISCHEL YEARBOOKS, INC.
P. O. Box 36 Marceline, Missouri 64658
Telephone (816) 376-3523

MEMORIES OF A LIFETIME
IN THE
PIKE'S PEAK REGION

BY

IRVING HOWBERT

❧

The Rio Grande Press, Inc.

GLORIETA, NEW MEXICO · 87535

First edition from which this edition was reproduced
was supplied by
LOUIS V. BOLING, Books
3413 Tiger Lane
Corpus Christi, Tex. 78415

Rare photographs in folio supplied by
CHAMBER OF COMMERCE
Colorado Springs, Colo.,
and by
STEWARTS COMMERCIAL PHOTOGRAPHERS, INC.,
P.O. Box 1064
Colorado Springs, Colo.

A RIO GRANDE CLASSIC
First published in 1925

LIBRARY OF CONGRESS CARD CATALOG 73-115107

I.S.B.N. 87380-044-3

First Printing 1970

The Rio Grande Press, Inc.
GLORIETA, NEW MEXICO · 87535

Publisher's Preface

We are simultaneously reprinting in this troubled summer of 1970 both of the titles written by the late great citizen of Colorado Springs, Irving Howbert--this title, first published in 1925, and *Indians of the Pike's Peak Region,* first published in 1914. Both are solid items of Coloradiana (is there such a word?), both have been out of print for generations, and both are great books to read. While the title of each book has a tendency to appear to focus the book on that particular region dominated by Pike's Peak, the reader might be gently reminded that the Pike's Peak region dominates the whole state. Within this region lies Denver and Pueblo, as well as Colorado Springs. This trio of urban centers constitutes by and large the heart of lovely Colorado. So the story of Colorado Springs, is in the largest sense, the story of Colorado itself.

In this book, which relates the story of a young frontiersman in an untamed land, the pages reveal the essential story of the birth of a great city and some of its great institutions. One of these latter was the First National Bank. It was founded by the author in 1874. His grandson, another Irving Howbert, is now a board member and a famed Colorado attorney. When we decided to re-publish the Howbert books, we sought the cooperation of the First National Bank. Through Vice President Gordon

Culver, we obtained all kinds of help in the way of research. On behalf of the bank, he also supplied some of the pictures we have added in the photo portfolio at the back of this book.

We included this portfolio of new pictures and old to show some scenes from here and there in Colorado Springs years ago and today. The only picture in the first edition is a photoengraving of Pike's Peak. That scene hasn't changed much for a million years, and not at all since Irving Howbert came to the Colorado frontier. Nearly everything else has, though. Space requirements did not permit us to show more than a few samples of "then and now", but what we show is typical.

Few mere hotels anywhere ever become national institutions, but in Colorado there are three (at least, and probably others) that did. One of these was the famous old Antlers Hotel. Another was the Broadmoor. Both are in the Springs. And within sight from Pike's Peak, the elegant Brown Palace in Denver.

There are some interesting comparisons in the folio. The present Antlers is a gleaming palace of modern conveniences. Its clean and lovely horizontal lines counterpoint the vertical lines of the famous mountain behind it. The Broadmoor is so very large it is nearly a city within a city. The elegance and stately setting of the Broadmoor still reflects the decor, the motifs and the atmosphere of quiet serenity so characteristic of elegant places in the 1880s and 1890s. Since World War II, serenity has been hard to come by. Young folks of today hardly know what the word means.

Anyway, the photo portfolio is our idea. It is new in this edition. What we picture as of 1970 will no doubt be the curiosities of A.D. 2070--a century hence. We might suggest, with a bit of cynicism, that by A.D. 2070 there may not be anything left at all but Pike's Peak; worse, if the government spendthrifts ever think of the idea, they'll dig that mountain up and move it to Chicago just for the sake of spending the taxpayer's dollars. One could assume that these days the only qualification for a job with the federal government is that you know how to waste money; if you do, and can throw it away with both hands (it doesn't matter what for), you're in. You can even get to the White House with a qualification like that; the last six presidents did.

Something else is new in this edition, too--the index. There was none in the first edition. A book like this, without an index, is comparable to a rubber crutch. We asked our indexing friend in Albuquerque, former librarian Katherine McMahon, to prepare an index for us and she did a great job.

The original of the foldout map at the back of this book is one of the treasures of the great Western History collection of the Denver Public Library. We appreciate the cooperation of Collection Librarian Alys Freeze, who provided the negative we used in producing the map.

We are grateful to the Colorado Springs Chamber of Commerce, too, for the considerable help and old pictures they came up with. We have yet to find a Chamber of Commerce anywhere that isn't ready to just about break its collective back to be of help when requested.

Oddly enough, our colleague in Corpus Christi, Tex., Mr. Louis V. Boling, Bookseller, provided the first edition we used to reproduce this edition, and also the impetus to do it. Copies of the first edition are quite rare, a fact as true of author Howbert's other book *(The Indians of the Pike's Peak Region)* as it is of this one. Anyway, early in 1970 Mr. Boling sent his copy to us and suggested it as a beautiful Rio Grande Classic.

We're always after free advice (although we do not always take it when we get it), so we wrote to the beautiful, beautiful new Penrose Public Library in Colorado Springs requesting comment and opinion from the librarian. Mrs. Margaret Reid replied promptly and enthusiastically, very much in favor of bringing the book back into print. Other librarians in Colorado were just as enthusiastic. We sought the opinion of Dick Noyes at the Chinook Book Shop and of Henry Novak at Levine's Book Store, and they were eager to see the book back in print again. We got back to Mrs. Reid eventually, and at our request, she graciously supplied the introduction on the ensuing pages.

She also supplied, from the library's microfilms, the author's obituary clips we have reproduced facsimile on the endsheets at the back of this title and likewise at the back of the other Howbert title. Everyone seems to like this device, and we do, too. We have used it on *Tombstone's Yesterday, Helldorado* and *Law & Order. Ltd.* The Facsimile clips are poor quality to start with, being out of a newspaper, but the story they tell is more authentic and interesting than something we might write. In this case, the clips are from the Colorado Springs *Gazette Telegraph* of December 22, 1934.

In this project we had the cooperation, which we greatly appreciate, of Clarence Coil and Floyd Brunson, professionals who own and operate Stewarts Commercial Photographers, Inc., of the Springs. They supplied some of the old photos of the First National Bank used in this book, as well as the foldout Indian picture and early view of Colorado Springs in the other title.

This is the 63rd beautiful Rio Grande Classic--a magnificent reprint of distinguished Western Americana. Our books are source books of American history.

Robert B. McCoy

Glorieta, N.M.
October 1970

Introduction

It is my pleasure to introduce this long-needed new
edition of Irvin Howbert's *Memories of a Lifetime
in the Pike's Peak Region*. For the first time this
invaluable historical information was authentically recorded by a man who participated in all of the events
whereof he wrote.

While the book, because of the course of events, is
partially biographical, it places more emphasis on the
trials and tribulations of the settlers, their efforts and
achievements in that time before, during and after Colorado became a state or Colorado Springs an incorporated
city in El Paso County.

He saw the several Indian tribes at war with one
another, the attacks on individuals and the thievery. He
was a member of the Third Colorado Cavalry when the
so-called Sand Creek massacre took place. He wrote of
these events without malice, or prejudice, and was considered by all who knew him as a fair, compassionate,
quiet man. His sincerity, lucidity and exactness of statement compel one's interest and acceptance of the account
as altogether dependable.

His entire career was identified with the financial,
educational and social interest of the city, the county
and the state. As a young man, he engaged in freighting,
herding cattle, farming and clerking. In 1869, he was
elected by acclamation Clerk of El Paso County, an
office he held for five terms. As county clerk, he issued
the certificate legally incorporating Colorado Springs as
a city. He resigned to assume his duties as cashier of
the First National Bank, where within two years, he became president. He played a vital role in mining, banking,

railroading and politics--activities which did much to develop the state. He served a term of four years as a state senator, was a trustee of Colorado College, a regent of the University of Colorado and one of the directors of the Chamber of Commerce. Irving Howbert died December 21, 1934.

At the time Mr. Howbert's *Memories of a Lifetime in the Pike's Peak Region* was published, Colorado Springs had a population of 34,000. That population is now estimated (1970) at 129,167. There are few residents of any age who are not interested in the history of this region. Visitors to the area also enjoy delving into its enthralling story. Copies of the first edition of this book are scarce indeed, and highly treasured by the proud possessors. To satisfy the interests of all, this much-needed new edition will be our best source of historical information about the Pike's Peak region, and we are happy to have it available again as a Rio Grande Classic.

(Mrs.) Margaret Reid
Librarian, Penrose Public Library

Colorado Springs, Colo.
October 1970

PIKE'S PEAK

MEMORIES OF A LIFETIME
IN THE
PIKE'S PEAK REGION

BY

IRVING HOWBERT

G. P. PUTNAM'S SONS
NEW YORK AND LONDON
The Knickerbocker Press
1925

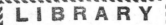

LIBRARY

| JUN 2 0 1979

UNIVERSITY OF THE PACIFIC

361030

Western
Americans
F
776
H84
1970

Copyright, 1925
by
Irving Howbert

Made in the United States of America

PREFACE

In this book of Memories I have endeavored to trace through my own experiences and observations the early history and growth of this immediate Pike's Peak region, particularly during the years before the railroads reached the Rocky Mountains. I came to this section with my father in 1860 when fourteen years of age and have lived here, at the eastern base of Pike's Peak, almost continuously since that time. My experiences have covered a wide field and brought me into contact with many phases of the early as well as the later life of the region.

I still have a distinct memory of the scenes and events connected with our five weeks journey of six hundred miles across the great plains to the Rocky Mountains, a stretch of country that, aside from the narrow fringe of settlements adjacent to the Missouri River and another along the eastern base of the mountains, was at that time inhabited solely by nomadic Indians and ranged over by great herds of buffalo and other wild animals.

It has been my privilege to watch the wonderful transformation that has since taken place, not only on the plains, but also in the mountainous sections of Colorado, as it has progressed year by year. The great plains that once looked so desolate to me, now are covered by innumerable productive farms; the few remaining Indians are on reservations; and the buffalo, antelope, and other wild animals of that period are virtually extinct. Where the savages roamed, towns and cities have arisen, and farmhouses dot the great plains in every direction.

Although the recollections of the first years of my life in this Pike's Peak region are vivid, as I then was at an impressionable age, I have not depended solely on my memory in writing this book. Many years ago I began to secure dictations from the more prominent of the original settlers, and from time to time I made written records of interesting events that came under my observation. My memory has been further refreshed at the yearly meetings of the "Half Century Club," a gathering of old settlers who came to this region prior to 1870, who meet to renew friendships and exchange reminiscences. I also have the diary that my father kept during our first trip across the plains and the remainder of that year. And for a long time, it has been my hobby to collect books pertaining to the history of the Rocky Mountain region and the entire southwest.

In order to make my story complete, I have found it necessary to include several chapters from my book, *The Indians of the Pike's Peak Region*, published in 1914.

IRVING HOWBERT.

COLORADO SPRINGS,
    March 31, 1925.

CONTENTS

CHAPTER   PAGE

I.—Across the Great Plains to the Rocky Mountains 3

II.—A Boy's Summer in a Placer Mining Camp 21

III.—The Pike's Peak Region Becomes My Permanent Home 35

IV.—The Territory of Colorado Formed and its Government Organized . 60

V.—Interesting Incidents Connected with the Early History of the Pike's Peak Region 78

VI.—Indian Troubles of 1864 . . . 95

VII.—With the Third Colorado Cavalry at the Battle of Sand Creek . 115

VIII.—Defense of the Battle of Sand Creek 134

IX.—A Week at Maxwell's Ranch in New Mexico—Experiences Along the Union Pacific 163

X.—Beginning of the Indian War of 1868 177

Contents

CHAPTER   PAGE

XI.—More Details of the Indian War of 1868 193

XII.—Elected County Clerk—Founding of Colorado Springs 215

XIII.—Early Ventures in Banking and Mining 238

XIV.—Settlement of Eastern Colorado—Experiences in Politics—Cripple Creek—Waite Campaign 257

XV.—Building the Cripple Creek Short Line—Colorado College—Park System . 280

Memories of a Lifetime in the Pike's Peak Region

Memories of a Lifetime in the Pike's Peak Region

CHAPTER I

ACROSS THE GREAT PLAINS TO THE ROCKY MOUNTAINS

PRIOR to the year 1848 agriculture was the only industry of any importance in the United States. There was little manufacturing and the mineral resources of the country were negligible. It is true that placer gold was found in North Carolina as early as 1799, and in Georgia a few years later, but the entire production of gold in the United States from the discovery of America to 1848, was less than $12,000,000, while in the five years following that date, the mines of California alone yielded $258,000,000 worth of the precious metal.

This great production of gold had a marked effect upon every part of the United States. It quickened the economic life of the nation and was to a great extent the impelling force that started the wonderful development, industrial and otherwise, which has taken place since that time.

3

The discovery of gold in California greatly stimulated the search for that metal elsewhere, especially in the mountainous districts of the west, and finding it in the Pike's Peak region ten years later, was one of the direct results.

Among the multitudes that went to California in 1848, were a number of semi-civilized Cherokee Indians who had become familiar with placer mining in the state of Georgia before their removal, some years before, from that state to the Indian Territory. These Indians, in going to and coming from California, followed the Arkansas River to the mouth of the Fontaine-qui-Bouille, and from that point used an old trail which ran northwesterly parallel to the mountains through the present state of Colorado.

For some years prior to 1857, there had been unconfirmed reports of gold having been found in the Rocky Mountains near Pike's Peak. However, it appears that the first definite information concerning these discoveries came from Cherokee Indians returning from California in the fall of 1857, who, on their arrival at Kansas City, reported that they had found placer gold in Cherry Creek, a tributary of the Platte River. This story is only one of the many handed down concerning the discovery of gold in the Pike's Peak region, but my impression is that, while others may have found gold at about the same time, the Cherokees were the first to make the fact definitely known.

This reported discovery was given widespread

publicity through the newspapers, and, although the reports were indefinite as to the extent and value of the placers said to have been found, the story attracted much attention throughout the country, especially in the west. As a result, in the spring and summer of 1858, three large and well equipped parties were formed in western Missouri and Kansas, in addition to various smaller ones from other localities, to explore the region where the new gold mines were supposed to be.

The first of the larger organizations, known as the "Green Russell Party," that being the name of its leader, started from Manhattan, Kansas, in May, 1858. In this party were a number of semi-civilized Cherokee Indians, which caused it to be spoken of by many as the "Cherokee Party." The second company was organized at Lawrence, Kansas, and was known as the "Lawrence Party," while the third one was designated as the "Kansas City Party," having been formed at that place. This last expedition was made up of fifty men and one woman. Among its members were Anthony Bott and George A. Bute, afterwards prominent citizens of the Pike's Peak region.

All these companies came up the valley of the Arkansas River and the Fontaine-qui-Bouille to the mountains, and each of them explored the country around the eastern base of Pike's Peak, later doing the same thing along the South Platte River and its branches in and adjacent to the South Park. The Green Russell Party reached the mountains in June,

1858; the Lawrence Party arrived in July; and the Kansas City Party, in September of that year. The Green Russell Party found a little gold in the sands of Cherry Creek about thirty miles from its mouth, and also washed a small amount out of the gravel along the banks of the Platte River near the present site of Denver, but did not find gold anywhere in paying quantities.

The three parties that I have mentioned were followed by others later in the year. Thus the population of the Pike's Peak region steadily increased until during the winter of 1858–59 it was estimated to be from six to eight hundred, the larger part of the people being temporarily settled at the mouth of Cherry Creek—now the site of Denver. Among them were very few women, the female members of the population probably not numbering more than one in twenty at that time and never exceeding the ratio of one in six during the next half dozen years.

There were no gold discoveries of great importance during the year 1858, but early in 1859 two small finds were made, one at Gold Hill in what is now the County of Boulder, and the other on Chicago Creek near the present town of Idaho Springs. However, on the 10th of May, 1859, the Gregory diggings were found in what is now Gilpin Country. This was the first important discovery of placer gold in the Rocky Mountain region.

These discoveries aroused great interest throughout the country and were the magnet that drew many to the Pike's Peak region during the summer of

1859. But later in that year, there was much disappointment when the comparatively limited extent of the productive diggings was realized, and many returned to their homes in the east, spreading the news that the reported discovery of gold in paying quantities in the Pike's Peak region was a fraud. However, before the year 1859 was ended, it was proved that there was much gold in that territory, as during that period placer mines were found at Tarryall, Fairplay and Buckskin Joe, on the western border of the South Park, and later rich diggings were located in the gulches near the present town of Breckenridge, these discoveries much more than doubling the gold producing area.

Reports of these later discoveries, which were spread all over the United States during the winter of 1859–60, were supplemented by news that early in May, 1860, the richest placers so far found had been opened up in California Gulch, where the town of Leadville afterward was laid out. News of these discoveries caused a veritable stampede to the Pike's Peak region from every part of the country during the spring and summer of this last named year. The United States had not yet recovered from the effects of the panic of 1857. Hard times still existed in all sections of the country; consequently, the people were in a receptive mood for anything that promised financial relief.

The journey to California, where the first important discoveries of gold had been made ten years before, was a formidable one, whether made by sea around Cape Horn, by way of the Isthmus of Panama with its lesser sea voyage, or across the great plains, mountains, and deserts intervening between the Missouri River and the Pacific Coast. On the other hand, a trip from the Missouri River to the Rocky Mountains, only six hundred miles, could be made without having to undergo any great hardships or discomforts. Therefore, it was not surprising that news of gold discoveries in a region comparatively so accessible should have created wide-spread interest and have attracted to the new mines large numbers from every part of the United States.

At that time, our family home was in Quincy, Adams County, Iowa, where my father, a Methodist minister, and member of the Des Moines, Iowa, Conference, was stationed. During the previous winter, news of the discovery of gold in the Pike's Peak region had furnished the principal topic of conversation in that community; and consequently, toward spring when the reports had been verified, a number of people decided to visit the new mining country. Among these were several prominent members of father's church. This aroused his interest in the movement to such an extent that he finally concluded to apply to the church authorities for a six months' vacation, that he might join a party that was forming. His request was granted and he at once began making preparations for the journey. A little later, it was decided that I should accompany him, which pleased me very much. At that time I had just passed my fourteenth birth-

day. I had heard and read a great many tales of
adventure in the Rocky Mountains and on the great
plains, which told of the trappers, Indians and buffalo, and described the wild and unusual features of
the country. My imagination had been fired by
these stories to such an extent that the region we
would pass through on our journey and the mountains beyond, were pictured in my young mind as
a veritable wonderland. That I was to have an
opportunity of seeing all these things seemed almost
too good to be true.

After many busy days of preparation on father's
part, including the purchase of two yoke of oxen
and a wagon, fitting up the latter with bows and
cover, and loading it with food supplies of every
kind sufficient for our needs during the next six
months—as we had no thought of remaining longer
—father, two friends and myself, in company with a
number of others from our community likewise
equipped, started on our journey May 4, 1860.

By this time, the roads throughout the west that
converged in the valley of the Platte River, were
lined with ox teams, traveling toward the Rocky
Mountains. Oxen were used for this work in pref-
erence to horses because oxen by nature were better
able to stand the long journey without other feed
than the grass of the plains, grain being unobtain-
able after leaving the settlements along the Missouri
River.

Our party crossed the Missouri River at Plattsmouth, Nebraska, and by this time had been joined

by other groups journeying towards the same destination. From the beginning we deemed it prudent to favor our oxen as much as possible in view of the long journey ahead of us. Consequently, we moved along leisurely, traveling fifteen to twenty miles a day, and at night, when possible, camping at some favored spot where wood, water, and grass were plentiful—these elements and the absence of alkali ponds being among the essentials of a good camping ground.

Two of our party slept in the wagon at night while the others made beds under it or out in the open. Sleeping out was not a hardship as no rain of consequence fell during our entire trip. The road we were following led across the country about fifteen miles north of the place where the city of Lincoln, capital of Nebraska, afterwards was located. During the first thirty or forty miles of travel after leaving Plattsmouth, we passed an occasional farmhouse, but from there on we saw none until nearing Denver, the frontier settlements of Nebraska at that time extending but a short distance west of the Missouri River.

Five or six days journeying over good roads, through an attractive, rolling country brought us to the valley of the Platte River. The Platte from this point to the Rocky Mountains is broad and shallow, having many islands. As a rule, there was a wide, grassy valley on each side of the stream, which afforded good pasturage for our cattle, when it had not already been grazed too closely by teams ahead of us. The wagon road then used ran along the south side of the river for the entire distance to the Rocky Mountains, sometimes close to its banks and again a mile or so away. From Fort Kearney to the junction of the North and South Platte Rivers, the road was the same as that used by travelers bound for California and Oregon.

On the 23rd day of May we reached Fort Kearney, at that time one of the frontier outposts of the Government. The Fort was without walls and consisted of the usual barracks, with a number of cannon placed around a square. The garrison was made up of two or three companies of regular army soldiers who, of course, were clothed in the blue uniform and armed and equipped in a manner peculiar to the period prior to the Civil War. This being my first glimpse of military life, I observed all these details with very great interest.

At or near Fort Kearney, the wagon roads from St. Joseph, Missouri, and other points along the Missouri River in that direction, and also from Council Bluffs, and other places to the north of Plattsmouth, all converged in the valley of the Platte River, along which we had been traveling for several days, thus bringing together a vast throng of men and teams having a common destination in the gold mines of the Rocky Mountains. From that time on until we reached the mountains, we never lacked for neighbors when camped at night, at which times, groups of wagons and camp fires could be seen dotting the valley of the Platte in every

direction. After passing Fort Kearney, oftentimes
when observing from high points overlooking the
country, I saw an almost continuous procession of
white covered wagons, extending for miles in front
and as far to the rear down the level valley of the
Platte River as the eye could reach. I am sure that
never in the history of this country has there been
another such scene presented. It is estimated that
from sixty to seventy thousand people went to the
Rocky Mountains during the summer of 1860, more
than ninety-five percent of whom traveled by way of
the Platte River; and that there were at least eleven
thousand wagons on the road between the Missouri
River and Denver during the months of May and
June of that year. If one could have taken in the
entire scene from Fort Kearney to Denver, a distance of some four hundred miles, during the latter
half of May and the first half of June, he would
have beheld a line of wagons sufficient to have made
a continuous procession covering at least a fourth
of the distance. These people were from all parts
of the United States and even from foreign countries.
Many were from New England, the eastern and
middle states, and considerable numbers from Vir-
ginia, Georgia, and other southern sections, with
throngs from every part of the west.

The morning after leaving Fort Kearney, I had
my first sight of a buffalo. We had camped the
night before on the bank of the Platte and had
driven our cattle across a shallow channel to one of
the islands opposite, in order to secure better graz-

ing than could be obtained nearer the road. Early
the following morning I went to the island with one
of the men to bring the oxen to camp. We found
them some distance away, and were starting to drive
them back when we heard a number of shots, and at
the same time our attention was called to a buffalo
galloping along in his clumsy fashion, coming almost
in our direction. I knew from the actions of the
beast that he had been wounded, and I had read
that a wounded buffalo was a very dangerous animal. As neither of us had a gun, the man with me
suggested that I go to camp as quickly as possible
and get one, and I needed no urging on that point.
So I started for camp as fast I could run, and it soon
came into my mind that the wounded buffalo might
turn in my direction. I was so alarmed by the time
I reached the stream that instead of stopping to take
off my shoes and stockings, I rushed through the
water to the camp and breathlessly told them what
I had seen. Even before this, I had heard numerous
shots in the direction of the buffalo, so that long
before our people arrived, the animal had been
killed. Our crowd secured a share of the meat, but
it was not at all what I had anticipated. The buffalo
evidently was an old one, for its meat was tough and
not at all palatable. This was the only buffalo I
saw on the entire trip, but hunters told us that they
were plentiful a few miles back from the river, having been frightened away by the crowds of people
overrunning the valley.

By this time we had reached the region designated on maps of that period as the "Great American Desert," but we saw little to make us think we were in a desert except an occasional stretch of sandy road that made hard pulling for our oxen. It is true that the grass on the higher land away from the river had a dried-up look, and even the land adjacent to the stream lacked the rich, productive appearance of the prairies in Illinois and Iowa, yet the landscape in no way resembled a desert waste.

During the entire trip our party made it a rule to rest on the Sabbath, and we did so excepting on one or two occasions when it became necessary to drive a few miles on Sunday morning to secure better grazing for the cattle. There were many others among the gold seekers who, from religious or other motives, adopted the same policy; consequently, every Sabbath we found a considerable number of people camped near us. Usually on Saturday night arrangements were made to hold morning and afternoon religious services the following day at some convenient point. Sometimes the meetings in our vicinity would be conducted by my father, and at other times by some one of the other ministers who happened to be in that locality.

In the great procession headed for the Rocky Mountains there were few families, but occasionally a wagon would be seen with a man, woman and children in it, perhaps a coop of chickens on the rear end and a milk cow or two being driven along, indicating that these people expected to remain a considerable time in the Pike's Peak region. Many of the wagons had the words: "Pike's Peak or Bust" painted in large letters on the wagon cover, and occasionally one would see peculiar traveling outfits. More than once we saw people pushing hand-carts on which were their belongings, and one day two men passed us in a light spring wagon, their motive power being a large sail stretched out to catch the breeeze that was blowing up the Platte valley that morning. They made great speed while the wind continued in that direction, but in a few days our slow-moving ox teams passed the dry-land sailors waiting for another favorable breeze.

Before reaching Fort Kearney we passed through the country of the Pawnee Indians, but evidently these savages were keeping away from lines of travel, as we failed to get a glimpse of them. However, between Fort Kearney and the Rocky Mountains, the country of the Sioux, Cheyennes and Arapahoes, we saw many members of these tribes camped at various places along the river. They showed no disposition to molest us, as at that time all these tribes were supposed to be peaceable, but their looks and general manner indicated that they were not pleased with the presence of this great throng of white people.

Among the things that attracted my attention, just outside of several of these Indian camps, were rude platforms supported by long posts. On each of these lay a dead warrior, wrapped mummy-like in skins. This, apparently, was the manner in which these Indians laid away the more prominent of their dead. At other places I saw their dead on small platforms placed high up in the big cottonwood trees that grew along the banks of the Platte. Some of these bodies undoubtedly had been placed there many years before, as under the trees I often picked up beads which had dropped from the decayed wrappings.

It was almost a month after crossing the Missouri River before we came in sight of the Rocky Mountains. However, by the time we arrived at the place known as "Frémont's Orchard" the mountains began looming up like a great wall to the westward, Long's Peak, with its snow white cap, being the most prominent point. I was greatly impressed by their mysterious grandeur, as these were the first mountains that I ever had seen.

On the 12th of June, we passed near St. Vrain's Fort, one of the old trapper stations founded many years before. Since 1840 this and Fort Lupton, not many miles away, had been Indian Trading Stations and important points of rendezvous for the trappers and adventurous explorers of the plains and mountains. The high walls of Fort St. Vrain were built of sun-dried bricks, and enclosed a space from 150 to 200 feet square, with buildings of the same material constructed around the inner side.

Many stories are told of interesting events connected with the history of these outposts. It was at Fort St. Vrain that Frémont waited in 1843 while Maxwell went to Taos, in New Mexico, to obtain horses and pack animals for the notable exploring expedition that was made by the former westward through the Rocky Mountains to California. It was here also that many other explorers of the then wild and comparatively unknown western portion of the United States rested and recuperated on their way through this interesting region.

These forts were connected with Taos, New Mexico, by a well worn trail, which ran up the Platte River to the mouth of Cherry Creek; thence along Cherry Creek to the head of one of its eastern branches, near the present town of Eastonville; then by way of "Jimmy's Camp" to the Fontaine-qui-Bouille at the present town of Fountain; down the Fontaine-qui-Bouille to its mouth; and finally, southwesterly, skirting the Spanish Peaks on the easterly and southeasterly sides, to Taos, New Mexico. During the first half of the Nineteenth Century there was more or less trading between the residents of Taos and the various Indian trading stations to the northward along the eastern base of the Rocky Mountains. Taos then was the winter home of many of the trappers of that period.

On the afternoon of June 14, 1860, we arrived at Denver. When nearing the town we noticed that there was a large encampment of Indians down near the Platte River, at a point probably not far from the present Union Railway Station, and, just as we were entering the outskirts, a very considerable number of Indians came from the village on horseback, riding in great haste up Cherry Creek. Many of them were squaws and old men. The squaws were crying and seemed very much distressed. We could not imagine what was the matter, but later learned that a war party had gone to the mountains from this Indian camp a few days before, and, in a battle with Utes, had suffered defeat, news of which had just been received. The squaws and old men that we had seen probably were relatives of the dead and wounded who were being brought in by the returning warriors.

Denver was a disappointment. At this time it was a comparatively small town, composed of a lot of shacks and the cheapest kind of frame buildings. There were only two well defined streets—Blake and Wazee—and even these were not very busy thoroughfares. The principal town was Auraria, on the western side of Cherry Creek, which contained a good many more houses than did Denver. There was intense rivalry between the two places, which later in that year was settled by a consolidation of the two under the name of the latter, making a town with approximately four thousand inhabitants.

We drove through the town and camped near the Platte River, in what is now West Denver. All of the land in the surrounding country, except that immediately contiguous to Denver and Auraria, was unclaimed and unoccupied territory. After making camp and turning the cattle out to graze, our party hurried back to town to learn the latest news from the mines, as that was the topic in which we were most interested. Of course the strange surroundings, the manner of life, and exciting stories that were being told of the mining regions, were of intense interest to me. The principal topic of conversation in every group on the streets was concerning developments in the older mining camps around Black Hawk, Central City, and Boulder, and touching the newer discoveries at Hamilton and Fairplay, on the head waters of the Platte; at California Gulch, on one of the upper branches of the Arkansas River; and at French, Georgia and other gulches on the Blue River in the vicinity of Breckenridge.

None of our party definitely knew the location of the different mining camps, how to reach them, nor as to their production, and this was the information that they sought to obtain as quickly as possible, in order that a prompt decision might be made as to the particular one that should be their objective point. The urgency of deciding this question was evident, as every day during our stay in Denver long lines of wagons could be seen moving out in the direction of one or the other of the mining camps I have mentioned, making it apparent that each day's delay lessened our chances of securing desirable claims.

The larger part of the Pike's Peak region east of the main Continental Divide and north of the Arkansas River, which included most of the towns and mining camps, belonged at that time to the state of Kansas, but being so distant from the settled part of that state, no effort had been made to organize a local government under its laws. Instead, there had been formed in many localities what were known as "People's Courts" for the trial of criminal cases, and recorders' offices had been established in which locations, deeds, and other transfers of title could be made a matter of record.

In cases of crime, the accused was promptly brought before the local court and a speedy trial given, the juries usually being a mass meeting of people of the community. If found guilty, the criminal was punished without delay. There being no jails, the only methods of punishment existing at that time were the lash, banishment from the locality, or hanging. The promptness and effectiveness of this method was demonstrated during our stay in Denver. A German in camp near Golden, who had killed one of his fellow-travelers, was promptly taken in charge and brought to Denver. The trial was held the next day. He was found guilty and hanged that afternoon.

CHAPTER II

A BOY'S SUMMER IN A PLACER MINING CAMP

IN so far as father and I were concerned, the question of our destination was decided for us within three or four days after we reached Denver, in a manner both satisfactory and far reaching in its effect. Shortly after our arrival father met Rev. John M. Chivington, Presiding Elder of the Methodist Church, who had recently been given supervision of the interests of that denomination throughout this Rocky Mountain region, with authority to establish missions wherever he deemed best. At this time Reverend Mr. Chivington was in need of some one to take charge of missions that he planned to establish in the mining camps around South Park and in the valley towns of Colorado City, Pueblo and Cañon City. This position he offered to father and strongly urged him to accept. Possibly it had dawned on father by this time that placer gold mining was rather more uncertain than he had been led to believe. No doubt this, as well as his sense of duty as a minister, influenced him to undertake the work, after having given the matter a few days' consideration. The acceptance of this position, of course, made it necessary that he sever his connection with the Des Moines, Iowa, Conference, which he did a little later. The matter having been settled, we left Denver on Monday, June 18, for Hamilton, in the South Park, which was to be father's headquarters.

We were accompanied by the other members of our party who, after investigation, had decided that the mining opportunities of the South Park region probably were more favorable than those of the older camps around Idaho Springs, Black Hawk, Central City and Boulder. Our road led us south-westerly to the foot hills, up and over the low mountains around the head of Bear Creek, and then southward down to the South Platte River a good many miles above Platte Cañon. From this point the road followed up the river for miles, crossing and recrossing it many times. The Platte River at that point is a stream of considerable size at all seasons of the year, but in late spring, at the time of melting snows, which was the period when we were there, it becomes a raging torrent. The road had been only recently constructed and was exceedingly rough, although passable. As no bridges had been put in, we had to ford the Platte, as well as every other stream along the route, and often it seemed to me that surely we would lose both cattle and wagon; but somehow or other we pulled through in safety.

The road finally left the Platte and went southerly over Kenosha Hill into the north end of South Park. My first view of the Park was from the top of this hill, and, young as I was, it made a lasting impression upon my mind. Spread out before me as far as the eye could reach, was a beautiful valley in which were occasional wooded hills that stood above the surrounding level, giving an appearance of a sea or vast lake dotted with timbered islands, the whole completely framed by rugged mountains. Far above the western boundary loomed the great Snowy Range, extending away to the southward. It was a scene I never have forgotten.

Saturday night we camped in a small aspen grove, five miles north of the town of Hamilton, our destination, and, in accordance with our established rule not to travel on the Sabbath, remained there until Monday morning. We had been a whole week making the trip from Denver, which now is made in a half day or less by railway or automobile.

On Sunday morning, noticing that there was a large snow bank on a mountain to the west which appeared to be not far distant from our camp, some of the party, myself included, decided to visit it. Our belief was that the round trip could be made in an hour or two, but it proved a case of deceptive vision such as so often fooled the "tenderfoot" unaccustomed to this clear atmosphere. We reached the snow, but only after nearly a half day of hard climbing, and were almost exhausted when we arrived back at camp late in the afternoon. After that experience we knew better how to judge distances in high altitudes.

Monday afternoon our party drove into Hamilton, which then was the principal town of the

South Park region. It was located on the western side of the Park along the north bank of the Tarryall branch of the South Platte River, just below Tarryall Gulch. This gulch is about six miles east of the Continental Divide. Hamilton, Tarryall, and the adjacent country, at that time had a population of about five thousand people. Large numbers of gold seekers were arriving every day, and, at the same time, many disappointed ones were leaving for other mining camps. Tarryall Gulch was alive with people washing gold from the sands and gravel along the creek, a mountain stream of considerable size.

A day or two after our arrival, father started out seeking members of his denomination, with the view of establishing a mission at that point, as he had been instructed to do. He was so successful in his efforts that within a week or two he had found enough Methodists to make a fairly strong organization. Soon after this was perfected, it was decided to erect a church building which, necessarily, had to be made of logs, the only building material at hand. Subscription papers were circulated and sufficient money was secured in a few days to warrant beginning work on this primitive structure.

All this occurred within two or three weeks after our arrival, showing that things moved rapidly in this new country. Meanwhile, the other members of the party had been prospecting, and, after examining a good many locations, had succeeded in securing a claim near the lower end of the main

Tarryall Diggings. It was arranged that I should join them and help in any work that a boy could do. It took some little time to get out lumber for the sluice boxes, as it had to be whip-sawed from logs cut in the vicinity, there being no sawmills in that part of the country. These sluice boxes usually were from twelve to fifteen feet in length and from fourteen to eighteen inches wide, with sides six to eight inches high. In some of these boxes strips were nailed fairly close together across the bottom, making the riffles necessary to catch the gold. Six to eight lengths of these sluice boxes were then joined together on the ground to be worked, making a continuous sluice of seventy to one hundred and twenty feet in length. This was placed at a pitch sufficient to cause the water to flow through it rapidly, a ditch from the creek previously having been made to conduct water into the upper end. After all this had been done, the next work was to dig up and throw into the sluice boxes the gravel on either side, which was supposed to contain gold. The rapid flow of water would carry off the gravel and small stones, leaving the gold, which was heavier, to settle on the bottom and be caught by the riffles.

The richest gravel lay close to bed rock, which was from four to twenty feet below the surface. Owing to the unevenness of this bed rock, there was a great difference in the value of the claims. A smooth bed rock caught and held little gold, but one with depressions or pockets often caught a great deal. Usually, placer claims were about two hundred feet in length, up and down the creek, and extended across the valley from bluff to bluff.

When all was ready, work was started on our claim with high hopes, but, after throwing gravel into the sluice boxes for two or three days, we concluded to turn off the water and clean up the gold from behind the riffles in order to ascertain the result of our labors. Much to our disgust the complete clean-up showed only $6.00 worth of gold for three days' work of three men and a boy. This was so disappointing that at once the party abandoned the claim and quit mining in that locality. Not all of the claims in the gulch proved as unprofitable as this one, for a number of those above our location were yielding from $100.00 to $500.00 a day per man. The owners of those claims had drawn the prizes, but apparently we had drawn a blank.

Hamilton was the point at which the roads branched to the various mining camps of that section. A road extending westward over Boreas Pass, as it was called, led to Breckenridge, French and Georgia Gulches; and one to the southeast led by Fairplay to Buckskin Joe and California Gulches. Each of these gulches was producing gold in large quantities. I have heard father tell of having seen a clean-up in California Gulch of nearly a quart of gold, mostly nuggets, as the result of three or four days' work of a few men. This was exceptional, but there were many claims in that and other mining camps that were producing exceedingly well. Besides the gulches that I have mentioned, which were the principal producers, there were numerous other smaller ones in out of the way localities on both sides of the Continental Divide from which a good deal of gold was being taken.

At this time, gold dust was the principal medium of exchange throughout all the region now embraced in the State of Colorado. Almost every one had a small buckskin bag in which he carried his gold, and every merchant owned small scales on which was weighed the gold dust taken in payment for merchandise. The gold of the various camps differed in value according to its purity. That from some districts was worth only $16 an ounce, and from others it ran as high as $18 an ounce. Gold from Tarryall Gulch was about the purest of any in the Pike's Peak region and was valued at the latter rate.

While I was making my initial attempt at mining, father was busy adding to his church membership and trying to raise the necessary funds with which to complete the church building, which already had been started. After the building was well under way, he made a tour of the mining camps in his circuit, organizing churches wherever the number of Methodists would warrant. A little later, we began construction of a dwelling for ourselves on a lot which father had secured not far from the center of town. Hamilton, a long, narrow town with one principal street, was located on the edge of a pine forest and as it grew extended back into the timber. Our lot was on the edge of this forest, and on and around it were numerous tall white pine trees. It was from these that we cut logs with which to erect our house, that being the only kind of structure it was possible to build at the time.

As I have said before, there were as yet no saw-mills in the country, and the only lumber obtainable for sluice boxes and building purposes was the product of whip-saws. This lumber was selling at $150 per thousand. Whip-sawing was an arrangement by which a log was placed horizontally on trestles eight to ten feet high, and sawed by two men, one on the platform and the other on the ground, who operated a saw six or eight feet in length, having a handle at each end. In this slow and laborious way planks were sawed, which were somewhat uneven as to thickness, but answered fairly well for sluice boxes, rough doors, and door and window frames. The supply being limited, none could be had for any other purpose. As there was no way of making shingles except by hand, which was a slow and costly method, dirt roofs were almost universal.

After we had the walls of our log house up to the proper height, a large log was placed on the top lengthwise, in the center of the building, to serve as a ridgepole. Then we placed small poles close together extending from this ridgepole to each side, the ends projecting over the sides to give proper eaves; and on these poles we put a thick covering of pine boughs. This foundation was covered with earth and gravel to a depth of eight to ten inches, which, when properly tamped, made a fairly good fair-weather roof, but was rather inefficient in a heavy or long-continued rain. The work of cutting the logs and putting them in place was done by father and myself, but, when the time came to dig and shovel earth and gravel to the roof, we hired men to do it. One of the men whom we employed on this work was a young university graduate, who afterwards became a prominent lawyer, and later, was elected a Justice of the Supreme Court of Colorado.

Soon after we reached Hamilton there was a devastating fire in the forest adjacent to the lot on which later our home was built, and on the mountain side just beyond. To me it was one of the most terrifying sights that I have ever seen. As I have said, the trees were very tall and had a thick growth of branches beginning a few feet above the ground. The fire, which probably was started by some careless camper, spread from tree to tree, usually catching in these lower branches, and in an incredibly short time flames would reach the top, shoot up one to two hundred feet in the air and in a few minutes subside. A moment later flames from another tree would flash up, and in this way the fire went through the entire grove. After having seen this fire, we would not have dared build in a forest that had not been burned over.

On account of the lack of lumber, we had only a dirt floor in our house at first, and, of necessity, our furniture was of the rudest kind, manufactured from poles and split logs. We secured enough whip-sawed lumber for doors, and door and window frames;

and in one corner we built a large fireplace out of small pieces of stone, which were abundant nearby. In this rudely constructed and primitively furnished house, father and I spent a comfortable summer. We were not ashamed of our habitation nor of its furnishings, for few of our neighbors had anything better.

Although we started construction of our house early in July, it was not finished until about the middle of August. Meanwhile, father made a two weeks' trip to Denver, returning by way of Colorado City. While he was away and until our house was finished, I boarded with a Cornish family, recently from across the sea. The family consisted of father, mother and three or four children. They were kindly people, but their language bothered me very much, being a dialect which I had great difficulty in understanding. I put in the time while father was away cutting poles for the roof of our house.

By this time the population of Hamilton had materially decreased, as, owing to the disappointingly limited area of profitable placer diggings in that vicinity, a large number of its inhabitants had moved away to other mining camps. Two or three times that summer, there was what was known as a "stampede," from Hamilton to reported new discoveries. These stampedes usually originated from some prospector coming to town and telling a friend, as a great secret, of rich placers he had discovered. Sometimes these were near, but more often many miles away. This friend would tell another, magnifying the reported find, and this would continue until many people knew the "secret." Some of the impatient ones would shoulder their picks, shovels and blankets, and, with a little food, steal off at once, while others waited until nightfall; and then it would become a race to see who would reach the supposed location first and thereby secure choice of claims. Generally, the reported discovery proved to be a fake, in which case, a weary, disappointed lot of men could be seen straggling into town a few days later, in an unobtrusive way so as to avoid being jeered at by those who had not been taken in. The man who started the report causing a stampede usually disappeared before the duped ones returned. If not, he was sure to be roughly handled, if not hanged, by the disappointed prospectors.

Father's missionary work covered a wide extent of country, and he necessarily was absent a good deal of the time, visiting churches that he already had established, and organizing others at various points in that region. There were twelve mining camps in his circuit, which extended from Fairplay and California Gulch on the south, to Hamilton, Breckenridge and adjacent gulches on the north, lying on both sides of the main Continental Divide. He had a regular church organization in six of these places to which he gave special attention, and visited and preached at the other camps as often as his time would permit. In making these visits to different settlements, he had to cross the main Continental

Divide many times, often by trails that were almost
impassable for horses.   Father conducted the first
religious services ever held in the South Park and his
work at Breckenridge and adjacent gulches, according to church authorities, was the beginning of
Methodism on the Pacific slope in Colorado.   The
same authorities say that his effort to build a church
at Hamilton was the first attempt of that kind in all
this Rocky Mountain region.   The foregoing will
give something of an idea as to the extraordinary
amount of church work father did that summer.

The other members of our party from Iowa, after
their disappointing experience in mining, left Hamilton and went elsewhere, and father often was away;
consequently, much of the time that summer I was
indeed a stranger in a strange land.   However, my
impression is that I did not mind it very much,
except when I was left alone in our house in the
woods, which I did not particularly enjoy.   I was
too much absorbed in the novelty and beauty of my
surroundings to become lonesome.   To one coming,
as I had, from a comparatively level country in the
middle west, where farming and stock raising were
the principal industries, directly to a busy placer
mining camp in the heart of the Rocky Mountains,
almost two miles above sea-level, the contrast
presented was very great.   Each day during that
period seemed to bring forth something new and
interesting.

The main street of Hamilton was without side-
walks, although by common consent a space next

to the row of houses was used for that purpose. It
was not an uncommon sight to see a horseman ride
up to the front of a store and give his order through
the open door without dismounting. Along this
street there were many saloons, but very few
stores. And the latter had only an occasional cus-
tomer owing to the fact that most of those who came
to the Rocky Mountains in the migration of 1860,
brought at least a six months' supply of flour and
groceries with them, not many planning to remain
longer. While the traffic on the main street was
heavy at times, it consisted mostly of slow moving
ox-teams and therefore there was little danger of
being run over.

I remember that one day while out on this street
I saw a procession of forty or fifty burros coming
from the south, driven by three Mexicans. Each
burro had a sack of flour strapped on its back. On
inquiry, I found that the men were from New Mexico
and had brought the flour to Hamilton hoping to
find a market for it. This they succeeded in doing
with little delay, as the supply was short at that
time. However, on eating bread made from this
flour an unpleasant quantity of grit was found in it.
The explanation as to the source of the grit was,
that, there being no threshing machines in New
Mexico, the separation of the wheat from the straw
had to be done by burros tramping it out, usually
on a dirt floor. After this, the wheat was winnowed
by hand to remove the chaff, which process served
well enough except when little particles of gravel and

sand, that happened to have worked up out of the
floor during the tramping, remained with the grain
and were ground up with it in the mill.   During
periods of scarcity this flour could be sold to Americans, but at any other time no one but a Mexican
would buy it.

When father was at home, he and I often went
fishing in a trout stream about five miles south of
Hamilton.   This creek was not large, but there
were many holes in it four or five feet deep where the
trout congregated in great numbers.   It was not
very exciting sport, as dip nets were the only things
needed to catch all the fish one wanted.   Mountain
trout were plentiful in all streams of that locality
excepting those where placer mining was carried on.
The muddy water resulting from this either killed
the fish or drove them to clearer streams.

Food supplies were fairly plentiful in Hamilton
all that summer; moderately good beef was obtainable, and deer and antelope meat was abundant.

CHAPTER III

THE PIKE'S PEAK REGION BECOMES MY PERMANENT HOME

LATE in the summer of 1860, father and I, accompanied by Mr. Girten, a friend of ours, made a trip to Colorado City, father having been favorably impressed with that locality at the time of his visit there a month previously. Our traveling equipment consisted of two horses and a light wagon with the necessary provisions and camp outfit. We necessarily camped out every night, as at that time there were no inhabitants in all the region between Hamilton and Colorado City.

Our route from Hamilton was easterly down Tarryall Creek across the South Park, over the low mountains on the south side of Tarryall Creek to the Platte River; then up Trout Creek, following a road located substantially as is the present one that passes through the town of Florissant; and then eastward across the Divide and down Fountain Creek to Colorado City.

The first night out of Hamilton we camped near one of the small branches of Tarryall Creek. While Mr. Girten and I were preparing the evening meal, father took his rifle and went off to a rocky hill near by, hoping to find game of some kind. In less than an hour he returned with a two-year-old mountain sheep, which he had killed not far away. We delayed supper that we might have some of the meat. I thought it the best flavored and tenderest I ever had eaten.

The region through which we were traveling, from the South Park to the eastern base of the mountains, had been aptly described by Ruxton, an English traveler, who visited this section in 1847, as "a veritable hunter's paradise," for in addition to many antelope, deer, mountain sheep, wild turkey and grouse, there were numerous herds of elk and mountain buffalo. The latter commonly were spoken of as "bison" in order to distinguish them from the buffalo of the plains. Instead of being brownish in color as the latter were, these bison of the mountains were black and somewhat smaller.

On account of the great quantity of game in this attractive region, its possession had been contended for by the Indians of the plains and the Utes of the mountains for ages before white men came. Every year, as far back as history or tradition goes, as soon as spring opened and grass was abundant, large parties from different tribes of the plains came marching in, and, after making their usual offerings at the "Boiling Springs," continued on up through Ute Pass into the mountains. There the Utes usually were waiting for them, whereupon a succession of battles between the contending tribes

would take place, with success generally on the side
of the Utes, who were the better fighters.   However,
by the middle of summer the Indians from the plains
often became so numerous in and around the South
Park as to greatly outnumber the Utes, forcing these
mountain tribesmen to retreat beyond the Continental Divide, where they would remain until the cold
weather of fall and early winter had driven their
enemies back to the plains.   Probably there are
few valleys in all the region to the westward of
Pike's Peak that have not been the scene of a battle
between these contending tribes at some time during the long period that this warfare was carried on.

In 1860 the Ute Pass wagon road was located
substantially as it is now, excepting that just below
the present town of Cascade it left the Fountain
and ran over the hills from a quarter to a half mile
south of the creek, closely following the old Ute
Indian trail down to the upper end of the present
town of Manitou.   This old Indian trail undoubtedly
had been used by the tribes of both mountains and
plains for hundreds of years prior to the coming of
the white settlers.   Dr. James, historian of Long's
Expedition, which visited this region in 1820, records that it was a well worn trail even then.   At
the time of our visit the only house in what is now
known as Manitou, was a rude shanty without a
roof, said to have been built by Dick Wooten, the
noted hunter and trapper, who was a contemporary
of Kit Carson.

Manitou's springs then were known by some as the

"Soda Springs" and by others as the "Boiling Springs." The only spring to which any attention was paid was the large one on the south side of the creek, now covered over and used by the bottling works. The wagon road from the mountains to Colorado City ran close to this spring. Attracted by it, we remained there an hour or more drinking the water and watching the great volume of gas coming from its depths. Scattered around the spring we saw many beads and Indian trinkets that had been left as an offering by some recent war party.

All of the Indians of this region believed that the "Great Spirit" dwelt in this spring, that the bubbles coming up through the water were the result of his breathing, and that it was necessary for them to make offerings to Him whenever they passed by to insure success in warfare and in the pursuit of game, and no Indian ever failed to do so. Oftentimes in the early days, after a war party of Indians from the plains had gone up Ute Pass, children from Colorado City would visit the springs to pick up beads and other things which they knew would be left as offerings by the savages, and sometimes they would dip the water out of the larger spring to obtain the beads and other articles that had been thrown into it.

Ruxton gives the following legend connected with the springs:

"Many hundreds of winters ago, when the cotton-woods on the Big River were no higher than an arrow, and the red men, who hunted the buffalo on the plains, all spoke the same language, and the pipe of peace breathed its social cloud of kinni-kinnik whenever two parties of hunters met on the boundless plains—when, with hunting grounds and game of every kind in the greatest abundance, no nation dug up the hatchet with another because one of its hunters followed the game into their bounds, but, on the contrary, loaded for him his back with choice and fattest meat, and ever proffered the soothing pipe before the stranger, with well-filled belly, left the village,—it happened that two hunters of different nations met one day on a small rivulet, where both had repaired to quench their thirst. A little stream of water, rising from a spring on a rock within a few feet of the bank, trickled over it and fell splashing into the river. To this the hunters repaired; and while one sought the spring itself, where the water, cold and clear, reflected on its surface, the image of the surrounding scenery, the other, tired by his exertions in the chase, threw himself at once to the ground and plunged his face into the running stream.

"The latter had been unsuccessful in the chase, and perhaps his bad fortune and the sight of the fat deer, which the other hunter threw from his back before he drank at the crystal spring, caused a feeling of jealousy and ill-humor to take possession of his mind. The other, on the contrary, before he satisfied his thirst, raised in the hollow of his hand a portion of the water, and, lifting it towards the sun, reversed his hand and allowed it to fall upon the ground,—a libation to the Great Spirit who had vouchsafed him a successful hunt, and the blessing of the refreshing water with which he was about to quench his thirst.

" Seeing this, and being reminded that he had neglected the usual offering, only increased the feeling of envy and annoyance which the unsuccessful hunter permitted to get the mastery of his heart; and the Evil Spirit at that moment entering his body, his temper fairly flew away, and he sought some pretense by which to provoke a quarrel with the stranger Indian at the spring.

"'Why does a stranger,' he asked, rising from the stream at the same time, 'drink at the spring-head, when one to whom the fountain belongs contents himself with the water that runs from it?'

"'The Great Spirit places the cool water at the spring,' answered the other hunter, 'that his children may drink it pure and undefiled. The running water is for the beasts which scour the plains. Au-sa-qua is a chief of the Shos-shone; he drinks at the headwater.'

"'The Shos-shone is but a tribe of the Comanche,' returned the other; 'Waco-mish leads the grand nation. Why does a Shos-shone dare to drink above him?'

"'He has said it. The Shos-shone drinks at the spring-head; other nations, of the stream which runs into the fields. Au-sa-qua is chief of his nation. The Comanche are brothers. Let them both drink of the same water.'

"'The Shos-shone pays tribute to the Comanche. Waco-mish leads that nation to war. Waco-mish is chief of the Shos-shone, as he is of his own people.'

"'Waco-mish lies; his tongue is forked like the rattlesnake's; his heart is black as the Misho-tunga (bad spirit). When the Manitou made his children, whether Shos-shone or Comanche, Arapahó, Shi-an, or Pā-né, he gave them buffalo to eat, and the pure water of the fountain to quench their thirst. He said not to one, Drink here, and to another, Drink there; but gave the crystal spring to all that all might drink.'

"Waco-mish almost burst with rage as the other spoke; but his coward heart alone prevented him from provoking an encounter with the calm Shos-shone. *He*, made thirsty by the words he had spoken—for the red man is ever sparing of his tongue—again stooped down to the spring to quench his thirst, when the subtle warrior of the Comanche suddenly threw himself upon the kneeling hunter, and, forcing his head into the bubbling water, held him down with all his strength, until his victim no longer struggled, his stiffened limbs relaxed, and he fell forward over the spring, drowned and dead.

"Over the body stood the murderer, and no sooner was the deed of blood consummated than bitter remorse took possession of his mind, where before had reigned the fiercest passion and vindictive hate. With hands clasped to his forehead, he stood transfixed with horror, intently gazing on his victim, whose head still remained immersed in the fountain. Mechanically he dragged the body a few paces from the water, which, as soon as the head of the dead Indian was withdrawn, the Comanche saw suddenly and strangely disturbed. Bubbles sprang up from the bottom, and rising to the surface, escaped in hissing gas. A thin vapory cloud arose, and gradually dissolving, displayed to the eyes of the trembling murderer the figure of an aged Indian, whose long snowy hair and venerable beard, blown aside by a gentle air from his breast, discovered the well-known totem of the great Wankan-aga, the father of the Comanche and Shos-shone nation, whom the tradition of the tribe, handed down by skillful hieroglyphics, almost deified for the good actions and deeds of bravery this famous warrior had performed when on earth.

"Stretching out a war-club towards the affrighted murderer, the figure thus addressed him:

"'Accursed of thy tribe! this day thou hast severed the link between the mightiest nations of the world, while the blood of the brave Shos-shone cries to the Manitou for vengeance. May the water of thy tribe be rank and bitter in their throats.' Thus saying, and swinging his ponderous war-club (made from the elk's horn) round his head, he dashed out the brains of the Comanche, who fell headlong into the spring, which from that day to the present moment, remains rank and nauseous, so that not even when half dead with thirst, can one drink the foul water of that spring.

"The good Wan-kan-aga, however, to perpetuate the memory of the Shos-shone warrior, who was renowned in his tribe for valor and nobleness of heart, struck, with the same avenging club, a hard flat rock, which overhung the rivulet, just out of sight of this scene of blood; and forthwith the rock opened into a round, clear basin, which instantly filled with bubbling, sparkling water, than which no thirsty hunter ever drank a sweeter or cooler draught.

"Thus the two springs remain, an everlasting memento of the foul murder of the brave Shos-shone, and the stern justice of the good Wan-kan-aga; and from that day the two mighty tribes of the Shos-shone and Comanche have remained severed and apart; although a long and bloody war followed the treacherous murder of the Shos-shone chief, and many a scalp torn from the head of the Comanche paid the penalty of his death."

The wagon road from the Soda Springs to Colorado City followed an old Indian trail most of the way. This trail had been widened where it ran through thickets of choke-cherry, currant and other bushes, and was a fairly good road.

On reaching Colorado City we went into camp at the upper end of the town near Camp Creek. Colorado City was a place of somewhat more than three hundred houses, most of which were built of logs, some hewed, but a majority in the rough. However, many of the business houses had square fronts made of lumber, which gave the principal street a more attractive appearance than was usual in a frontier town. The main business street was Colorado Avenue, the residences being located along parallel streets. As I recall it, the town covered much the same ground that it did at the time of its consolidation with Colorado Springs in recent years, excepting that in the early days the houses were more widely scattered.

The first formal action toward locating the town of Colorado City was taken August 13, 1859, by M. S. Beach and R. E. Cable, acting for the Colorado City Town Company which had been organized in Denver the day before. The town site covered about twelve hundred acres on the north side of the Fountain between Camp Creek and the Monument. The town had a boom during the remaining months of the year, about two hundred houses were built that fall and winter and half as many more the following spring; but that marked the apex of Colorado City's growth for many years thereafter.

On our arrival in Colorado City we were not long in discovering that the town was on the wane. Prior to the year 1860, most of the travel from the east to the Pike's Peak region had come by way of the Arkansas Valley to the mouth of the Fountain, then northward to Colorado City and Denver by roads that ran parallel to the mountains. However, in the spring of 1860, the border war in southern

Kansas, together with threatened Indian troubles
along the Arkansas River, turned the larger part of
the Pike's Peak travel to the valley of the Platte,
leaving the towns in southern Colorado virtually
stranded. Up to that time these places had been
supported in large measure by the gold seekers passing through them. Nevertheless, Colorado City
maintained its importance a little longer than the
other towns by reason of having a fairly good wagon
road into the mining regions in and around the
South Park, but this advantage was soon ended.
During the winter of 1859 and '60, the people of
Colorado City materially improved the road through
Ute Pass and on to the mining regions and hoped by
this means to attract travel that way; but, the distance being so much greater than by the direct road
from Denver,—which I have described heretofore—
the effort was a failure and Colorado City lost what
little prestige it had, never to regain it to any great
extent.

In Colorado City and the country adjacent to it,
substantially the same form of government had
been established as was in force at Denver. The
authorities of Kansas, to which this region belonged,
having made no effort to assume jurisdiction, the
people had come together and formed what they
called a Claim Club. This organization had adopted
a method of procedure for locating and recording
farming claims and transfers of title, and had elected
a recorder whose office was in Colorado City. Anyone taking up a farming claim was required to file a

description of it in this office before the location became valid. After he had done this, the claimant was entitled to the protection of the Claim Club as against any later filings.

Informal as was this procedure, that of the courts for trial of criminal cases was even more so. In a general way these tribunals were made up, as in Denver, of all the men of the vicinity who could be brought together on short notice. The crowd elected from one to three of their number to act as judges for each special case. These judges called witnesses, took evidence in the presence of the assembled crowd, and this gathering then decided by vote as to the guilt or innocence of the accused.

An instance of this kind had occurred in Colorado City a month before, at the time father was there. As he and Reverend Mr. Johnson were riding into town they saw a large crowd around a pile of lumber, adjacent to the principal street. They rode over to find out what was going on, and ascertained that a Mexican was on trial for theft of a horse the previous night. It appeared that the Mexican had stolen the horse from the outskirts of town and then started with it for New Mexico, but had been followed and captured before he reached Pueblo. The people assembled to try him had elected three persons to act as judges, one of whom was Benjamin F. Crowell, afterwards one of the most prominent citizens of the county. These judges had appointed a sheriff for the occasion, who had charge of the prisoner. In addition they named one of the bystanders, who was supposed to have some knowledge of the law, as a prosecuting attorney, and still another to defend the prisoner. When father and his companion arrived, the evidence was being taken. A short time after, there being no further witnesses to examine, the judge submitted the matter to the crowd, asking all who believed the Mexican guilty and were convinced that he should be hanged, to walk across the street. This everyone did, excepting the two ministers. Whereupon, the judges pronounced sentence of death and instructed the sheriff to see that the prisoner was hanged forthwith. At this juncture the ministers asked the privilege of saying a few words, which was granted. They called attention to the fact that hanging a man was a serious affair, and sought to hold religious services before the execution took place. This the crowd refused, saying that they would finish the matter in hand first and attend services later. Without further delay the Mexican was marched off to a tree that stood in a gulch on the south side of the Fountain, just above the mouth of Camp Creek, and in less than thirty minutes from the time of his conviction, he was executed.

Another instance illustrating these summary methods of procedure occurred a little later. What has been known during recent years as the Pope Ranch, near Pike View station on the Denver & Rio Grande Railroad, was owned at that time by two men, Pat Devlin and Jim Laughlin, both of whom were rather tough characters. Trouble having arisen between them concerning some matter connected with their partnership, they became bitter enemies, and each swore to kill the other on sight. From that time on until the occurrence which I am about to relate, both men went armed and were constantly on the lookout for each other. One day while both were in Colorado City, Laughlin, who had a double-barreled shot gun in his hands, seeing Devlin coming down the street, lay in wait for him behind an adjacent building, and as the latter passed by, fired a heavy load of buckshot into him. Devlin fell mortally wounded, and it was supposed that his death would follow quickly. He was carried off by bystanders and Laughlin was placed under arrest. A jury of the people immediately assembled, representatives of which visited Devlin and on their return, reported that he was badly wounded and could not recover. On hearing this, the jury decided that it would be a useless waste of time to wait for his death and at once proceeded with the trial, taking the testimony of persons who had witnessed the affair. After full consideration of the evidence the jury determined that, as Devlin was a tough character, his death would be a good riddance, and that Laughlin was to be commended instead of censured for the shooting. Consequently, without further delay, they brought in a verdict of justifiable homicide. This decision was somewhat premature, as Devlin lived more than two weeks after the verdict was rendered, but such things cut little figure in those early days.

The instances given may indicate a too summary way of executing justice, yet under the conditions existing at that time, the method adopted appeared to be absolutely necessary for the protection of life and property. It certainly is true that both were as safe, if not safer, then than at the present time. With scarcely an exception, the men in mining camps of the Pike's Peak region, wherever thrown together for any length of time, instituted and maintained some kind of local organization to control matters of public interest and for the protection of life and property, which was another evidence of the inherent capacity of American people for self government.

The show place of Colorado City at the time of our arrival was a small tract of land east of town in the valley of the Fountain, that was under cultivation by irrigation, a method of farming unknown to the people of the regions whence most of the gold-seekers came. Only recently had it dawned upon any of those who had come to the Rocky Mountains seeking gold, that there might be other industries in the Pike's Peak region besides mining. Few of them had the least idea that the lands of this arid section could be made of any value agriculturally, but those who visited the garden tract and saw corn and all sorts of vegetables growing luxuriantly as a result of irrigation, came away with new ideas as to the possibilities of this country. Already they had discovered that these great plains were admirably adapted to stock raising, and now it was proved that by irrigation methods, they could be made great agriculturally as well.

While here on his visit a month before, father had taken up a tract of land east of Monument Creek in what is now a part of Colorado Springs. This land, as I remember, extended from the lower end of the present Colorado College grounds northward, paralleling the creek to what is now the town of Roswell. It is my impression that he had no definite idea at the time as to what he would do with the claim, but a visit to the irrigated garden tract having shown him the possibilities of agriculture here, he decided to secure title to land somewhere in this vicinity. He believed that owing to the fertile soil of its valleys, its mild climate, and scenic attractions, there was a great future for this immediate region. However on this later trip, a visit to the Monument Creek claims and inquiries concerning the flow in that stream, convinced him that the water supply was too limited and uncertain and that, even if it were abundant, ditches to conduct it to the land on which he had filed would be very expensive to construct. Having reached this conclusion, he abandoned the Monument Creek claims and a few days later found a vacant tract of land along Cheyenne Creek, about half way between its mouth and Cheyenne Cañon, which he filed upon and arranged for the construction of a claim cabin. This was necessary in order to show the public that the tract had been taken up in good faith. At approximately the same time that we took up our Cheyenne

Creek claim, others were doing the same thing at
various places along the Fountain and its tributaries, wherever water for irrigation purposes could be
obtained and brought to the land without too much
cost. Within the next year or two a large acreage
of land along these streams was brought under cultivation. This was fortunate for Colorado City, as
the development of this agricultural industry was
the principal thing that kept it from dropping out of .
existence.

After all preliminaries connected with taking up
our claim had been attended to, we started on the
return trip to Hamilton, traveling leisurely and hunting on the way. The only incident of interest on
this trip occurred during the afternoon of the first
day out from Colorado City, when father and I,
taking our rifles, left Mr. Girten with the wagon
near where the town of Woodland Park now stands,
and started across the country, intending to meet
him again at some point on the road near the present town of Florissant. We had not gone far before
we came upon a large herd of elk grazing in a little
valley near the edge of the forest. Evidently they
saw us first, for before we had time to shoot they
started up and in their fright went crashing through
the forest, making a sound like a tornado passing
through dead timber. When running, elk lay their
antlers back on their shoulders and point their noses
straight ahead. This prevents the prongs of the
antlers from catching in branches of the trees. The
sight of those big animals and their stampede was

most interesting, as well as thrilling, during the few minutes it lasted.   After a long, weary walk we reached the wagon at the point agreed upon without having seen any other game.   Two days more of travel through the interesting region beyond the Platte brought us to our home at Hamilton.   Father had to leave the next day for appointments at various places in his circuit, and I was left alone in our house in the woods most of the time for the next three weeks.   While we were at Colorado City, father had decided that he would remain in the Rocky Mountain region for the next few years. This decision having been reached, it was arranged that I should return to our home in Iowa as soon as any one was found with whom I could go, that I might attend school during the winter.   Father was to follow a few months later for the purpose of bringing the entire family to the Pike's Peak region the following spring.

Few letters from home had reached us during the summer as they were rather expensive luxuries.   For a United States mail route to this Rocky Mountain region was yet to be established, and all letters that we received came by express at a cost of twenty-five cents each.   Although I had never been away from home so long before, I seldom had the least tinge of homesickness.   However, I was greatly pleased when it was decided that I should return. I thought of my many novel and interesting experiences which I should enjoy telling to mother, the family, and the neighborhood boys, and, in addition, father had just had a pair of buckskin trousers made for me, with fringe down the sides such as the trappers wore, and I was sure that these would excite the envy of all my schoolboy friends.

On the 18th day of September, 1860, arrangements having been made covering my passage, I started for home in company with three old friends of father's. We made the trip in a light wagon drawn by a span of horses. Our route from Hamilton followed the same road that father and I had taken in going to and from Colorado City in August. Several other persons whom we knew traveled in company with us. Almost every one in the party had met with interesting experiences during the previous summer, which were related as we sat around the camp fire at night. On this trip we saw the usual amount of game, then so abundant in that region. In addition, soon after we came over the Divide on the head of Fountain Creek, we saw a large flock of wild turkeys, which were the first and only wild turkeys that I ever have seen in the Rocky Mountains.

After passing Colorado City, our route led up Monument Creek and down Plum Creek to Denver; then down the valley of the Platte River along the same road that we had followed coming to the mountains the spring before. Nothing of especial interest occurred on the trip eastward, except that when we were two hundred miles or more from the Missouri River, our horses began to give out. The lack of grain or other suitable feed had begun to tell on them, and from that time on until the Missouri River was reached we had to travel slowly.

When I left Hamilton father entrusted to my care all of the gold dust that he had accumulated during the summer, as well as his surplus cash, which I was to take home to mother. The responsibility of this was a cause of considerable anxiety to me all the way. I had been instructed to turn the gold dust into money when I reached the town of Plattsmouth, on the Missouri River. Although unable to get as good a price as I thought the gold should bring, I finally sold it and reached home safely with the proceeds on the 18th of October, just one month after leaving Hamilton. Of course I was happy to be at home again, and mother, my brothers and sisters were overjoyed to see me, and were much interested in the experiences I had to relate. School was in progress and I started in immediately, attending regularly during the following winter. Soon after reaching home I was caught out in the rain with my buckskin trousers on, and, to my great regret, they shrank so much that they were useless thereafter.

About the middle of the following February father reached home. He had made the trip from Denver to the Missouri River by stage coach in a little less than six days' continuous traveling. The coach stopped neither night nor day, excepting to change horses at stations—which were about twelve miles apart—and at eating stations, where stays were made just long enough for passengers to get their meals. Otherwise the coach went along steadily, and the only sleep that passengers obtained during the entire trip was such as they were able to snatch sitting up in their seats.

Soon after arriving at home my father began making arrangements for the family's journey to the Rocky Mountains in the spring. He secured two yoke of oxen and a large covered wagon, and equipped the latter with a good many conveniences for traveling, in order to make the trip as comfortable as possible for my mother and sisters. Fitted in the rear end of the wagon was a large cupboard that had shelves and a door that could be let down to form a good-sized table. In this cupboard all our cooking equipment and food for the day were kept. We also had a sheet iron camp stove for cooking purposes, which was set up at night, either in the tent or outside, as the weather might make desirable. This outfit was something rather unusual at that time.

We started from our home in Quincy, Adams County, Iowa, early in May, 1861, and traveled over the same route that father and I had followed the previous year, reaching Denver in about thirty-five days, after an uneventful trip. A good many Indians were seen, but fortunately they were not hostile at that special time and gave us no trouble. The journey was a tiresome one for mother and my sisters, but, as they were strong and healthy, they stood it fairly well. For my small brothers, it was a perpetual picnic.

Denver had grown a great deal since the year before and had thrown off much of its frontier appearance. From Denver to Hamilton our route was the same that father and I had gone over the year before, but in the meantime the road had been materially improved. It was not nearly so rough, and many bridges had been put in, which made travel much pleasanter. The only unusual incident during that part of the trip occurred one day after we had reached the Platte River. As we were plodding along, there suddenly came a large number of mounted Indian warriors trailing single file down the road toward us. When they were nearer, we saw that two of the warriors had squaws astride behind them. Some of the Indians could speak a little English, and from them we ascertained that they were Arapahoes and had been in a battle with the Utes in the South Park. The two squaws were Utes who had been captured during the engagement and now were being taken to the Arapahoe camp near Denver. The squaws were stolidly riding along and did not seem to mind their plight very much, or if they did, they were not showing it, apparently being resigned to their fate.

In the course of two or three days we reached Hamilton and settled down for the summer in the house that father and I had erected the previous year. Since that time, a sawmill had been put in operation at Hamilton, and lumber now was abundant. This enabled us to put in a good floor and to partition the house into several rooms, which made it a comparatively comfortable dwelling place for a pioneer mining town, although my mother and my sisters thought it still somewhat primitive.

Father was compelled to be away most of the summer, carrying on his church work in the various towns and mining camps of his circuit. Soon after we arrived, with father's aid, I secured employment for myself and our team in hauling logs to a sawmill near town. Experience had shown that lumber made from spruce timber, a kind that predominated immediately around Hamilton, was too soft for durable sluice boxes and that yellow pine was much better. The nearest supply of the latter kind of timber was about ten miles away, and owners of the sawmill were anxious to procure teams to haul the logs from that point to their mill. The remuneration offered being attractive, it was arranged that I should enter their employ, and on the following day I made my first trip. I started out with my two yoke of oxen and wagon and without difficulty reached the point where the logs had been cut. As I had just passed my fifteenth birthday and was rather small for my age, the men at the logging camp necessarily had to do the loading for me. Three large-sized yellow pine logs were put upon my wagon and I started back with the load. I had gone only a few hundred yards when, in crossing a small but rather deep gully into which the front wheels went down suddenly and then up as quickly, one of the logs, that had been loaded too far forward, struck the wagon tongue and snapped it in two. Of course there was nothing to do but have the logs unloaded and take the wagon to town for a new tongue. This I did, and in a day or two when the repairs had been made, returned to the timber for another load which was properly placed upon the wagon and I again started for the mill. I reached the main road without trouble, but had gone only a few yards further when one of the tires ran off, resulting in smashing a wheel. Again I had the wagon unloaded and took it to town for repairs. A day or two later I went out the third time, but by now I had become so thoroughly awakened to the possibilities of trouble that, after the wagon was loaded, I kept close watch of every part of it and came through successfully. Thereafter I made my daily regular round trip during the remainder of the summer without any further accident or mishap. The work was not hard, as I generally left home around eight o'clock in the morning and arrived back with my load of logs about half past four in the afternoon, for which the pay was five dollars. My earnings during that summer seemed a small fortune to me; and, looking back, I have no doubt that the experience obtained was of the greatest value to me in after years. It sharpened my wits and taught me to think for myself in every emergency, and to look ahead and try to avoid possible trouble. This training, doubtless, has enabled me to escape many difficulties that I would otherwise have encountered, while the outdoor work hardened me for the strains of later years.

Hamilton was not as large a town as it was the previous summer. Many of its inhabitants had gone to the newer mining camps, others had moved to valleys outside of the mountains to engage in agriculture and stock raising; and still others, whose homes were in the South, had returned to take part in the Civil War, which was just beginning. The population of Hamilton continued to decrease until within a few years the town was virtually abandoned. At the present time only one house remains on the site.

Between people from the South who remained in Colorado and those of the North, much bitterness existed. The spirit of war was prevalent here as elsewhere, and there were frequent clashes of a serious nature between the contending factions. During the summer of 1861 recruiting for the First Regiment of Colorado Volunteers was under way at Hamilton. Although I was somewhat undersized and probably would not have been accepted, I was anxious to enlist in this Regiment, but on broaching the subject to my parents, they at once vetoed it, and I had to wait until later for my military experience.

CHAPTER IV

THE TERRITORY OF COLORADO FORMED AND ITS GOVERNMENT ORGANIZED

ABOUT the middle of October, 1861, our family packed its belongings and started from Hamilton for Colorado City, which locality was to be our future home. By this time snow had fallen to a considerable depth throughout the mountains, which made the journey a disagreeable one.

Upon arriving at Colorado City little difficulty was found in securing a fairly good house, and soon we were comfortably located for the winter. It was apparent that Colorado City had continued to decline since our visit the preceding summer. The town presented a deserted appearance; many houses had been moved away to farming claims down the Fountain valley, and a considerable number of those remaining were vacant and in a dilapidated condition, the result of heavy wind storms during the previous winter.

Referring to wind storms, one occurred soon after our arrival at Colorado City that was particularly terrifying to us, this being our first experience with the Colorado variety. It came straight off the mountain with terrific force and continued without let-up for forty-eight hours. A part of the roof of our house became loosened and we expected it to go almost any minute during the last twenty-four hours of the storm. Often in those days, hours before a gale of this kind made its appearance, people would be warned of its approach by the roaring of the wind in the dead timber of the adjacent mountains. During these wind storms many of the men of Colorado City who had no families to look after, carried their blankets down into the brush along the Fountain and slept there at night until the gale was over.

While the outlook for the future of Colorado City was not at all promising, its founders had not given up hope of making it a place of importance, and, in furtherance of their efforts in that direction, they established a weekly newspaper called *The Colorado City Journal*, the first number of which appeared in May, 1861. B. F. Crowell was its editor. Fortunately I have a copy of the issue of November 28, of that year, which, although a small affair of four pages, much of it taken up by patent medicine advertisements, contains many items of interest. The paper had three columns of war news which came by telegraph to Julesburg, two hundred miles east of Denver, and by mail from that place to Colorado City. Much of its telegraphic news relates to the arrest of Slidell and Mason, who were on their way to England, as representatives of the Confederate Government, and to the complications with England that were sure to follow.

An article of interest in it tells of the capture on the Arkansas River east of Pueblo, of a company of forty-three Southern sympathizers who were attempting to join the Confederate army. I may add that in their march southward from Denver this party seized horses wherever they found them. Two fine animals were taken from a Mr. Bowlby on his ranch south of the Fountain, opposite the present city of Colorado Springs. They forced him to bring the horses in from the pasture for them, threatening to kill him if he refused.

Among the local items I find the following:

"Arrivals. Dr. Garvin from French Gulch and John Addleman of Delaware Flats have appeared as residents among us for the winter. Also Rev. Wm. Howbert and family, accompanied by several other families from Buckskin Joe, Tarryall and other places in the mines; all to spend the winter and many to make their permanent abode in our romantic young city."

On the same page is the following:

"Quite a severe blow occurred on Tuesday night during which two buildings were overturned, one belonging to Gerrish & Co. and the other to Judge Petit. Both were very poorly constructed or they would have withstood the storm."

The advertisement of the "General Store" of Tappan & Co. is the most prominent one in the paper. The members of this firm came from Boston direct to the Pike's Peak region in 1859, and founded stores in both Denver and Colorado City.

Directly under this is a notice asking for recruits for Company A, 1st Regiment, Colorado Volunteers. This regiment later acquired great renown by doing the major part of the fighting that resulted in defeating and driving from New Mexico a Confederate army under General Sibley after that army had overrun more than half of the Territory. It was said that General Sibley planned to take possession of Colorado after the conquest of New Mexico had been completed.

Among the advertisements on the first page is one of the Central Hotel, kept by Mrs. Maggard— the only hotel in town. Another is of the Colorado City & Denver Express Line, which states that coaches ran every week between the above points, carrying the U. S. mail, express matter, and passengers, leaving Colorado City Sunday morning, arriving in Denver Monday afternoon, starting back Thursday morning, and reaching Colorado City Friday afternoon.

Another announcement is that of Harper & Brothers, Publishers, stating that in the *Harper's Weekly* of November 24 a new novel by Charles Dickens entitled "Great Expectations" was commenced.

According to an article in this same paper the first

lode mines in the Pike's Peak region were discovered near the head of Blue River in August of the year 1861. This was news of vital importance to the Territory, as placer mining was on the wane at that time.

That winter father and I made the cabin on our Cheyenne Creek claim habitable and in March, 1862, our family moved into it. Previously that winter, which had been a very mild one, we had spent a good deal of time in constructing a ditch from Cheyenne Creek, building fences and putting our land in shape for cultivation. We had purchased a number of cattle, a team of horses and the necessary farming implements. Therefore when spring came, we were in fairly good shape to start our ranch life. Father retired from the active ministry that year, but continued during the remainder of his life to take a great interest in church matters and frequently, in the absence of the regular minister, conducted services in the Methodist Church in Colorado City.

On the 14th of April we were surprised by a snowfall that exceeded anything we had ever seen. In twenty-four hours, more than two feet of heavy snow fell, covering everything excepting the bushes along the creek and the tall shrubs of the higher land with a thick white blanket. We gave up hope of saving our stock, as it seemed impossible for the animals to survive until the snow should disappear. However, it soon began to melt, and in a few days the hillsides were bare, the cattle having suffered but little in the meantime. When the snow had gone the ground was in good shape for plowing, and I then had my first experience in farming. I must say that I did not enjoy the work. Plowing was not so bad, but when it came to following a team of horses and a harrow over rough plowed ground, I thought it the hardest work that I ever had done, and I quickly made up my mind that I was not going to be a farmer.

When the ground had been made ready for seeding, it became necessary to consider the new problem of irrigation. Laterals or furrows that would conduct water to the different parts of the field had to be located properly in order to secure good results. To insure this, the contour of the ground was carefully studied and laterals laid out accordingly. Father having been raised on a farm, was well acquainted with ordinary methods of agriculture, and had learned much through observation since coming to this arid region. Therefore, by following the advice of farmers familiar with the new method, he was able to plan his irrigation system in a way that brought satisfactory results. We raised and harvested a good crop of wheat, oats, and corn that season and sold at a fair price the part of it that was not needed for our own use.

Several times that summer when my services were not required on the farm, I took a yoke of oxen and wagon and made trips to the Finley sawmill in the Pinery on the Divide for lumber to be used in building a new and better dwelling house on our ranch.

The road from the ranch to the sawmill was down
Cheyenne Creek to its mouth, thence across the
Fountain, over the present townsite of Colorado
Springs to Templeton's Gap, and on to the Pinery.
It took me all day and until after dark to reach the
mill, where I stayed that night.   Loading the lumber the following morning would delay me in starting back, and on my return trip it often happened
that darkness came before I reached the place where
Colorado Springs now stands.   There I had to pass
close to an old cemetery that occupied a part of the
southern end of the present townsite.   Being still
a mere boy and having heard and read a great many
stories of ghosts, I was always on the lookout for
one to appear among the graves, and was much
relieved when I was safely by the dreaded place.
After harvest, we proceeded to erect a dwelling on
our ranch that was comfortable and compared favorably with those of our neighbors.

By this time, much of the cultivatable land along
the Fountain and its branches had been taken up,
temporary improvements made, and a considerable
acreage brought under cultivation.   The first year,
there was little fencing and the houses were cheap
and crude structures.   But after the first crop was
harvested, more substantial buildings were erected
and permanent improvements began to take the
place of the temporary ones.

A large majority of the first settlers of El Paso
County were men and women of more than average
intelligence, with only a few of the shiftless class

often found on the frontier. Virtually everyone
who came to the Pike's Peak region prior to the
summer of 1860, had come as a gold seeker and had
brought along supplies sufficient for the period he
expected to be away from his home. But many of
these people, after seeing the grand Rocky Mountains and the beautiful valleys along their eastern
base and hearing from the few who came in 1858 and
1859 of the mild climate and the great productive-
ness of the lands when irrigated, changed their
minds, brought their families here, and remained.
Few ever regretted it. At no time were there many
of the typical frontier class here, and the small
number there were soon left for newer regions. I
remember one of this class, a resident of Colorado
City, who with his family left here in 1862 for some
point farther west on account of this locality being
too crowded for them.

Of the permanent settlers of this immediate Pike's
Peak region in 1860 and 1861 a very considerable
number were from the New England and middle
states. The man having the greatest influence in
Colorado City from the time it was founded was
M. S. Beach, who was from New Jersey. The person most influential in El Paso County affairs during the twenty-five years following its organization
was Benjamin F. Crowell, a native of Massachusetts.
And one of the most efficient County Commissioners
that El Paso County ever had was J. C. Woodbury,
also born in Massachusetts.

A movement to secure the passage of a bill by

Congress forming a Territory that would take in the
Pike's Peak region and adjacent country, was
started at Denver early in the year 1860, but nothing definite came of it until February of the following year. Meanwhile, the founders of Colorado City,
knowing that the new Territory would be formed
sooner or later, had a representative in Washington lobbying to have it named "Colorado," hoping
in this way to promote Colorado City's chances of
securing the capitol. This representative was instructed also to have the southern boundary of the
new Territory pushed as far south as possible in
order to make Colorado City more nearly in the
center of it. While the measure was being considered by Congress, various names for the proposed
Territory were suggested such as Tahosa, Lafayette,
Columbus, Franklin, Idaho, San Juan, Colona, and
one or two others. Hon. Schuyler Colfax, afterwards
Vice-President, who introduced the bill, was said
to have favored the name "Colona." However,
the name "Idaho" had been virtually decided upon,
when, through the influence of Colorado City's representative, it is said, "Colorado" was substituted
just before the final passage of the bill on February
26, 1861. Naturally the people of Colorado City
were much elated over this result of their efforts.

The Territory of Colorado was formed out of
country taken from the adjacent state of Kansas and
the territories of Nebraska, Utah, and New Mexico. The Arkansas River had been the northern
boundary line of New Mexico previous to that

time; and, prior to the treaty made with Mexico in 1848—just twelve years before our arrival—it was the northern boundary line of the Republic of Mexico.

Soon after the passage of the Colorado Enabling Act by Congress, William Gilpin of Missouri, a veteran of the Mexican War, was appointed Governor of the new Territory. On his arrival in Denver two or three months later, Governor Gilpin caused a census to be taken, which showed that the Territory had a total population of 25,331, consisting of 20,758 white males, 4,484 white females, and 89 negroes of both sexes. He then divided the Territory into Districts, from which members of the Legislature soon after were elected. This first Legislature met in Denver on the 9th of September, 1861, and spent the next sixty days enacting laws for the government of the Territory, creating the various counties and providing for their organization. Shortly before the adjournment of the Legislature, an Act was passed locating the capital of the Territory at Colorado City. Soon thereafter Governor Gilpin appointed M. S. Beach, Henry S. Clark and A. D. Sprague, Commissioners of the new County of El Paso, charged with the duty of organizing a county government.

The County of El Paso, as originally laid out, was about forty by sixty miles in extent, and comprised the territory around Pike's Peak—west of that mountain almost as far as the Platte River and east for approximately thirty miles on the plains.

Through the center of it, east and west—north of Pike's Peak—runs the famous Ute Pass, from which came the Spanish name of the county, El Paso.

The Commissioners appointed by the Governor met on the 16th day of November, 1861, divided the county into precincts, and named judges for the election soon to be held. This election was for the purpose of choosing the various territorial, legislative, county, and precinct officers that had been provided for by the laws recently enacted. At this election Benjamin F. Crowell, A. D. Sprague and John Bley were elected County Commissioners; Scott Kelly, Sheriff; and George A. Bute, County Clerk. All these officials qualified early in 1862, and soon thereafter the County Commissioners proceeded to perfect the precinct organization throughout the county. These Commissioners were the actual founders of established government in this county. All the county officers elected at that time were men of more than usual efficiency and business ability. Although little revenue was at their disposal, they managed the affairs of the county during the next three years without incurring any indebtedness whatever. Naturally, after organized government had been established throughout the Territory, Peoples' Courts and Claim Club organizations went out of existence.

The second Legislature of Colorado met at Colorado City, July 7, 1862. There was but one cheap, primitive hotel in the town, of such limited capacity that it could accommodate only a small proportion of the members of the legislative body, not to mention its numerous employees. This made it necessary for many members to camp out during their stay. Naturally, under such conditions the legislators were much dissatisfied, and, after convening, did not long delay in enacting legislation changing the capital to Denver. Thereupon its members quickly departed, journeying to their new place of meeting on horseback and in wagons, some of them camping out along the way.

An amusing account of this event was given by Judge Wilbur F. Stone in an address at a meeting of the El Paso County Pioneer Society held September 25, 1906. Judge Stone was a member of the House of Representatives from Frémont County in the Legislature referred to and took an active part in its proceedings. His account was as follows:

"The first Territorial Legislature of Colorado, which consisted altogether of but twenty-two members, thirteen of the House and nine of the Council, located the capital of the Territory at Colorado City. This was done chiefly on the ground that it was the geographical center of Colorado, and the gateway to the mountains. There was also a poetical idea associated with the Garden of the Gods. Perhaps, too, some may have entertained a prosaic notion that Pike's Peak as a landmark would serve to guide the wayward members from the remotest camp to that valley of wisdom. So there in July, 1862, the lawmakers met for the second session. The number had been increased by act of Congress to twenty-six members of the House and thirteen of the Council, but by a misunderstanding as to the time of meeting, a number were not present, there being only seven or eight of the Council in attendance.

"A more unique gathering together of a legislative assembly probably never before presented a subject for chronicle. They came in wagons, ambulances, horseback and on foot. Two old overland stage coaches, with four mules each, brought loads from Denver and Gregory diggings. George Crocker and his fellow member from California Gulch footed it all the way over the snowy range, across the South Park and down through the mountains, one hundred and forty miles, carrying each a blanket on which they slept beside the trail wherever night overtook them. They started with grub enough to last them through as they supposed, but having taken a wrong trail, lost a day in wandering about the wilderness and were nearly starved when they arrived at the capital. I shall never forget the aspect of that brilliant man and lawyer, George Crocker, when he walked up and laid down his blanket at the door of the House of Representatives. He had been mining and possessed no other clothes than those he wore at his sluice box in the gulch. His dress was a blue flannel shirt, trousers patched with buckskin, an old boot on one foot and a brogan on the other, an old slouch hat that he had slept in, the brim partly gone. His face was blackened by the smoke of the campfire and furrowed by perspiration, his eyes hollow with fatigue and hunger, feet blistered by walking, hair tangled and beard yellow with dust; this was the picture of a statesman of the new west in the genesis of our generation. The next day we elected this same George Crocker speaker of the House, and his speech on taking the chair would have done credit for polished oratory to a Massachusetts Cicero at the foot of Bunker Hill.

"The hall of the House of Representatives was a log room twenty by fifteen feet in size. The furniture was a bare pine table with a stool behind it for the speaker, and some rough boards laid across boxes served as benches for the members.

"The Council assembled in the kitchen of old Mother Maggard's log tavern. The body took a recess while the cooking was in progress. No sufficient preparations had been made to entertain the Legislature, and anticipating this, most of the members had brought a store of grub along with them.

"The members of the House batched in their little assembly room, took turns at cooking at the fireplace—a delightful recreation in July—carried water in pails from the creek, and slept at night on the floor. The gay season at the capital was opened by not only the Legislature but the Supreme Court.

"Chief Justice Hall drove down from Denver in a buggy, and another two-seated buggy brought Amos Steck and Dick Whitsitt, accompanied by their wives, dressed in the fashion of the Cherry Creek metropolis. Daniel Witter, my fellow member from Park County, brought his family with him and set up housekeeping in a tent.

"At the end of two or three days the charm of this sort of life began to wane, the bloom was no longer on the rye. In fact the rye itself was almost gone and this bred a potent element of discontent. There was not enough of paper, ink, pens or postage stamps in the capital for a day's business, no printing press nearer than Denver, and typewriters were not then invented. So the House passed a joint resolution to adjourn to Denver. This was opposed in the Council by two or three southern members, the leader of whom was the Honorable Bob Willis of El Paso County, who held a large number of shares of stock in the Colorado City Town Company, and this move threatened a fall in capital stock. The opponents of the move were in a minority, but it required their presence to make a quorum. A brilliant scheme was hatched and executed—the obstructionists, before a final vote was taken, fled from the capital and secreted themselves at Willis' ranch, a dozen miles down the Fountain. At the end of a day or two a more brilliant coup d'état was devised by the majority. Two members were sent down to the ranch with a flag of truce, and proposed a treaty whereby, in consideration of a certain number of shares of capital stock, they agreed to vote against the resolution, if the absentees would return and allow the vote to be taken. The bait was swallowed, though it grieves me to say that these two ministers plenipotentiaries wilfully lied to the party of the second part. No sooner was a quorum counted than the doors were locked, the question put to vote and carried, ayes five, nays three. The three were soon laughed into submission, and in less than twenty minutes teams were hitched up, mules saddled, and the gay capital was moving from the mouth of Camp Creek to the mouth of Cherry Creek. We felt sorry for Mel. Beach and the other nice fellows who had laid out the town originally, and now the legislature had 'laid it out' completely."

In making up the organization of the House of Representatives before leaving Colorado City, father was elected Chaplain of that body, and as the Legislature at once moved to Denver, he necessarily was away from home most of the time during the remainder of the summer. This put the burden of taking care of the ranch upon myself and a man whom we had in our employ.

In those early days all necessities of life not produced in the Territory had to be brought by team from towns along the Missouri River. If the Denver merchant sent his order by mail to a wholesale house in St. Joseph, Missouri, which was a favorite point for purchases, it took about six days by coach for the letter to reach its destination, and at least a month, and frequently longer, for the goods to arrive in Denver. The length of time between mailing an order and receiving merchandise, if there happened to be unavoidable delays, as sometimes occurred, often led to a serious shortage in some articles of daily use. Due to this condition, it happened more than once that salt sold at from fifty cents to one dollar a pound, potatoes twenty-five cents a pound, flour twenty dollars per hundred pounds, and other articles in like proportion. Fortunately, wild meat was plentiful and cheap at all times, as game of various kinds was sufficiently abundant at no great distance from any of the settlements to meet every demand. Later on, the increasing herds of cattle supplanted the buffalo, antelope, and deer, on the ranges, and beef took the place of wild game in the markets.

During the first years of Colorado City's existence, its merchants brought their goods directly from Missouri River towns, but this was abandoned a little later and Denver became the supply point, not only for the merchants of Colorado City, but for many of the ranchmen of the Fountain valley as well. By reason of the fact that Denver was the supply point for Government forts, it usually afforded a good market for the produce of the farmer, while at Colorado City there was little or no market at all. For that reason, many ranchmen of this county hauled what they had to sell to Denver and made their purchases there at the same time.

The trip to Denver could be made with a team of horses in two days, if the wagon was not heavily loaded. The ranchman or freighter usually started from Colorado City early in the morning and by noon would reach the Holcomb Ranch, which was on the county road near the present town of Monument. Here he would feed his horses, eat his noon meal, and then go on to the Coberly Ranch, located on the west side of Plum Creek about one and a half miles north of the present station of Larkspur on the Denver & Rio Grande Railroad, where he would stay all night. The next forenoon's drive took him to the Richardson Ranch, on Richardson Hill, about ten miles north of Castle Rock. The stop here would be to feed his horses and get lunch, after which he would leisurely drive on to Denver, reaching there in the evening. The wagon road from Castle Rock to Denver then ran down Plum Creek for about five miles from the former place, then directly north across the hills to Denver, instead of around by Sedalia as at present.

I spent the winter of 1862–63 in helping to fence our land, in enlarging ditches, and in preparing to plant a larger crop the following season. While getting out fencing material on the side of Cheyenne Mountain, I noticed hundreds of stumps of small trees which undoubtedly had been cut down for lodge poles by the Indians. And at various places along Cheyenne Creek, I saw where these poles had been shaved down to the proper size. Scattered about lay many abandoned ones, worn out by long use and being dragged around over the plains.

CHAPTER V

INTERESTING INCIDENTS CONNECTED WITH THE EARLY HISTORY OF THE PIKE'S PEAK REGION

EARLY in the spring of 1863, the people of this region had an experience that was unusual, and for a time, most terrifying. Men were murdered at various places and for no accountable reason. The assassins were not known, and for two weeks or more following the first crime, they were not seen. The first murder was committed at a sawmill ten or twelve miles south of Cañon City; however, owing to the fact that there were no telegraph lines in southern Colorado at that time, the news did not reach Colorado City until two or three days later. The murdered man had been found a short distance from the mill, having been killed by a gunshot, but he had not been robbed, and nothing had been taken from the sawmill excepting some food, which made it apparent that the motive was not robbery. As the dead man had no known enemies, the whole affair was most mysterious. While the news was still being discussed by the people of El Paso County, word came that another man had been killed in what is now known as "Dead Man's Cañon" between

78

the Little Fountain and Turkey Creek, about twelve miles south of Colorado City. Apparently, he had been dispatched in the same manner and by the same assassins as the Cañon City victim. Again none of his belongings had been taken, which still further mystified the people of Colorado City and vicinity, and all sorts of motives were imagined. This was during the time of the Rebellion, and many thought that the murderers were Confederate guerillas, who, in this way, were attempting to intimidate the people of Colorado, with the ultimate intention of taking possession of the Territory.

The day following this second killing, two mounted men, acting peculiarly, were seen in what was known as the Big Hollow, two or three miles south of Cheyenne Creek, who no doubt were the murderers, although the man who saw the suspects was too far away to give an accurate description of them. By now, the people of this community had become so thoroughly alarmed that they hardly dared to step out of their houses after dusk, as it was impossible to tell where the assassins would appear next. Two or three days after the murder in Dead Man's Cañon word was received indicating that the assassins had left this immediate region and were operating elsewhere. The mail carrier coming in from the South Park, reported finding the dead body of John Addleman, a well known man of this region, lying near the house on his ranch west of the Platte River, a few miles from the present town of Florissant. The mail carrier said that he was so greatly alarmed by the discovery that he had not stopped to bury the body or investigate the case further than to decide that Addleman had been murdered. John Addleman was the son of a Chief Justice of the Supreme Court of Pennsylvania, and had been a well-known and popular resident of Colorado City until a short time before, when he had taken up and moved to this ranch. Miners who came by Addleman's house a day or two later found the body and buried it. These miners said that judging from the tracks found around the house, they were of the opinion that there were two men engaged in the affair and that the murderers had surprised Addleman early in the morning and had marched him around in his bare feet for an hour or two before killing him.

Soon after this, the assassins appeared in the northern end of the South Park, and, for some time, each day brought news of the murdering of one or more persons. In every case the only motive seemed to be a desire to kill. Some two weeks after the first murder, the assassins shot at a ranchman who was driving along the road between Alma and Fairplay, in Park County. He escaped injury only because the bullet happened to hit a book that he had just received in the mail at Fairplay and had put in the breast pocket of his coat. At the sound of the shot, his team took fright and ran away, carrying him out of range of the assailants before they could shoot again. While this was going on, the teamster saw that his would-be assassins were two Mexicans. On reaching Fairplay, he reported these facts, whereupon a posse was quickly organized and started in pursuit of the murderers. The pursuing party had no difficult in finding the trail, which was followed over rough country to a point a few miles northwest of Cañon City, where the Mexicans were surprised in camp. Apparently the assassins had started for New Mexico as soon as they realized that their identity had been discovered and that they were being followed. When surprised, both made strenuous efforts to get away, but one of them was killed before he had gone very far. The other was seriously wounded, but escaped, and, as was ascertained later, returned to his home near Fort Garland in the San Luis Valley. Later on, he induced his nephew, a mere boy, to join him, and these two again took to the mountains and began waylaying and killing white people along the roads crossing the Sangre de Cristo Range.

After this had been going on for some time, the authorities, by offering a large reward, induced an old-time trapper and hunter by the name of Tom Tobin, to run down the assassins. Tobin secured the aid of another man, and the two, having ascertained the neighborhood in which the Mexicans were concealed, trailed them to their hiding place, which was in fallen timber on the side of a mountain not many miles distant from Fort Garland. Under cover of this fallen timber, Tobin and his comrade crawled close to the assassins' camp without being discovered. Before the Mexicans were aware of his presence, Tobin, who was a dead shot, had killed the elder, and succeeded in dropping the younger a moment later. It was said that Tobin cut off the head of the elder one, preserving it in alcohol, and afterwards took it to Denver to prove his right to the reward.

It had been known for some time that the two original assassins were brothers named Espinosa, as was also the nephew. On the body of the elder one—killed by Tobin—a memorandum was found showing that they were religious fanatics and had killed thirty-one white people in all. They had done this, as they claimed, because the Virgin Mary, in a vision, had ordered them to kill Americans as long as they lived. Naturally, the people of southern Colorado were greatly relieved when news came that these assassins had been definitely put out of the way and were no longer a menace to the traveler and isolated settler.

In the fall of 1863, we disposed of our ranch on Cheyenne Creek and purchased cattle with the proceeds. Having previously acquired a considerable number, this addition made our herd one of the largest in El Paso County. After the sale of the ranch we moved to Colorado City, where we remained until the following spring. During the winter we bought and later moved to a ranch on Camp Creek, just above Colorado City; and afterwards, by location and purchase, we acquired the remainder of the valley up to what is now known as Glen Eyrie. All of the region around the Garden of the Gods and west of the valley of Camp Creek was

vacant land at that time, and it was in these hills
that we kept our stock during the next year or two.

My principal occupation during that time was
looking after our herd; but this did not require
very close attention, and many were the days in
which I sat on the rocks with a book on geology or
some other subject of interest to me, reading as I
watched the cattle. At one time, I thought of pre-
empting the Garden of the Gods and even went so
far as to comply with the preliminaries necessary
to establish a legal claim, but later forfeited my
right, thinking the tract of little value.

According to M. S. Beach, principal founder of
Colorado City, the Garden of the Gods was so named
by R. E. Cable, a lawyer from Kansas City, here
on a visit in August, 1859. Mr. Beach states:
"Cable was then a young and poetic man, and when
we visited the site together I suggested that it
would be a capital place for a beer garden when the
country grew up. He exclaimed, 'Beer garden!
Why, it's a fit place for the Gods to assemble. We
will call it the Garden of the Gods,' and by that
name it was known from that date. No one should
endeavor to take that honor from Rufus Cable."
Although this name was universally recognized
from that time, the locality was more often spoken
of by the early settlers as the Red Rocks.

From the time I first came to the Pike's Peak
region, I was continuously impressed by the unusual
interest of the country—its scenic beauty, its strange
animal life, and the foreign touch left by its con-

tact with the French trappers, Spanish explorers, and Mexican laborers. There were a great number of Spanish words in general use which were due to our proximity to New Mexico where Spanish was the language of the people, and to the fact that a large percentage of the farm laborers, cattle and sheep herders, and sheep shearers of this region were Mexicans. Many of the farmers who located here had never heard of irrigation, and virtually none of them were familiar with its use; while the Mexicans had known no other way of raising crops. It is true that many of their irrigation methods were crude and soon were materially improved by the Americans, but they answered for the time being. As farm hands the Mexicans, on account of their indolence, did not last long in this country, but as sheep herders and shearers they were in demand for many years.

Another thing that attracted my attention was that a large percentage of the streams had either Spanish or French names, and some had both. For instance, the French knew the Arkansas River by that name, while the Spaniards of New Mexico called it Rio Nepesta. Our own Fontaine-qui-Bouille was known to the people of New Mexico as Rio Almagre. The reason for these names lay in the fact that Spain had claimed the ownership of this region for more than a century before the United States acquired it, and during that period many Spanish people had explored it; and that the French names had been given by trappers of that nationality who roamed over this country in considerable numbers during the early part of the last century and the latter half of the preceding one.

The early history of this Pike's Peak region was connected with that of Mexico and Spain rather than with that of the United States. Prior to 1820, Spain claimed a stretch of country of indefinite width east of the Rocky Mountains extending from Mexico north to the Yellowstone River. The records of New Mexico show that there was a military expedition through the country north of the Arkansas River and east of the mountains in 1719, and another the following year. Although it is difficult to trace accurately from the reports obtainable the route taken by these expeditions, there is good reason to believe that one or both of them passed over the present town site of Colorado Springs. We know that many other Spanish parties visited this Pike's Peak region between that time and 1820, when Spain finally waived its right to this section.

In corroboration of the claim that Spanish expeditions passed over the town site of Colorado Springs at a very early date, is the following incident. While digging a cellar at 529 East Pike's Peak Avenue in June, 1894, workmen uncovered, some six feet below the surface, an iron box four by six inches in size, which was rusted to the point of disintegration. This iron box held a crucifix, attached to which was a Maltese cross having a small erect cross as a pendant. The two crosses were made of dark colored stone resembling chalcedony, while the crucifix was of solid brass hammered. All these articles were hand made showing the hammer marks and filed edges. None of the three bore any inscription or date, but evidently had been lost by some priest accompanying one of the early Spanish exploring expeditions.

Van E. Rouse, secretary of the Board of Education in Colorado Springs at the time of the discovery, happened to be watching the excavation when the iron box containing the crosses was uncovered, and obtained possession of them. It was Mr. Rouse's purpose to give them to the El Paso County Pioneer Association for its historical collection, but before this was done they had mysteriously disappeared. However, they had been seen by many people, myself included. The loss was most unfortunate, for these old Spanish crosses were relics of great historical value.

It is known that one of the principal trails north and south along the eastern base of the Rocky Mountains crossed the present town site of Colorado Springs. And the place where the iron box was dug up would have been a natural camping ground, as water was accessible in Shooks Run, a few hundred feet away, and from this camp the country was clearly visible in every direction. This was necessary as attack from hostile Indians had continually to be guarded against. The surface of the ground at that point might easily have been built up five or six feet during the two centuries that probably elapsed between the time the crosses were lost and discovered again, the frequent high winds from the west during the winters being sufficient to account for the accumulation.

Up to the time of the founding of Colorado Springs, there were large herds of wild horses in the eastern part of El Paso County and adjacent country. Many attempts were made from time to time to capture them by use of pitfalls and other devices, but these efforts seldom were successful. One method tried with some success was to have mounted men stationed in relays at intervals of several miles over a long distance, to run down the wild horses. One of the horsemen would start the herd running at full speed in the intended direction and follow it; as the herd passed by the first relay man, the pursuer would drop out and the other, with a fresh horse, would take his place. This continued until the end of the line was reached. Then, if possible, the herd was turned back and the men who had dropped out would take up the pursuit again. This would be continued for hours with the hope of tiring the wild animals until they could be lassoed, but it never was entirely successful, for as a rule only weaklings were captured, and they were of little value.

Many stories were told of magnificent stallions leading the various herds; of their remarkable speed, and the strict discipline they maintained by continually rounding up their charges, punishing by bites and kicks the laggards and those disposed to wander away from the main body. General Palmer, the founder of Colorado Springs, in a letter written in September, 1869, says that on a trip taken that year from Fort Sheridan, terminus of the Kansas Pacific Railway, directly across the country to the present town site of Colorado Springs, he saw many buffalo, three herds of wild horses, and antelope in such numbers that he was seldom out of sight of them.

In the early days, game was abundant on the plains and in all this Rocky Mountain region, consequently there were unlimited opportunities for those who enjoyed hunting. Deer were plentiful along the foothills and in the mountains, and antelope were so numerous on the plains and so easily killed that this meat could be had for almost nothing. Explorers passing through this country prior to 1843 reported buffalo plentiful along the valley of the Fountain. However, at the time I came here the plains buffalo had disappeared from this immediate region, although they were abundant on the plains from eighty to one hundred miles eastward. The great number of buffalo skulls and bones that were scattered everywhere over the country adjacent to the mountains and for fifty to sixty miles out on the plains, proved that buffalo had been numerous here at some previous time. Sage, a New Englander, who was here in 1842, tells of killing buffalo near Jimmy's Camp; while Ruxton, the English traveler, in the part of his book entitled *Mexico and the Rocky Mountains*, describing a visit to the Pike's Peak region, says:

"It is a singular fact that within the last two years the prairies extending from the mountains to a hundred miles or more down the Arkansas River, have been entirely abandoned by buffalo. Indeed in crossing from the settlements of New Mexico, the boundary of their former range is marked by skulls and bones."

We who came here twelve or thirteen years later found the same evidence of great destruction of these animals in all the country adjacent to the mountains. It was the opinion of many that an epidemic had broken out among the buffalo which had resulted in their virtual extinction in this region; while others claimed that these animals starved to death after a great snowfall in the early part of some winter. The latter explanation seems to me to be the more probable. An aged trapper of those early days told me that there was a snowfall six or seven feet in depth—probably an exaggeration—in the early winter of 1843 or 1844, covering all this region for a considerable distance out on the plains, the larger part of which remained on the ground until the following spring, and that most of the buffalo, antelope, and other wild animals starved to death during the winter. Having seen since I came here two or three deep snows in the early fall and the disastrous effect they had on the antelope and range cattle, I am inclined to believe the starvation theory.

In the summer of 1864, accompanied by two

friends, I made my first ascent to the summit of Pike's Peak, arriving there the morning of July fourth. We had started on foot from Colorado City the day before, each carrying a blanket and food sufficient for our need for the two days we expected to be absent. As there was no trail we, like everyone who made the ascent at that time, had to pick out our own route. We followed up the north side of Ruxton Creek to a point near the present Half-Way House, then went northwesterly for several miles through a perfect maze of fallen trees, reaching timberline about sundown. Here we built a fire, ate our supper, then smoothed off as well as we could the rocky surface of the place selected for our bed. This consisted of the three blankets that we had brought along, one to sleep on, the other two for covering, all three of us sleeping together. The night was cold, ice formed on the stream nearby; consequently, soon after going to bed we found that the man in the middle had much the best of it, and so we decided that each man should occupy that place an hour in turn. In this way we all secured a little sleep, notwithstanding the uneven nature of the ground under the blanket on which we lay. About three o'clock the next morning we arose, hoping to reach the summit in time to see the sunrise. In order to wash our hands and faces we had to break the ice in the creek, and to save time we ate our breakfast cold, and resumed our climb before daylight. A short distance below the summit, on the eastern face of the Peak, we crossed a snow drift, left over from the preceding winter, that was at least a quarter of a mile wide. I do not remember ever to have seen since that time such a large snow bank at that place in midsummer. We reached the top a few minutes after sunrise and, as the sky was clear, we had an excellent view in every direction. To the north we saw smoke in what is now known as Manitou Park, which we supposed came from an Indian camp. The only indication of others having been on top of the Peak before us were a few small piles of rock, which presumably covered cards bearing the names of persons who had preceded us. After spending about an hour on the summit, we started on our return trip. In our descent we followed a different route from that taken in going up, our course being northeasterly to the Ute Pass, a mile or two below Cascade Cañon. We did not find this way any improvement over the direct one, but it gave us a chance to go through a section then unexplored, in which there was much less fallen timber, more open valleys, and quantities of bright colored flowers. We reached Colorado City that evening, very tired, but well satisfied with our experience.

In reference to the flowers of this region, M. S. Beach says that in 1861, Professor Parry, of Harvard University, pressed him into service as guide to the summit of Pike's Peak. The professor had two assistants with him, and the purpose of his visit was to gather specimens of plants and flowers for his department of the college. He spent two and a half days in the woods along the slopes of the Peak, getting to the summit in the pursuance of his purpose. He informed Mr. Beach afterwards that during the trip he had found and noted eighteen new plants and flowers not then known to the science of botany. In this connection, Dr. James, the botanist of Long's expedition to this region in 1820, in his report says that in crossing the divide between the Platte and Arkansas Rivers he found a columbine, a flower hitherto unknown in the flora of America.

The population of El Paso County slowly increased from 1861 to 1864, and an additional number of acres were placed under cultivation in the valley of the Fountain during each year of that period. At the same time, the cattle industry was growing rapidly. In 1862, the first flour mill was erected in Colorado City, and for a time wheat from distant points in the northern and southern parts of the Territory was sent here to be ground. A second and larger mill was built a year or two later, and, as the area sown to wheat increased in the county, a third was erected farther up Fountain Creek, near what was known in later times as the Becker place. However, the latter mill never was used to any great extent, but the two at Colorado City were operated to their full capacity much of the time for a number of years, grinding wheat raised in El Paso and adjacent counties. Crops were large in 1862, and would have been much larger in 1863 had it not been for the drouth of that year and the lack of adequate irrigation facilities.

The year 1864 was a trying one for the people of El Paso County, as well as for those of the entire Territory of Colorado. Following the dry summer of 1863, excessive snowfalls came during the next winter, and in the spring of 1864, before the snow had entirely melted, there were heavy rains that filled the Fountain to flood proportions. Later on, cloudbursts followed at frequent intervals, with the result that the stream was scarcely fordable between Colorado City and the Pueblo County line for weeks at a time. A cloudburst on the head of Cherry Creek that summer did great damage to the City of Denver, and, at about the same time, one occurred on the headwaters of Monument Creek and the Fountain, which swelled the latter stream to such an extent as to wash away many houses and drown ten or twelve persons in the lower end of El Paso County.

Another cloudburst on the head of Cheyenne Creek that summer brought down a flood of water that covered the valley—a width of several hundred feet at places—all the way from the Cañon to the mouth of the creek. The present site of Stratton Park and the valley below it were covered at one time to a depth of from two to six feet. A mile or two east of the mountains the channel of Cheyenne Creek was changed by this flood for half a mile or more, and just below the point where the Broadmoor branch of the street railway crosses Cheyenne Creek, people climbed into the big cottonwood trees to escape the rush of water. In addition to the trouble and loss occasioned by excessive rains and floods, grasshoppers appeared in swarms and were a source of much annoyance and further loss to many farmers.

CHAPTER VI

INDIAN TROUBLES OF 1864

ONE might suppose that the people of Colorado had been scourged enough already, but it soon became apparent that further calamities awaited them. During the early summer of 1864, rumors of an impending war with the Indians of the plains were current throughout the Territory. Although these Indians had been committing depredations along the lines of travel between Colorado and the Missouri River almost continuously during the previous year, the possibility of trouble with them here at the base of the mountains had given our people little concern. However, the serious nature of information now received indicated that the inhabitants of El Paso and adjoining counties on the north were in great danger of attack by the savages, and this news alarmed the people very much.

Prior to 1863, the Indians of the plains as well as those of the mountains, had been on fairly friendly terms with the settlers of this section. Once or twice a year a war party of Cheyennes and Arapahoes would come in from the plains, pass on through Colorado City, stop at the Soda Springs to make their offerings, as I have described in an earlier chapter, and then disappear up Ute Pass into the mountains. A few days later, usually after a battle with the Utes, they came marching back and, after again paying tribute to the springs, continued out on the plains to the eastward.

These war parties seldom gave any trouble here except in the way of begging food; consequently, their appearance occasioned no alarm. Before the whites and Indians of the plains became involved in warfare, the Utes seldom came down out of the mountains in summer time, but occasionally appeared during the winter months. The condition that in a measure protected the settlers of the Pike's Peak region in those early days, was the fact that the country between the base of the mountains and the Continental Divide was disputed territory, the Utes insisting that their country extended to the eastern base of the Rocky Mountains, while the Indians of the plains claimed the main Continental Divide as their western boundary. Each of the contending tribes knew that a visit to this locality meant a possible fight with its enemies. Consequently, when any of the bands appeared we knew their stay here was not likely to be long. The perpetual warfare waged between these tribes probably was in a great measure due to race enmity, the Sioux, Cheyennes, and Arapahoes being of an entirely different origin from the Utes. The former tribes had originated on the Altantic coast, while the Utes evidently had had their beginning somewhere in the northwestern part of the continent. It is known that the Utes were occupying the mountainous regions of Colorado long before the Sioux, Cheyennes, and Arapahoes had reached the Missouri River in their gradual migration to the west.

The plains Indians were a tall, athletic people while the Utes were directly the opposite, being short and heavy set. The Ute language is in no wise related to that of any of the Indians of the plains, excepting the Comanches, who are a kindred people. The Cheyennes and Arapahoes were virtual interlopers in this region. Both tribes were of the Algonquin stock whose original home was in the New England States and southern Canada. When first heard of about 1750, the Cheyenne Indians were located in northern Minnesota. In 1790, they were living on the Missouri River near the mouth of the Cheyenne. A little later they moved west into the Black Hills, having been driven there by the Sioux. Here they were joined by the Arapahoes and from that time on the two tribes were bound together by the closest relations. They lived in the same villages and roamed in company over the great plains.

Beginning about 1800, these two federated tribes, accompanied for a time by some of the Sioux with whom they were now on friendly terms, gradually moved southward along the eastern base of the Rocky Mountains. Later, after many years' warfare with the Kiowas—who were the earlier occupants of this Pike's Peak region—the Cheyennes and Arapahoes were victorious and, by a treaty made in 1840, secured undisputed possession of the territory north of the Arkansas River and east of the mountains. As this was only eighteen years before the coming of the whites, the Cheyennes and Arapahoes could not rightfully claim this region as an ancestral possession. The country acquired by the Cheyennes and Arapahoes through their victory over the Kiowas embraced more than eighty thousand square miles of territory. This area was out of all proportions to their numbers as in the two tribes there were never more than five thousand men, women, and children all told.

Early in 1861, the Government made a treaty with the Cheyennes and Arapahoes by which these tribes gave up the larger part of the lands claimed by them in the new Territory of Colorado. For this they were to receive $450,000, which was to be paid in fifteen yearly installments, the tribes retaining as a reservation for their own use a tract of about seventy miles square located on both sides of the Arkansas River in the southeastern part of the Territory.

From the time of their first contact with the whites, the Cheyennes and Arapahoes were alternately friendly and hostile, just as their temper or whim dictated on any particular occasion. With the old trappers and hunters of the plains, the Cheyennes had the reputation of being the most treacherous and untrustworthy of any of the tribes in the west. The Arapahoes, while occasionally committing depredations against the whites, were said to be somewhat different in temperament, in that they were not so sullen and morose as the Cheyennes, and were less treacherous and more open and trust-worthy in their dealings. This estimate of the characteristics of the two tribes was fully confirmed in our contact with them in the early days of Colorado.

The Cheyennes were continuously hostile during the years 1855, 1856 and 1857, and during that period killed many whites and robbed numerous wagon trains along the Platte River. Finally in 1857, they were severely punished in a number of engagements by troops under the command of Colonel E. V. Sumner, and, as a result, gave little trouble during the next five or six years.

In early days the Arapahoes came in touch with the whites to a much greater extent than did the Cheyennes. Members of the latter tribe usually held aloof, and by their manner plainly expressed hatred of the white race. Horace Greeley, in a book describing his trip across the plains to California in 1859, tells of a large body of Arapahoes who were encamped on the outskirts of Denver in June of that year, as he says, on account of the protection they thought it gave them from their enemies, the Utes. This was the band which I have already mentioned as being in camp at Denver when we passed through there in June, 1860. Their relations with the whites could not have been very unpleasant or they would not have tarried so long. With the exception of a few scattered settlements of white people along the base of the mountains, the country for several hundred miles to the east was open to them. I am reciting all these facts as preliminary to my account of our war with these tribes which was soon to come, that the reader may know something of the savages with whom we had to deal.

From the year 1859 to the beginning of 1863, wagon trains that brought supplies from the Missouri River to Colorado continued to come and go without molestation, but from the latter part of 1862 on, it was noticed that the Indians of the plains were acquiring more guns and ammunition than was necessary for their ordinary hunting. Early in 1863 they began to attack and rob wagon trains, steal horses and threaten exposed settlements. However, nothing occurred to cause great alarm in this immediate Rocky Mountain region until in the summer of 1864. About the 20th of June of that year, word reached Colorado City that a day or two previously the Hungate family, living on Running Creek about forty miles northeast, had been murdered by Indians. The father and mother had been shot down and mutilated with horrible brutality, and the children who had tried to escape by running, were pursued and killed, so that not one of the family was left alive.

This news made the residents of Colorado City, and the settlers along the Fountain and on the Divide exceedingly uneasy, and thereafter they were constantly on the lookout, not knowing where the savages might next appear. Two or three weeks after the murder of the Hungate family, some cattle herders came into Colorado City late one evening and told of having seen near Templeton's Gap half a dozen mounted Indians who were acting suspiciously. Following the killing of the Hungate family and other acts of hostility at various places along the eastern frontier of our settlements, this was most alarming news. Early the next morning an armed party went to the point where the Indians had been seen, found their trail, and followed it. In this way it was discovered that at some time during the previous night the Indians had been on the hill that overlooks Colorado City on the north, evidently for the purpose of ascertaining the strength and preparedness of the settlement, with the view of a future attack. Their trail from that point led into the mountains west of the Garden of the Gods.

It was a well known fact that the tribes of the plains, taking advantage of the war of the Rebellion—which then was at its critical stage—had been attempting during the previous winter to make a coalition for the purpose of wiping out the settlements along the eastern base of the mountains. This fact and the mysterious movements of these Indians, taken in connection with their recent acts of hostility, seemed convincing proof that the band was here with evil intent.

At that time we were living on the west side of Camp Creek about half way between Colorado City and the Garden of the Gods. I had heard the alarming news while in town that morning and as a result was keeping a sharp lookout for the savages all the afternoon. However, the day passed without anything further having been seen or heard of them. Shortly after sundown, my brothers Edgar and Frank, who at that time were small boys, brought our stock in from the neighborhood of the Garden of the Gods. While I was helping them drive the cattle into the corral adjacent to our house, I happened to look up the valley of Camp Creek, and there about half a mile away, I saw six mounted Indians leading an extra horse. They were going easterly along an old Indian trail that ran across the hills just south of the Garden of the Gods and out into the valley of Camp Creek through a gap in the ridge at what was afterwards known as the Chambers Ranch, then across Camp Creek and over the Mesa, crossing Monument Creek just above the present town of Roswell. As soon as I saw these Indians I felt sure they were the party that had been trailed into Colorado City the night before. Without delay, I strapped on a revolver, took my gun, and rode to Colorado City as fast as my pony could travel, to report what I had seen. The people of that town had been greatly agitated during the day, and the news I brought added much to their excitement.

It was at once decided that the Indians must be followed and, if possible, the purpose of their visit here ascertained. In less than three-quarters of an hour, ten mounted and well armed men were ready for the pursuit. Those forming the party were Anthony Bott, Dr. Eggleston, William J.

Baird, A. T. Cone, Rensselaer Smith, William Garvin, myself, and three others whose names I do not recall. By eight o'clock we were crossing the Mesa along the trail followed by the Indians. We appreciated the necessity of making as little noise as possible, and all talking was carried on in an undertone. The trail led from the Mesa down to Monument Creek and then across the stream and northward parallel to it over a bed of gravel, through thick clumps of willows which enclosed it on both sides. It was a starlight night without clouds, but not light enough to see an object any distance away. Not expecting to find the Indians so soon, as we believed them to be far ahead of us, we were startled, just as we came up on the first rise out of the willows, to see them huddled together to the left of us under the bank apparently preparing to start a small camp fire. To the right of us were their ponies, which had been turned out to graze, we being directly between the Indians and their mounts. The Indians were just as surprised as we were, and for an instant, the situation was extremely tense. However, as we refrained from firing, the Indians, evidently realizing that they were at a disadvantage in not being able to reach their ponies, and hoping to make us believe that they were friendly, began calling out, "How! How!" as Indians usually do on meeting white people. Knowing that this probably was only a subterfuge, we kept our guns ready for instant use, while we tried to ascertain the object of their presence in this locality. Some of our people had a

slight knowledge of Spanish with which the Indians
seemed somewhat conversant, and by the use of
this language and by signs, we tried to let them know
that we were there only to learn their object in visiting this region and not to do them harm. We explained that if they could show that they were here
for no hostile purpose, they would be allowed to go
on their way unmolested, but in order to establish
this fact, it would be necessary for them to go with
us to Colorado City where competent interpreters
could be found; meanwhile, they must give up their
arms. Apparently they assented to this proposition, and at once surrendered such of their arms as
were in sight. Six of our party then dismounted,
and each took an Indian in charge while he was bringing in his pony. The Indian assigned to me was a
tall, slim fellow, fully six feet in height, and probably not much over twenty years of age. He appeared to take the situation quietly, and I had no
reason to apprehend any trouble with him. I allowed
him to lead his pony to the camp, where he mounted,
as all were permitted to do. We then formed the
savages in ranks of twos, placing a file of our men
on either side of them, each white man having charge
of the Indian next to him. This left two extra men
for the front and two to guard the rear. I was
in charge of the Indian on the left side of the rear
rank and had hold of his bridle with my right hand.
The order was given to march, and we started south,
but had proceeded only a few yards when the Indians
suddenly halted. From the time they had mounted

they had been talking animatedly with one another in their own language, which none of us understood. While this was going on, one of our men happened to see that an Indian had a knife in his hand. This was taken from him, and then we made a systematic search of the others and found that most of them had knives, and one a spear concealed under his blanket. It was with great difficulty that these weapons were twisted from their hands, but finally we thought that we had them completely disarmed. Then the order to move was given once more. Instantly, the Indians gave a tremendous war-whoop, shook their blankets, and were out from between us before we realized what was happening. The bridle rein that I was holding was jerked from my hand before I knew it. We were so dazed for the moment, that the Indians probably were seventy to one hundred feet away before our men began shooting. Meanwhile, my pony, which was of Indian breed, had become almost unmanageable; he seemed determined to go along with the Indian ponies, and I had great difficulty in restraining him. Before I succeeded, the animal had carried me so far in front that I was in great danger of being shot by my comrades. By the time I could get my pony under control, the Indians were too far away for me to shoot with hope of doing any execution, but in the meantime the others had been making such good use of their weapons that in a few minutes the affair was over, and five Indians had fallen from their ponies. Whether they had been killed or wounded we did not learn until some years later. When the occurrence ended, we could dimly see five of their ponies running riderless over the plains. It was now about ten o'clock, so we made little effort to locate the dead and wounded. After rounding up the ponies and gathering such of the belongings of the Indians, dropped in their flight, as were visible in the darkness, we started on our return to Colorado City, taking the ponies with us.

The whole occurrence was one of the weirdest scenes that I ever have witnessed. First, the sudden discovery of the Indians in the darkness of the night, to their surprise as well as ours; the group formed of the Indians with the whites surrounding them; the bringing in and mounting of the ponies; the start of the party and sudden halt, followed by the forcible taking of weapons from the Indians; the shrill war-whoop of the six savages ringing out in the solitude, followed by shots; and then the dim outline of riderless ponies running here and there over the plain. This dramatic scene, full of action, was completed a few minutes later by rounding up the riderless ponies, and beginning the march back to Colorado City. Our chosen route home took us over the present townsite of Colorado Springs, the only inhabitants of which at that time were antelope, coyotes and prairies dogs. On our way we passed over the present Colorado College reservation, then down what is now Cascade Avenue to a ford crossing Monument Creek about a quarter of a mile below the

present Rio Grande passenger station, then westerly
to Colorado City.

On the way home the question came into our
minds, whether we could have acted differently
under the circumstances. We knew that the tribes
to which these Indians belonged were at war with
the whites, and that, unless they were on their way
to fight the Utes, they were here on no peaceable
errand so far as our people were concerned. Their
course in going only to the foot of the mountains
showed that they were not seeking the Utes, and
their actions under cover of the previous night and
afterward, up to the time they were captured,
proved conclusively that they were here as scouts
of a larger party, to ascertain and report the strength
of the town and its surrounding settlements. When
first discovered they were in an out-of-the-way spot
and, from that time on until their capture, they
traveled over abandoned roads and trails, probably
hoping in this way to fulfil their mission without
detection. These things convinced us that we had
accomplished an important work, and the only regret
we had was that we had not been able to bring in
the captives.

Early the next morning several of our party returned to the scene of the occurrence, expecting to
find the bodies of the Indians that unquestionably
had been killed while trying to escape, but there
was nothing to indicate a struggle excepting a few
articles of clothing and personal adornment, and
marks upon the ground that showed where the

dead and wounded evidently had lain. Several years afterwards it was learned from members of the Cheyenne tribe, that three of this scouting party had been killed outright, one was so badly wounded that he died shortly afterward, and another was slightly wounded, and one had escaped unhurt. The last, with the aid of the one slightly wounded, had carried off and hidden the dead during the night. Many years afterwards a skeleton was found in a cleft of the rocks in a gulch not far from the place of this occurrence, which undoubtedly was the remains of one of the savages killed at the time referred to.

News of our evening's experience spread rapidly and created intense excitement in Colorado City and throughout this section. The people of El Paso County now realized that they were face to face with Indian troubles of the most serious nature, and that arrangements for defense of the town and surrounding country must be made immediately. The fighting strength of the whole region was exceedingly limited compared with the great horde of savages occupying our eastern frontier. Probably there were not over three hundred men of all ages in El Paso County at that time. And, as further showing the precarious position of the community, I wish to call attention to the fact that the inhabited part of the United States in 1864 extended but little west of the Missouri River, leaving our narrow strip of settlements along the eastern base of the Rocky Mountains in Colorado separated

from the nearest civilized communities to the east
by a stretch of the great plains approximately four
hundred miles in width, inhabited by wild and
savage tribes of nomadic Indians. This same condition existed northward all the way to the British
possessions, and to the west the Ute Indians held
undisputed sway to the border of the Great Salt
Lake Valley. On the south, with the exception of
a small part of New Mexico which was sparsely
settled by feeble and widely scattered communities
of Spanish speaking people, wild tribes roamed
over every part of the country for hundreds of miles.
From the foregoing it will be seen that the settlements of Colorado at this time were but a small island
of civilization in a sea of savagery. These settlements at times were completely cut off from civilization in every direction by this cordon of savage
tribes. Their very existence now was threatened,
with no hope of assistance from our national Government, because the Civil War was then at its most
critical stage, demanding elsewhere every resource of
the nation.

Threatened as they were by hordes of hostile savages, and surrounded by conditions that would have
had a disheartening effect upon any people not inured
to frontier life, the settlers of El Paso County had no
thought of allowing themselves to be driven out or
overwhelmed. Warning was sent at once to every
family throughout the county, with the result that
within a day or two, virtually all ranches were
abandoned. People from fifteen miles down the

Fountain valley below Colorado City, came to that town for protection. Those living below that point gathered at the extreme lower edge of the county and there built a place of defense. In Colorado City the work of constructing a fort around the Anway Hotel, an old log building, was started at once. Green pine logs, ten to fifteen inches in diameter and about fifteen feet long, were cut on the adjacent mountains, brought in, and set on end in the ground close together, entirely circling the hotel, making an enclosure considerably larger than that building. Portholes were cut in these logs at intervals for use in repelling an attack. During the next month or two all the women and children were gathered in this fortification at night. Throughout this time a picket force of three or four mounted men, of whom I often was one, was maintained night and day on the flat east of Monument Creek, the present site of Colorado Springs. There was scarcely a day during this period in which Indians were not seen at various points in the country immediately to the east of Colorado City and along the Fountain, but, as the people everywhere were watchful, the savages had slight opportunity for catching anyone unawares.

About two weeks after the encounter on Monument Creek, a messenger arrived at Colorado City, who had been sent by Governor Evans to warn the people of an impending attack by the Cheyennes and Arapahoes upon all settlements along the eastern frontier of Colorado. It appeared that the Governor had received information from Elbridge Gerry, one of his secret agents, that eight hundred hostile Cheyenne and Arapahoe warriors in camp at the Point of Rocks, near the head of Beaver Creek in eastern Colorado, had planned a simultaneous attack upon all the frontier settlements of Colorado from a point in the valley of the Platte River, one hundred miles north of Denver, to the Arkansas River at the mouth of the Fontaine-qui-Bouille. According to the program agreed upon by the Indians, one hundred warriors were to go to the valley of the Platte, two hundred and fifty to the head of Cherry Creek, and the remainder of the eight hundred to the valleys of the Fountain and Arkansas Rivers. Upon reaching the appointed localities, these parties were to be divided into small bands, each one of which was to attack a farmhouse, kill its occupants, loot the property and run off stock.

Elbridge Gerry, from whom the information of this proposed raid was received, was the grandson of a signer of the Declaration of Independence, and although an educated man, had lived with the Indians for a good many years and married a Cheyenne woman. At this time he was living with his Indian wife on a stock ranch in the valley of the Platte River, sixty to seventy miles below Denver. It was here that the information reached him through two Cheyenne chiefs, who came to warn him of the impending danger. Gerry received the word about midnight and early the next morning started on horseback for Denver to notify Governor Evans, arriving there about eleven o'clock that night, having ridden the sixty or seventy miles without resting. As the date set for the raid was but a day or two distant, Governor Evans at once dispatched messengers in every direction to notify the people. The one sent to Colorado City reached that place the next afternoon, and warning was immediately sent to the few ranchmen down the Fountain and east of Colorado City, who, for urgent reasons, had been compelled to return temporarily to their homes.

The following day, small bands of Indians appeared along the whole eastern frontier of El Paso County, but their raid was a failure, as the warning given through the occurrence on Monument Creek, and that sent by the Governor, had put every one on guard. Consequently, the savages found that the settlers at every point either had fled, or were ready to defend themselves. That the information given by Gerry was absolutely correct was shown by the fact that the Indians appeared at the appointed time along the entire frontier of Colorado, from the Platte to the Arkansas River. However, since, in almost every locality, as in El Paso County, they found the settlers on the lookout, the wholesale slaughter planned by the savages did not take place. After killing one man near Fort Lupton on the Platte River below Denver, and two or three others near the head of Cherry Creek, besides stealing many cattle, the larger part of the Indians returned to their rendezvous out on the plains, leaving a few warriors along the borders to harass the settlers during the remainder of the summer.

The Point of Rocks on Beaver Creek, where the eight hundred Indians were in camp, is less than one hundred miles northeast of Colorado City. It is practically certain, as we assumed from the first, that the Indians we surprised on Monument Creek two or three weeks previously were from that camp, and had been sent out to secure information concerning the settlements of this region, preparatory to the raid they were then planning. There is every probability that an awful calamity would have befallen the settlers of El Paso County had not the Monument Creek occurrence aroused our people to a full realization of their impending danger. At that time, news traveled slowly; weekly mails then were the only method of disseminating news, as telegraph lines had not yet been built into this part of the Territory, and there was no newspaper published in the county. As a result, news of Indian raids and outbreaks in other parts of the Territory often were a week or more in reaching the people of El Paso County. Had the news brought by the messenger from the Governor been our first warning, it would then have been too late to gather in any considerable portion of our scattered settlers before the appearance of the Indians. Governor Evans, in his evidence before the Committee on the Conduct of the War, at Washington, in March, 1865, telling of this incident, expressed the opinion that had the plan of the Indians been carried out without previous notice to the settlers, it would have resulted in the most wholesale and extensive massacre that ever has occurred in this country.

CHAPTER VII

WITH THE THIRD COLORADO CAVALRY AT THE BATTLE OF SAND CREEK

EARLY in September, 1864, a company of the First Colorado Cavalry, on its way to Denver from one of the forts in New Mexico, stopped for the noon meal at Jimmy's Camp, about ten miles east of Colorado City. Not having seen any Indians on the march, both officers and men of the company were exceedingly skeptical as to there being any in this region, and made sport of the settlers for their apparently unnecessary alarm. Upon making camp the soldiers turned their horses out to graze, placing a trooper in charge of them. The animals gradually wandered farther and farther away from camp, and were about a half mile distant when a band of Indians suddenly came dashing out of the timber near by. Almost before the guard realized what was happening, the savages had rounded up the horses and were off over the hills with them, yelling back taunts as they rode away. The following day these soldiers came tramping into Colorado City on foot, a dejected lot. It gave the settlers great pleasure to jeer at them as they passed, knowing that the loss of the horses was due entirely to a lack of proper precaution on the part of the officers, who had refused to believe the information given them.

During the remainder of the summer following the Monument Creek incident, in addition to my picket duty, I helped harvest a field of wheat on our Camp Creek ranch. All crops down the Fountain and along its tributaries were harvested by armed parties that summer. In our case, father and I were assisted by two other men. On going into the wheat field we stacked our guns and never moved more than fifty feet away from them in our work, all the time keeping a sharp lookout for Indians.

Repeatedly during this period, the Governor of Colorado called the attention of our General Government to the helpless condition of Colorado's settlements and the inability of the Territory to protect them, and urged that national troops be sent here. However, this was virtually impossible, as the entire military force of the nation at that time was needed elsewhere in suppressing the Rebellion. It is true that the twelve companies composing the First Regiment of Colorado Cavalry were distributed along the frontier of the Territory, but these necessarily had to be scattered over such a wide extent of country that there seldom was more than one company in a place; consequently, they were of little use in the way of defense. The people of El Paso County realized all this and knew that they must depend in a large measure upon themselves for protection from the savages. Facing this predicament, apparently they took all necessary precautions and acted wisely in every emergency. Meanwhile, the Indians were in virtual possession of all lines of travel from the east and every coach that came through from the Missouri River to Denver had to run the gauntlet. Some arrived riddled with bullets, others were captured and their passengers killed. Instances were known where the victims were shot full of arrows, roasted alive, and subjected to every kind of cruelty a savage could devise.

Finally, after many urgent appeals, the Governor of Colorado was authorized to raise a regiment of one-hundred-day men, to be used in protecting the frontier settlements of the Territory and in punishing the hostile Indians. Lieutenant George L. Shoup, of the First Colorado, was commissioned Colonel of the new regiment, which was designated as the Third Colorado Volunteer Cavalry. Colonel Shoup, while serving as an officer of the First Colorado Cavalry, had proved himself to be very able and efficient. Afterwards, he was for many years United States Senator from the State of Idaho. From the day that he received his appointment, Colonel Shoup proceeded with great energy to organize his command. Recruiting officers were placed in almost every town in the Territory, and, in less than thirty days, between eight and nine hundred men had enlisted. A number besides myself from El Paso County joined this regiment at the first call. Among the El Paso recruits were John Copeland, Anthony Bott, Robert Finley, Henry Coby, Samuel

Murray, John Wolf, A. J. Templeton, Henry Miller, myself and several others whose names I have forgotten. The recruits from El Paso County were combined with those from Pueblo County and mustered into the United States service at Denver on the 29th day of August, 1864, as Company G, Third Regiment, Colorado Volunteer Cavalry. Our officers were O. H. P. Baxter of Pueblo County, Captain; Joseph Graham of the same county, First Lieutenant; and A. J. Templeton of El Paso County, Second Lieutenant. Within a short time after we had been mustered in at Denver, our Company marched back on foot through El Paso County to a point on the Arkansas River, five miles east of Pueblo, where we remained for the next two months waiting for horses and equipment. Meanwhile, we were being drilled and prepared for active military service.

On the last day of October and the first day of November of that year, there was a tremendous snow storm along the eastern base of the Rocky Mountains in Colorado. The snow fall at our camp was twenty inches in depth, at Colorado City it was over two feet on the level, and on the Divide, still deeper. All supplies for the Company had to be brought by teams from the Commissary Department at Denver. The depth of the snow on the Divide for a time made this impossible, and a food shortage at our camp soon was imminent. As there appeared to be little hope of relief in the near future, our Captain instructed every one who had a home within a reasonable distance, to go there and remain until further orders. In accordance with these instructions, myself and a half dozen others from El Paso County started out before daylight the next morning and tramped laboriously all day through deep snow along the Arkansas and Fountain valleys. For a part of the way a wagon or two had gone over the road since the storm, making it exceedingly rough, especially so after the sun had gone down and the snow had frozen. As a result, we were nearly worn out by dusk, and it was eleven o'clock that night before we found a place to stay, by which time we were utterly exhausted. Our tramp was resumed early the next morning, but I was only able to reach the home of one of my comrades, a few miles beyond. There I remained for the next two days, too nearly used up to proceed at once to my own home in Colorado City, six miles away. However, two weeks of complete rest at home put me in good condition again. At the end of that time we were notified by the Captain that supplies had been received and were ordered to return to camp at once.

Two or three weeks before we left camp, the company had been clothed in light blue uniforms such as were then worn by the cavalry branch of the United States Army, and soon after our return, equipment of arms, ammunition, and the necessary accoutrement was issued. The guns given us were old, out of date Austrian muzzle-loading muskets of large bore, and our ammunition consisted of paper cartridges from which one had to bite off the end when loading. These guns sent a bullet rather viciously, but one never could tell where it would hit.

A week or two later our horses arrived. They were a motley looking group composed of every kind of equine animal from pony to plow horse. The saddles and bridles were the same as those used by the regular cavalry service, and were good of their kind. I had the misfortune to draw a raw-boned, squarely built old plow horse, upon which I thereafter spent many uncomfortable hours. If the order came to trot, followed by an order to gallop, it took so long to get my steed well under way on a trot, that he would be going like the wind before I could bring him to a gallop. Meanwhile, his rough trot would be shaking me to pieces. From what I have said it will be understood that our equipment, as to arms and mounts, was of the poorest class, evidently from the reject of the armies in the east.

A majority of the Third Regiment had been in camp near Denver during all this time. This inactivity had caused a great deal of complaint among both officers and enlisted men. The regiment had been recruited principally from the business men, miners and farmers of the Territory, and the understanding was that they were to be given active service against the hostile Indians at the earliest possible moment. However, undoubtedly the delay was unavoidable, due to the fact that the necessary horses had to be driven to Colorado from east of the Missouri River, and this took more than a month. At last, about the middle of November, everything was ready and the main part of the Third Regiment, augmented by three companies of the First Colorado, all under command of Colonel Shoup, immediately started on its way south towards a destination known only to the principal officers. The expedition was under direction of Colonel John M. Chivington, Commander of the Military District of Colorado. Our company joined the regiment as it passed our camp about the 25th of November, and from that time its real hardships began.

We steadily marched down the valley of the Arkansas River, going into camp between seven and eight o'clock each night; but by the time we had eaten supper and cared for our horses, it was after ten o'clock. Reveille sounded at four o'clock the next morning and before daylight we were on the march again. In order that news of our approach should not reach the Indians, every man whom we met on the road was taken in charge, and guards were placed at all ranches for the same purpose. We arrived at Fort Lyons about four o'clock in the afternoon of November 28, to the great surprise of its garrison, as they were not aware that the regiment had left the vicinity of Denver. A picket was thrown around the Fort at once to prevent the trappers or Indian traders, who generally hung around such places, from notifying the savages of our presence.

Soon after arriving at Fort Lyon, we were informed that our wagon train now would be left behind, and each man was instructed to get from the commissary a few pounds of bacon and sufficient hard-tack to last three or four days, these articles of food to be carried along in our saddlebags. At eight o'clock that night, the regiment took up its line of march across the prairie in a direction almost due north from Fort Lyon. Each company was formed in ranks of fours, and we traveled rapidly from the start. It was walk, trot, gallop, dismount and lead, all night long. I had slept but little for two or three nights previous to this, and consequently, I found this all night marching terribly exhausting. During the latter part of the night I would willingly have run the risk of being scalped by Indians for a half hour's sleep. Sometime after midnight, the regiment's guide led us through one of the shallow lakes that are so plentiful on the plains of that region. He was suspected of being more friendly to the Indians than to the whites, and it was thought probable that he planned this purposely, hoping that the water would reach and spoil our ammunition, making it ineffective in the anticipated engagement. During the night, in order to keep awake, many of us had been nibbling on the hard-tack that had been issued to us, and were greatly disgusted in the morning when we found it very much alive.

It was a bright, clear, starlight night, the air crisp and uncomfortably cool, as might have been expected at that time of year. Just as the sun was coming up over the eastern horizon, we reached the top of a ridge, and away off down in the valley to the northwest, we saw a great number of Indian tents, forming a village of unusual size. We knew at once that this village was our objective point. Off to the left, between the place where we were and the village, there was a large number of Indian ponies scattered over the plain grazing. Two or three minutes later, orders came directing our battalion to capture this herd. Under command of a major of the regiment we started immediately on the run in order to get between the ponies and the Indian camp before our presence was discovered. We had not proceeded any great distance when we saw half a dozen mounted Indians coming from the direction of the camp, riding rapidly toward the herd. However, upon seeing our large force they hesitated a moment, and then started back to their village as fast as their ponies could take them. We were not long in securing the herd, which consisted of between five and six hundred ponies. The officer in command detailed a small force to take charge of the animals, with instructions to drive them away to some point where they would be in no danger of recapture.

The remainder of our battalion then started directly for the Indian village, which lay over a little ridge to the north. In the meantime, the main part of the command had marched rapidly northward down the slope to Sand Creek, along the northern bank of which, and a mile or more to the westward, the Indian camp was located. Crossing the creek, the regiment proceeded along the north bank until near the village, where they met the Indians, and then the battle began. At the same time our battalion, after capturing the horses, was coming in from the south. This left an opening for the Indians to the westward, up the valley of Sand Creek, and also to the northward, across the hills toward the Smoky Hill River. Before our battalion had crossed the low ridge that cut off a view of the village, the firing had become general. When we first sighted the Indian camp there were a good many ponies not far away to the north of it, and now as we came in view of it again, we saw a large number of Indians—supposedly squaws and children—hurrying northward on these ponies, out of the way of danger.

After the engagement began, the Indian warriors concentrated along Sand Creek, using its high banks on both sides as a means of defense. Sand Creek at this point is about two hundred yards wide, the banks on each side of which are almost perpendicular and from six to twelve feet high. The engagement later extended up this creek for three or four miles from the Indian encampment. Our capture of the ponies placed the savages at a great disadvantage, as an Indian is not accustomed to fighting on foot. The number of warriors in the village was about equal to our force, and, had they been mounted, we would have had great difficulty in defeating them, as they were better armed than we were, and the ponies were far superior for military purposes, to the horses of our command.

Throughout the engagement our battery did effective work, its shells, as a rule, keeping the Indians from concentrating in considerable numbers at any single point.   However, soon after the beginning of the fight, I saw a line of from seventy-five to one hundred Indians gathered at one place, receive a charge as steadily as veterans, and their shooting was so effective that the soldiers were forced to fall back for a time.   But returning to the charge soon after, the troopers forced the Indians to retire behind the banks of the creek, which they did in leisurely manner, leaving a large number of their dead upon the field.   The company to which I belonged became disorganized early in the fight, as did a number of others; and after that we fought in little groups wherever it seemed the most effective work could be done.   After the first few shots at the beginning of the engagement, I had no fear whatever, nor did I see others displaying the least concern as to their own safety.   The fight soon became general all up and down Sand Creek valley, the Indians constantly firing from their places of defense along the stream and a continuous fusilade being kept up by the soldiers, shooting at every Indian that came within range of their guns.   I think it was in this way that some of the squaws were killed, as it was utterly impossible at a distance of two hundred yards, to distinguish between the sexes, on account of similarity in their dress.

As our detachment moved up the valley, we frequently came in line of the firing and the bullets whizzed past us unpleasantly, but fortunately, not one of our group was hit. At one point we ran across a wounded man, a former resident of El Paso County, but serving in a company raised elsewhere. A short time previously, as he was passing near the creek, a squaw hidden behind the bank had shot an arrow into his shoulder, inflicting a very painful wound. He was being cared for by members of his own company. A bit further along we crossed over to the north side of the creek and then moved leisurely up the valley, shooting at the Indians whenever any were in sight. By this time most of them had burrowed into the soft sand of the banks, which formed a comparatively safe place of defense, and from which they could shoot at the whites with a minimum of exposure.

Soon after this we joined a detachment which was carrying on a brisk engagement with a considerable force of Indians who were hidden behind large piles of driftwood along the banks and out towards the center of Sand Creek, the bed of which was unusually wide at that point. Our men were posted in a little depression just back from the north bank, but a few of them had crawled forward as far as they dared go, and were shooting into the driftwood, trying to drive the Indians from cover. Soon after I reached this point, a member of the company from Boulder, having stepped out a little too far and then turned around to speak to one of us, was shot in the back, the bullet going straight through his chest. Realizing at once that he was badly wounded, probably fatally, he asked to be taken to his company. I volunteered to go with him and, after helping him on his horse, we started across the prairie to where his company was supposed to be. With every breath bubbles of blood came from his lungs, and I had little hope that he would be able to rejoin his comrades alive. As it was, just as we reached the company he fainted and was caught by his captain as he was falling from his horse. I returned at once to the place that I had left and found the action still going on. During my absence, our little force had been considerably increased by soldiers from other parts of the battlefield. It now was decided to make it so hot for the savages by continuous firing that they would be compelled to leave their places of cover. Soon two or three of the Indians exposed themselves and instantly were shot down. In a short time the remaining ones started across the creek towards its southern bank. They ran in a zigzag manner, jumping from one side to the other, evidently hoping by so doing that we would be unable to hit them, but by taking deliberate aim we dropped every one before any reached the other bank.

About this time orders came from the commanding officer directing us to return at once to the Indian camp, as information had been received that we were liable to be attacked by a large force of Indians coming from the Smoky Hill River where it was known they were congregated. Obeying this order, we marched down the creek, and as we went were repeatedly fired at by Indians hidden behind its banks. We returned the fire, but the savages were so well protected that there was no reason to believe any of our shots proved effective. At one place an Indian child three or four years of age ran out to us, holding up its hands and crying piteously. At first I was inclined to take it up, but changed my mind when it occurred to me that I should have no means of caring for the little fellow. I knew that there were Indians concealed within a couple of hundred yards of where we were, who certainly would look after him as soon as we were out of the way; consequently we left him to be cared for by his own people. Every one of our party expressed sympathy for the little fellow and no one dreamed of harming him.

As we neared the Indian camp we passed the place where the severest fighting had occurred earlier in the day, and here we saw many dead Indians, a few of whom were squaws. At the edge of the camp we came upon our own dead, who had been brought in and placed in a row. There were seven of them, and we were informed that there were forty wounded in a hospital improvised for the occasion. Among the dead I expected to find the Boulder man whom I had taken to his company, but, strange to relate, he survived his wound. I saw him two or three years afterwards apparently entirely recovered. The number of Indians killed has been variously estimated at from two hundred and fifty to five hundred. My own opinion is that two hundred and fifty to three hundred would cover all losses sustained by the hostiles.

We reached the Indian camp about four o'clock in the afternoon, the battle having continued without cessation from early morning until that time. The companies were immediately formed into a hollow square, inside of which our horses were picketed. I was so utterly exhausted from want of sleep and food, as were many others, that I hunted up a buffalo robe, of which there were large numbers scattered around, threw myself down on it and was asleep almost as soon as I touched the ground. The next thing I remember was being awakened for supper about dusk. We were told that we must sleep with our guns in our arms, ready for use at any moment. Near midnight we were aroused by a more than vigorous call of our officers, ordering us to fall in line immediately to repel an attack. We rushed out, but were in such a sleepy condition that we had difficulty in forming a line, as hardly any of us knew what we were doing. In the evening, by order of the commanding officer, all Indian tents outside of our encampment had been set on fire and now were blazing brightly all around us. We heard occasional shots in various directions, and out in the light of the fire could be seen what looked like hundreds of Indian ponies running hither and thither. Apparently there were no riders, but we knew that Indians, in an encounter, always try to conceal their bodies from the enemy by lying over on the far side of their mounts. From the number of what appeared to be horses that could be seen in every direction, it seemed that surely we were due to be overwhelmed.

However, after forming in line and while waiting for the attack, it was discovered that what we had imagined to be ponies, were only the numerous dogs of the Indian camp, which, having lost their masters, were runnning about wildly. Nevertheless, it was evident that Indians were all around us, as our pickets by this time had been fired upon and driven in from every side of the camp. As no attack was made, a little later, the regiment was divided into two lines, one of which was marched fifty feet in front of the other. Then, being instructed to secure blankets, we wrapped ourselves in them and, with our guns in our arms, lay down and slept the remainder of the night.

In the Indian camp we found an abundance of flour, bacon, coffee and other articles of food from which the regiment could have maintained itself for an indefinite length of time, had it been necessary. In many of the tents there were articles of wearing apparel and other belongings which evidently had been taken from wagon-trains and ranches that the Indians had looted. More than a dozen scalps of white people, some of them from the heads of women and children as evidenced by the color and fineness of the hair, were found in the tents. One of the scalps showed plainly by its condition that it had been taken only recently. Several members of the regiment found horses and mules in the Indian herd that had been stolen from them by the hostiles in their various raids during the preceding year. This Indian camp was overflowing with proof that these savages were among those who had been raiding the settlements of Colorado during the previous summer, killing people, robbing wagon-trains, burning houses, running off stock, and committing outrages of which only a savage would be guilty. This evidence only corroborated in the strongest possible manner what we already knew.

About noon on the day following the battle, our wagon-train came up and was formed into a hollow square in the center of the camp. Then the lines were drawn in so that the wagons could be used as a means of defense. Our officers were aware that the large body of Cheyennes and Arapahoes on the Smoky Hill River, from sixty to seventy-five miles distant, might attack us at any time. Throughout the day, many Indians were seen hovering around camp in every direction, and our scouting parties were seldom able to get far away without being fired upon by the savages. Several men were killed and a number wounded in skirmishes that took place. During the second night of our stay on the battleground, we were kept in line continuously, with our arms ready for use at a moment's notice, and at intervals during the entire night there was an exchange of shots at various points around the camp.

I never fully understood why we did not follow up our victory by an attack upon the hostile bands on the Smoky Hill River, but I presume that it was on account of the inferior horses, arms, and equipment of our regiment. Probably Colonel Chivington, taking these facts into consideration, decided that his force was not strong enough to fight successfully such large numbers as were known to be in that locality. The third day after the battle, the command took up its line of march down the Big Sandy and followed it to the Arkansas River, from which point we moved easterly along the north side of this stream to the western boundary line of Kansas.

Soon after reaching the Arkansas River we struck the trail of a large party of Indians traveling down its valley. The savages seemed to be in great haste, as they had thrown away their camp kettles, buffalo robes, and every other thing that might impede their flight. Realizing that the Indians could not be overtaken by the entire command on account of the poor condition of many of the horses, Colonel Chivington specially detailed three hundred of the best mounted and best armed men and sent them forward by forced marches in pursuit of the savages. But even this plan proved unsuccessful and the chase was finally abandoned when near the Kansas line.

The term of enlistment of our regiment having already expired, the command now was reluctantly faced about and the return march to Denver begun. From the time of leaving the Sand Creek battle-field the weather had been exceptionally cold and disagreeable; sharp piercing winds blew from the north almost incessantly, making us extremely uncomfortable during the day and even more so at night.

Being without tents and compelled to sleep on the open prairie, we found the cold at times almost unbearable. The thin, shoddy government blankets that had been issued to us at the time of our enlistment offered the slightest possible protection against the bitter winds; consequently those were fortunate indeed who could find a ravine or gully in which to make their beds.

At the time our non-commissioned officers were appointed, I was named as one of the corporals. The principal benefit that I received from the office was exemption, with one exception, from guard or picket duty. However, the only time I served as Corporal of the Guard came on one of the coldest nights of the winter.

Our march back to Denver was leisurely and uneventful. In due course of time we reached our destination, and were mustered out of service on the 29th day of December, 1864. We then dispersed to our homes, satisfied with the work that had been done, and convinced that it needed only a little further punishment of the savages to settle permanently the Indian troubles, at least as far as the Territory of Colorado was concerned.

CHAPTER VIII

DEFENSE OF THE BATTLE OF SAND CREEK

FEW events in American history have been the subject of so much misrepresentation as the Battle of Sand Creek. It has gone down into history as an indefensible massacre of peaceable Indians, and perhaps nothing that can now be said will change this erroneous impression in the world at large, notwithstanding the fact that the accusation is unjust and a libel upon the people of Colorado. Worst of all, this misrepresentation was given wide publicity through the reports of two Congressional Committees following unfair, one-sided and prejudiced investigations. Unfortunately, at that time Colorado was a Territory and had no Senators or Representatives in Congress to defend the good name of its people, its only representative being a Delegate in Congress without vote, consequently, without influence. To add to the bad features of the situation, our people at home realized but dimly what was taking place at Washington until after the mischief had been done; consequently, the Congressional investigations virtually went by default, so far as the people of Colorado were concerned.

It should be kept in mind that Colorado was at that time, comparatively speaking, more remote from the rest of the country than Alaska is today, and the means of disseminating news throughout the Territory were exceedingly limited. From early November, 1864, until March, 1865, the coaches that carried the mail between the Missouri River towns and Denver ceased running on account of the hostility of the Indians, and all this time Colorado was practically cut off from the rest of the world, except for limited telegraph service that did not reach any point in the Territory outside of Denver. Thus the enemies of Colonel Chivington had full sway in their efforts to blacken his reputation and that of the citizens forming the Third Colorado. I wish to emphasize the fact that a large majority of that regiment were high class representative men. Colorado had already contributed its full quota to the army fighting the Rebellion, and that without a draft having been made; but when the emergency arose caused by the defenseless condition of her settlements, numerous farmers, merchants, and professional men, many of whom would have been exempt in case of a draft, enlisted in the Third Colorado, making that regiment a more representative organization than any that had previously been raised.

It was a fact well known in Colorado that the accusations on which the various Congressional and military investigations were based had their origin in the petty jealousy of military officers. It was the same kind of spirit that caused the loss of more than one battle in the Civil War.   However, at Sand Creek, on account of the secrecy of preparations, the victory could not be prevented, but the good effects could be and were, in a large measure nullified, to the great detriment of the people of Colorado.   And this was done by officers who formerly were residents of the Territory and indebted to it for their official positions.   But to understand fully the animus of these men, it will be necessary for the reader to know something of their history, as well as that of the other officers involved in the controversy.

Colonel John M. Chivington, who was in command at the Battle of Sand Creek, and who was the principal target throughout the various investigations, was the Reverend John M. Chivington who was in charge of the Methodist Missions in Colorado at the time we arrived in 1860.   He was a member of the Kansas-Nebraska Conference, and had been selected for this mission work because of his unusual energy, ability and force of character.   The prominent position that the Methodist Church early assumed in the Territory under his administration, confirmed the wisdom of his appointment.

Upon the organization of the First Colorado Volunteer Cavalry in the early part of 1862, Rev. Mr. Chivington resigned his position as Presiding Elder of the Rocky Mountain District, and was commissioned Major of the new regiment.   He soon became the regiment's most influential officer.   He was the most prominent figure in its wonderful march to New Mexico, and the remarkable victories won by it over the invading Texan Confederates were largely due to his brilliant leadership. By the end of the active campaign, Major Chivington had become so popular with the officers and enlisted men that upon the resignation of John P. Slough, the Colonel of the Regiment, he was promoted to that position over Lieutenant Colonel Samuel F. Tappan on petition of a large majority of the commissioned officers of the regiment. This was the beginning of all his troubles, as will be seen further along in my narrative. Later Colonel Chivington was appointed by General Canby to the command of the Military District of New Mexico and was afterward transferred to the same position in Colorado, which office he held at the time of the Battle of Sand Creek.

Colonel Chivington was a man of commanding presence and possessed marked ability, both as a preacher and an army officer. I can do no better than quote what General Frank Hall says of him in his History of Colorado:

"Though wholly unskilled in the science of war, with but little knowledge of drill and discipline, Major Chivington, of Herculean frame and gigantic stature, possessed the courage and exhibited the discreet boldness, dash and brilliancy in action, which distinguished the more illustrious of our volunteer officers during the war. His first encounter with the Texans at Apache Cañon was sudden and more or less of a surprise. The occasion demanded not only instantaneous action, but such disposition of

his forces as to render it most effective against superior numbers and the highly advantageous position of the enemy.   He seemed to comprehend at a
glance the necessities of the situation and handled his
troops like a veteran.   His daring and rapid movement across the mountains and the total destruction
of the enemy's train, simultaneously with the battle
of Pigeon's Ranch, again attested his excellent
generalship.   It put an end to the war by forcing
the invaders to a precipitate flight back to their
homes.   He hesitated at nothing.   Sure of the de-
votion and gallantry of his men, he was always
ready for any adventure, however desperate, which
promised the discomfiture of his adversaries.

We cannot but believe that had his application for
the transfer of his regiment to the Army of the
Potomac, or to any of the great armies operating
under Grant, been acceded to, he would have made a
still prouder record for himself, the Regiment, and the
Territory.   That he was endowed with the capa-
bilities of a superior commander, none who saw him
in action will deny.   On a broader field, he might
have won imperishable renown."

The overshadowing reputation made by Colonel
Chivington in the campaign against the Texas invaders of New Mexico, and his subsequent promo-
tion to the Colonelcy of the Regiment over Lieutenant-Colonel Samuel F. Tappan, although apparently
acquiesced in at the time, aroused a spirit of jealousy, envy, and antagonism against him on the part

of a small group of officers headed by Lieutenant
Colonel Tappan and Major E. W. Wynkoop. This
antagonism manifested itself on every possible occasion. After their return from New Mexico, these
officers never allowed an opportunity to pass for
discrediting and injuring the "Preacher Colonel,"
and after the battle of Sand Creek, they never
tired of referring to it as an evidence of his un-
fitness.

Lieutenant-Colonel Tappan had been a professional newspaper correspondent in Washington before entering the army; consequently, he had no
trouble in filling the eastern press with exaggerated
and distorted accounts of the battle. In his crusade,
he had the active support of all the Indian traders,
interpreters, half-breeds, and others of similar character who congregated around an Indian agency. He
also had the sympathy of the Indian Bureau at
Washington, which usually took the sentimental
side of every question affecting the Indians.

Prior to 1864, the Indians of the plains that had
been on the warpath during the summer, were permitted to make peace in the fall, remain unmolested
during the winter, receive annuities, and accumulate
ammunition for the coming summer's raids; but in
that year the overtures of the Cheyennes and Arapahoes were rejected, except upon the condition that
they submit to the military authorities. This they
not only refused to do, but continued their depredations at places convenient to their winter camps, and
received from Colonel Chivington's command the

punishment they so richly deserved. This meant great financial loss to the traders and hangers-on around the Indian Agency at Fort Lyon; consequently, these people also actively joined in the attack upon Colonel Chivington.

This crusade resulted in two Congressional investigations of the battle and a hearing by a Military Commission. Before the Joint Special Committee of the two Houses of Congress, the principal witnesses were Major Wynkoop, Captain Soule, Lieutenant Cramer, two Indian agents, two Indian traders, two half-breeds, and one interpreter, to sustain the accusations, and only Governor Evans and three minor officers of the Third Colorado Regiment for the defense. Aside from Governor Evans and the three officers just mentioned, the witnesses were extremely hostile to Colonel Chivington, and apparently were ready to go to any length in their testimony in order to blacken his reputation and that of the Third Colorado. Neither Colonel Chivington nor Colonel Shoup was present or represented in any way. In the hearing before the Committee on the Conduct of the War, Colonel Shoup was not represented, and Colonel Chivington only by means of a deposition. As a result of these partial and one-sided investigations, both Committees condemned Chivington and pronounced the battle a massacre. The most unjust and absurd investigation of all was that made by a Military Commission which was composed of three officers of the First Colorado Cavalry, all subordinates of Colonel Chivington, headed by his inveterate enemy, Lieutenant-Colonel Samuel F. Tappan.

The accusation made at each hearing was that the Cheyenne and Arapahoe Indians attacked by Colonel Chivington's command at Sand Creek, were not only friendly to the whites, but were under the protection of the military authorities at Fort Lyon, and that the battle was, by the consent, if not by the direction, of Colonel Chivington, an indiscriminate massacre. All of this, I believe, is proved to be untrue to the satisfaction of any reasonable person, by the facts related in my account of the battle and of the Indian hostilities in El Paso County—where I resided— and elsewhere throughout Colorado, during the year and a half preceding this event. In corroboration of my statements as to the hostile character of the Indians punished at Sand Creek and to show the conditions existing elsewhere in the Territory previous thereto, I quote from Governor Evans' reply to the report of the Committees on the Conduct of the War, dated August 6, 1865.

In the Territorial days of Colorado, the Governor was ex-officio Superintendent of Indian affairs within its boundaries. At the time of the Sand Creek Battle, Honorable John Evans, formerly of Illinois, was Governor of Colorado, and had held that office since the spring of 1862. Governor Evans was a personal friend of President Lincoln and had been appointed Governor by the latter on account of his high character, great ability, and efficiency in administrative affairs. Governor Evans' supervision of Indian

Affairs in Colorado during 1862, 1863, and 1864, made him a better qualified witness as to the conditions existing among the various tribes during these years than any man of that period. The following extract from his reply to that part of the report of the Committee on the Conduct of the War, which, under the heading "Massacre of the Cheyenne Indians," refers to his responsibility in the matter, tells of the attitude of the Indians towards the whites during that period and of his own strenuous efforts to avert hostilities.   Among other things he says:

"The war opened early in the spring of 1864. The people of the East absorbed in the greater interest of the Rebellion, know but little of its history. Stock was stolen, ranches destroyed, houses burned, freight trains plundered, and their contents carried away or scattered upon the plains; settlers in the frontier counties murdered, or forced to seek safety for themselves and families in block-houses and interior towns; emigrants to our Territory were surprised in their camps, children were slain, and wives taken prisoners; our trade and travel with the States cut off; the necessities of life were at starvation prices; the interests of the Territory were being damaged to the extent of millions; every species of atrocity and barbarity which characterizes savage warfare was committed."

"The records of these offices also show that, in the autumn of 1863, I was reliably advised from various sources that nearly all the Indians of the plains had formed an alliance for the purpose of going to war in the spring, and I immediately commenced my efforts to avert the imminent danger. From that time forward, by letter, by telegram, and personal representation to the Commissioner of Indian Affairs, the Secretary of War, the commanders of the department and district; by traveling for weeks in the wilderness of the plains; by distribution of annuities and presents; by sending notice to the Indians to leave the hostile alliance; by every means within my power, I endeavored to preserve peace and protect the interests of the people of the Territory."

"I had appealed by telegraph, June 14, to the War Department for authority to call the militia into the United States service, or to raise one-hundred-day troops; also had written to our delegate in Congress to see why I got no response, and had received his reply to the effect that he could learn nothing about it; had received a notice from the department commander, declining to take the responsibility of asking the militia for United States service, throwing the people entirely on the necessity of taking care of themselves."

"The Third Regiment was organized under authority from the War Department, subsequently received by telegraph, and under a subsequent proclamation issued on the 13th of August, and was regularly mustered into the service of the United States about three months before the battle the committee were investigating occurred."

In summing up, Governor Evans says:

"First: The Committee, for the evident purpose of maintaining their position that these Indians had not been engaged in war, say the prisoners they held were purchased. The testimony is to the effect that they captured them.

"Second: The committee say that these Indians were and always had been friendly, and had committed no acts of hostility or depredations. The public documents to which I refer show conclusively that they had been hostile, and had committed many acts of hostility and depredation.

"Third: They say that I joined in sending these Indians to Fort Lyon. The published report of the Commisioner of Indian Affairs, and of the Indian council, show that I left them entirely in the hands of the military authorities.

"Fourth: They say nothing seems to have been done by the authorities to prevent hostilities. The public documents and files of the Indian Bureau, and of my superintendency, show constant and unremitting diligence and effort on my part to prevent hostilities and protect the people."

If anything in addition to Governor Evans' statement is needed to prove the hostility of the Indians attacked at Sand Creek, it will be found in the admission of the Indians themselves made at the council held by Governor Evans with Cheyenne and Arapahoe chiefs in Denver about sixty days prior to the battle. At this council there were present Black Kettle, White Antelope, Head Chief of the central band of Cheyennes, Bull Bear, leader of the Cheyenne Dog Soldiers, Neva, sub-Chief of the Arapahoes, and several other minor chiefs of those tribes. These chiefs admitted that their people had been and were still committing depredations, as the following extract from the report of the council, taken down at that time, conclusively shows:

Gov. Evans: Who committed the murder of the Hungate family on Running Creek?

Neva: The Arapahoes, a party of the northern band who were passing north. It was the Medicine Man, or Roman Nose, and three others. I am satisfied from the time he left a certain camp for the north, that it was this party of four persons.

Agent Whitley: That cannot be true.

Gov. Evans: Where is Roman Nose?

Neva: You ought to know better than we, you have been nearer to him.

Gov. Evans: Who killed the man and boy at the head of Cherry Creek?

Neva:	(After consultation.) Kiowas and Comanches.
Gov. Evans:	Who stole the horses and mules from Jimmy's Camp twenty-seven days ago?
Neva:	*Fourteen Cheyennes and Arapahoes* together.
Gov. Evans:	What were their names?
Neva:	Powder Face and Whirlwind, *who are now in our camp, were the leaders.*
Col. Shoup:	I counted twenty Indians on that occasion.
Gov. Evans:	Who stole Charlie Autobee's horses?
Neva:	Raven's son.
Gov. Evans:	I suppose you acknowledge the depredations on the Little Blue, as you have the prisoners then taken, in your possession?
White Antelope:	We (the Cheyennes) took two prisoners west of Ft. Kearney and destroyed the trains.

It will be seen from the foregoing that these Indians, although pretending to be friendly, had to admit that their people stole the horses from soldiers at Jimmy's Camp, near Colorado City, an account of which I have already given, and that the Indians who did it were in their camp at Sand Creek at the time the council was being held. They lied concerning the man and boy killed at the head of Cherry Creek, for they knew that the Kiowas and Comanches never came this far north, and that the murders were committed by their own people. Neva's admission that Raven's son stole Charlie Autobee's horses proved the hostility of the Arapahoes, as Raven was the head chief of that tribe.

At the time the council was being held General S. R. Curtis, commanding the military district, sent the following telegram to Colonel Chivington, evidently fearing that peace would be made prematurely:

"FT. LEAVENWORTH,
September 28, 1864.

"TO COLONEL CHIVINGTON:

"I shall require the bad Indians delivered up; restoration of equal numbers of stock; also hostages to secure. I want no peace till the Indians suffer more. Left Hand is said to be a good chief of the Arapahoes but Big Mouth is a rascal. I fear the Agent of the Indian Department will be ready to make presents too soon. It is better to chastise before giving anything but a little tobacco to talk over. No peace must be made without my direction.

"S. R. CURTIS, Major General."

On November 2, 1864, Major Wynkoop was relieved of the command at Fort Lyon, and Major Anthony of the First Regiment of Colorado Cavalry

was appointed his successor.   The reason given for
the removal of Major Wynkoop was that he was inclined to temporize with the hostile Indians, contrary to the orders of his superior officers.

In a report made by Major Anthony to his
superior officers from Ft. Lyon, under date of
November 6, 1864, he says:

"Nine Cheyenne Indians to-day sent in wishing
to see me.   They state that six hundred of that tribe
are now thirty-five miles north of here, coming towards the post, and two thousand about seventy-
five miles away awaiting for better weather to enable
them to come in.

"I shall not permit them to come in even as prisoners, for the reason that if I do I shall have to subsist
them upon a prisoner's rations.   I shall, however,
demand their arms, all stolen stock, and the perpetrators of all depredations.   I am of the opinion
that they will not accept this proposition, but that
they will return to the Smoky Hill.

"*They pretend that they want peace, and I think they
do now, as they cannot fight during the winter, except
where a small band of them can fight an unprotected
train or frontier settlement.   I do not think it is policy
to make peace with them until all perpetrators of depredations are surrendered up to be dealt with as we may
propose.*"

This report was dated only twenty-three days
before the battle of Sand Creek occurred.   The In-

dians Major Anthony mentions as camped thirty-five miles away, were the ones that were attacked by Colonel Chivington. That they were not and had not been under Major Anthony's protection, and that he considered them hostile, is clearly shown by the above report, as well as by the testimony given by him March 14, 1865, in an investigation of the battle of Sand Creek, made by the Joint Committee on the Conduct of the War, as shown by the following extracts:

"Did you not feel that you were bound in good faith not to attack those Indians after they had surrendered to you, and after they had taken up a position which you yourself had indicated?"

"I did not consider that they had surrendered to me; I never would consent that they should surrender to me. My instructions were such that I felt in duty bound to fight them wherever I found them, provided I considered it good policy to do so. I did not consider it good policy to attack this party of Indians at Sand Creek unless I was strong enough to go on and fight the main band at the Smoky Hill River, some seventy miles further. If I had had that force, I should have gone out and fought this band on Sand Creek."

In Colonel Chivington's deposition taken and presented at the same investigation, among other things, he makes the following statement concerning the

battle of Sand Creek and the conditions leading up
to it:

"On the 29th day of November, 1864, the troops
under my command attacked a camp of Cheyenne
and Arapahoe Indians at a place known as Big Bend
of Sandy, about forty miles north of Fort Lyon,
Colorado Territory. There were in my command
at that time about (500) five hundred men of the
Third Regiment Colorado Cavalry, under the immediate command of Colonel George L. Shoup of
said Third Regiment, and about (250) two hundred
and fifty men of the First Colorado Cavalry. . . .
I had four 12-pound mountain howitzers, manned by
detachments from cavalry companies."

"From the best and most reliable information I
could obtain, there were in the Indian camp at the
time of the attack about eleven hundred or twelve
hundred Indians; of these about seven hundred were
warriors and the remainder were women and children. I am not sure that there were any old men
among them. *There was an unusual number of
males among them, for the reason that the war chiefs of
both nations were assembled there, evidently for some
special purpose. . . .*"

"What number did you lose in killed, what number in wounded and what number in missing?"
"There were seven men killed, forty-seven
wounded and one was missing."

"From the best information I could obtain, I judge
that there were five or six hundred Indians killed; I
cannot state positively the number killed, nor can I
state positively the number of women and children
killed. Officers who passed over the field by my
orders, report that they saw but few women and
children dead, no more than would certainly fall in
an attack upon a camp in which they were. I myself passed over some portions of the field after the
fight and *I saw but one woman who had been killed,
and one who had hanged herself, I saw no dead children. From all I could learn, I arrived at the con-
clusion that but few women or children had been slain.
I am of the opinion that when the attack was made on
the Indian Camp, the greater number of squaws and
children made their escape, while the warriors remained to fight the troops.*"

"I do not know that any Indians were wounded
that were not killed; if there were any wounded, I
do not think they could have been made prisoners
without endangering the lives of the soldiers; Indians usually fight as long as they have strength to
resist. Eight Indians fell into the hands of the
troops alive, to my knowledge; these, with one exception, were sent to Fort Lyon and properly cared
for. . . ."

"My reason for making the attack on the Indian
camp was that I believed the Indians in the camp
were hostile to the whites. That they were of the

same tribes with those who had murdered many persons and destroyed much valuable property on the Platte and Arkansas rivers during the previous spring, summer and fall, was beyond a doubt. When a tribe of Indians is at war with the whites, it is impossible to determine what party or band of the tribe, or the name of the Indian or Indians belonging to the tribe so at war, are guilty of acts of hostility. The most that can be ascertained is that Indians of the tribe have performed the acts. During the spring, summer and fall of the year 1864, the Arapahoe and Cheyenne Indians, in some instances assisted or led on by Sioux, Kiowas, Comanches and Apaches, had committed many acts of hostility in the country lying between the Little Blue and the Rocky Mountains and the Platte and Arkansas rivers. They had murdered many of the whites and taken others prisoners, and had destroyed valuable property, probably amounting to $200,000 or $300,-000. Their rendezvous was on the headwaters of the Republican, probably 100 miles from where the Indian camp was located. I had every reason to believe that these Indians were either directly or indirectly concerned in the outrages that had been committed upon the whites. I had no means of ascertaining what were the names of the Indians who had committed these outrages other than the declarations of the Indians themselves; and the character of the Indians in the western country for truth and veracity, like their respect for the chastity of women who may become prisoners in their hands, is not of that order which is calculated to inspire confidence in what they may say. In this view I was supported by Major Anthony, First Colorado Cavalry, commanding at Fort Lyon, and Samuel G. Colley, United States Indian Agent, who, as they had been in communication with these Indians, were more competent to judge of their disposition toward the whites than myself. Previous to the battle they expressed to me the opinion that the Indians should be punished. We found in the camp the scalps of nineteen white persons. One of the surgeons informed me that one of these scalps had been taken from the victim's head not more than four days previously. I can furnish a child captured at the camp ornamented with six white women's scalps. These scalps must have been taken by the Indians or furnished to them for their gratification and amusement by some of their brethren, who, like themselves, were in enmity with the whites."

"I had no reason to believe that Black Kettle and the Indians with him were in good faith at peace with the whites. The day before the attack Major Scott J. Anthony, First Colorado Cavalry, then commander at Fort Lyon, told me that these Indians were hostile; that he had ordered his sentinels to fire on them if they attempted to come into the post, and that the sentinels had fired on them; that he was apprehensive of an attack from these Indians and had taken every precaution to prevent a surprise. Major Samuel G. Colley, United States Indian Agent for these Indians, told me on the same day that he had

done everything in his power to make them behave
themselves, and that for the last six months he could
do nothing with them; that nothing but a sound
whipping would bring a lasting peace with them.
These statements were made to me in the presence
of the officers of my staff whose statements can be
obtained to corroborate the foregoing."

"Since August, 1863, I had been in possession of
the most conclusive evidence of the alliance, for the
purpose of hostility against the whites, of the Siouxs,
Cheyennes, Arapahoes, Comanche, Kiowa, and
Apache Indians."

"Their plan was to interrupt, or, if possible, entirely prevent all travel on the route along the
Arkansas and Platte rivers from the states to the
Rocky Mountains, and thereby depopulate this
country."

"With very few troops at my command, I could do
little to protect the settlers, except to collect the
latest intelligence from the Indians' country, com-
municate it to General Curtis, commanding department of Missouri, and warn the settlers of the
relations existing between the Indian and the whites,
and the probability of trouble, all of which I did."

The testimony of Governor Evans, Major Anthony, and Colonel Chivington covers every phase
of the matter in controversy. Governor Evans'

statement proves beyond question that the Cheyennes and Arapahoes were viciously hostile during the
entire summer preceding the battle of Sand Creek,
and this was admitted by Black Kettle in his letter
to Major Colley, the Indian Agent, and by the other
chiefs in the council at Denver.

Governor Evans also makes it plain that, after
many futile attempts to induce the Indians to stop
their raids upon the settlements of Colorado and the
lines of travel thereto, he refused to consider the
matter further and turned the Indians over to the
military. The telegram of General Curtis, Commander of the Military Department, sent at the time
the council was being held, says: "No peace must be
made without my direction." And peace had not
been made when the battle of Sand Creek was
fought. Major Anthony, Commander of the Military Post of Fort Lyon, near the Cheyenne and
Arapahoe Agency, says that the Indians attacked
were hostile and not under his protection, and that
he would have punished them had his force been
strong enough to fight them and the large band on
the Smoky Hill River as well. Colonel Chivington's
testimony confirms the statement of Governor
Evans as to the hostility of both Cheyennes and
Arapahoes, and he says this was corroborated by
both Major Anthony and Major Colley, the Indian
Agent, each of whom told him, while at Fort Lyon
prior to the battle, that the Indians camped on Sand
Creek were hostile and should be punished.

The only Arapahoes that by any stretch of the

imagination could be said to have been under the protection of the military, were the small part of the tribe under the control of Left Hand, a sub-chief; while there is no doubt whatever as to the hostility of the head chief, Raven, and his followers, who constituted a large majority of the tribe. It is generally conceded that Chief Left Hand and a few of his band were peaceably inclined. But, unfortunately, he and the occupants of six or eight lodges of his people, about forty persons in all, including women and children, were in the camp of the hostile Cheyennes and Arapahoes at the time the attack was made and suffered accordingly. Left Hand knew that the Cheyennes and a very large part of his own people were at war with the whites, and of the chance he was taking by being in company with the hostiles. If it resulted disastrously, he had no one but himself to blame. It was utterly impossible to discriminate between Indians of different tribes in the midst of battle. In those days, Indians seldom permitted themselves to be taken prisoners, and an attempt to do so, even if the Indians were badly wounded, was a dangerous undertaking. This was the reason that no prisoners were taken at Sand Creek.

It is inconceivable to any one who knew the members of the Third Colorado that either its officers or enlisted men, with possibly a rare exception, would have approved, much less have participated in, the wanton acts of cruelty claimed to have been perpetrated. No unprejudiced person can believe a charge of such character against Colonel Shoup, afterwards for many years a United States Senator of high standing from the State of Idaho; or Major Hal Sayre, one of Colorado's most prominent mining engineers; or Captain Harper Orahood, who later was for many years a law partner of Senator H. M. Teller; or Captain Baxter of Pueblo, or Captain Nichols of Boulder, both afterwards members of the Legislature of Colorado; or in fact, against any of the officers of the Third Colorado, as practically all of them were men of high standing in their respective communities.

I was on the battlefield within fifteen minutes after the fight began, and during the day, with a part of our company, I went along the south side of Sand Creek from the scene of one engagement to another until I had covered the full length of the battlefield on that side of the creek. We then crossed over to the north side and followed up the creek as far as the engagement extended. On our return to camp we went over the entire length of the scene of the fighting on the north side of the creek, thus covering during the day almost the entire battlefield, as after the first half hour in the morning there was but little fighting except near the banks of the creek. During that time, I saw much of the battle, but not once did I see any one shoot at a squaw or a child, nor did I see any one take a scalp, although it is true that in some instances this was done, for, as I returned to camp, I saw a number of dead Indians whose scalps had been taken, among them a few squaws. They probably had been scalped by some irresponsible person, or possibly by some of the many men who had suffered from the Indian raids. Among the members of our regiment there were many who had had friends or relatives killed, scalped, or mutilated by these Indians, and almost every man had sustained financial loss, either directly or indirectly, by reason of their raids. After these experiences, it is not surprising that they should have been determined to inflict such punishment upon these savages as would deter them from further hostilities. I did not see a dead or wounded child, and it is inconceivable that any were killed during the fight except accidentally. The incident of the child who wished me to take it up, indicated the sympathetic attitude of our men towards the innocent non-combatants.

I think the proof I have presented shows conclusively that every one of the charges made by the enemies of Colonel Chivington was untrue; that, on the contrary, the Indians attacked at Sand Creek were, and had been during the previous summer, viciously hostile to the whites; that they were not under the protection of the military authorities at Fort Lyon; and that the battle was not a wanton massacre.

The adverse criticism of this whole affair was but one of the many acts of injustice experienced by the frontier settlers. From the formation of the Government up to the time when the Indians were finally placed upon reservations, the frontier settlers, in addition to defending themselves from the savages, always had to contend with the sentimental feeling in favor of the Indians that prevailed in many sections of the East. The people of the East had forgotten, or had never read of, the atrocities perpetrated on their ancestors by the savages, and resting secure in the safety of their own homes, they could not realize the privations and dangers that those who were opening up the frontier regions of the West had to endure. And to add further to the difficulties of the situation, the Indian Department usually was dominated by sentimental people who apparently had neither sympathy for the frontier settler, nor any conception of a just and proper method of dealing with the Indians.

No effort seems to have been made to study the inherited traits that governed the Indian in his dealings with others. The nomadic Indian of the central and western part of the United States was in most matters merely a child. His sole occupation from youth to old age was following the chase and fighting his enemies. Almost the only topics of conversation in the Indians' tents and around their camp fires were the details of their hunting expeditions and of their battles; and from his earliest days, every Indian boy was taught that his one hope of glory and of making a reputation depended upon his ability to kill his foes. Every one of the nomadic tribes had its hereditary enemies with whom it was in a perpetual state of warfare. During the summertime, it was one continuous round of war parties going out to attack their enemies and parties returning, bringing with them the scalps of those they had killed, together with squaws and children they had captured, and frequently with large herds of horses they had stolen.

The Indians could have been easily handled had the Government studied their nature and formulated a systematic policy for their control, compelling them to regard the rights of the whites as well as of their neighboring tribes, and had, at the same time, protected them from wrongs perpetrated upon them by thieving and disreputable white men; in short, had treated them with justice in all things and required the same from them in dealing with the whites. In this connection, I assert, from my personal knowledge, that more than ninety-five per cent of the frontier settlers treated the Indians with the utmost fairness and used every possible endeavor to avoid difficulties with them.

As I have said already, the Indians were greatly handicapped in carrying on warfare in the winter, as during that period their ponies became very much weakened through having to subsist entirely upon the dry grass of the plains. In this way, white people had a great advantage and it would have required only a few cases of summary punishment during the winter, such as we gave them at Sand Creek, to have settled Indian troubles in this region for all time. Had the battle of Sand Creek been followed up as it should have been, the frontier settlements of Colorado would thereafter have had little trouble with any of its Indian neighbors, and many lives of both Indians and white men would have been saved. The period I have referred to was certainly a "Century of Dishonor," not only because of the attitude of the Government in its dealings with the Indians, but also in the treatment of those of its own people who were opening up its frontier lands for settlement.

Four years later, the absurdity of the policy of permitting the Indians to murder and rob during the summer, make peace in the fall, and remain unmolested during the winter, accumulating ammunition for the following summer's warfare, finally dawned upon the authorities and a new plan was adopted. As a result, on the 27th of November, 1868, General Custer, under the direction of General Sheridan, Commander of the Military Division of the Missouri, made an attack similar to that at Sand Creek upon the Cheyennes camped upon the Washita, south of the Arkansas River, in which one hundred and three Indians—a number of whom were squaws—were killed, fifty-three squaws and children captured, and eight hundred and seventy-five ponies were taken and killed. As General Sheridan says in his report:

"The objects of the winter's operations were to strike a hard blow and force them on to the reservation set apart for them; or, if this could not be accomplished, to show to the Indian that the winter season would not give him rest; that he with his village and stock could be destroyed; that he would have no security winter or summer except in obeying the laws of peace and humanity."

As in the case of Chivington, Custer was attacked viciously for this affair, but, fortunately, Custer had the backing of the Commanding Officers of the Army and nothing his enemies could do affected him in the least.

What a fortunate thing it would have been for the people of the entire frontier, from Canada to Mexico, if this policy had been adopted a few years earlier!

CHAPTER IX

A WEEK AT MAXWELL'S RANCH IN NEW MEXICO—
EXPERIENCES ALONG THE UNION PACIFIC

THE winter of 1864–65 was one of the most severe in the history of this region. As I have stated before, a deep snow fell on the last day of October and the first of November. It turned severely cold afterwards and an unusually low temperature prevailed, with few interruptions, during the next two or three months. This prevented the snow from melting to any extent and, of course, made it very hard for the cattle on the range and the wild animals of the plains to get sufficient food to keep from starving.

The deep snow on the prairies to the east drove the antelope in large numbers to the country along the base of the mountains. The occasional warm days, followed by freezing weather, caused a thin crust to form on top of the snow, and this, not being strong enough to sustain much weight, made traveling over it difficult for both man and beast. Consequently, the antelope, as they ran, continually broke through the crust, and, when pursued, had little chance to escape—an ordinary dog could catch them without trouble.

On my return from the army, I assumed charge of our ranch and cattle, and spent most of the time during the remainder of the winter attending to the duties connected with that work.

While there were no Indian troubles in this vicinity during the summer of 1865, it was a period when constant watchfulness was deemed necessary. The Indians, as usual, were raiding stage stations and attacking mail coaches and wagon trains along the lines of travel between the Rocky Mountains and the Missouri River, but made few attacks upon the frontier settlements of this Territory. Doubtless, the lesson given them at Sand Creek the previous year caused them to be wary of again arousing the people of Colorado.

One morning late that summer our two horses, which had been picketed out near the house, were missing. For reasons that follow, we at once concluded that they had been stolen and that Mexicans were the thieves. As I have stated before, Mexicans were much in demand here in Colorado as farm hands and sheep herders. The high wages given here, as compared with those paid in New Mexico, made it an attractive field for them, and, as a result, large numbers came every spring, seeking employment in the lines I have mentioned. Most of them came on foot, and as a rule worked faithfully and efficiently during the summer, but seldom remained longer. Almost without exception, they drew their wages in the fall and returned to their homes in New Mexico. Generally, these Mexicans started back on foot, as they had come, but frequently, before they had gone far, this method of travel became too tiresome and somebody's horses were appropriated. By the year 1865, this method of procedure had become alarmingly frequent; consequently, whenever horses were missing, the blame was instantly placed on the Mexicans, and generally the accusation was well founded.

Naturally, that September morning, when we found that our ponies were gone, we at once decided that Mexicans had taken them. Upon investigation, we learned that in addition to our ponies, two other horses and three mules had been stolen from people in the adjacent country. By following the trails of the missing animals, it was found that, after having been brought together a few miles down the Fountain, they were taken in the direction of New Mexico.

With little delay, a party of fifteen men, all well mounted and armed, of whom I was one, started in pursuit of the thieves. The trail made by the seven stolen animals was plain and easily followed. It led down the west side of the Fountain for about eight miles, then across that stream, and on in a southeasterly direction over an uninhabited part of the plains. The trail showed that the stolen animals were being pushed at a good speed. After continuing the pursuit all day at as rapid gait as our horses could stand, darkness found us on the plains about fifteen miles north of the Arkansas River, and fifty miles from Colorado City. Here we camped for the night, on the open prairie, when it became too dark to see the trail. There was no water near, but, fortunately, the grass was good. After picketing our horses with long lariats, we lay down upon the bare ground, with our saddles for pillows, and tried to get a little sleep; but, being without blankets, we spent a most uncomfortable night. At dawn the next morning, we saddled our horses and started out again. Our leader, Dan Gessinger, formerly belonged to the regular army and had seen much frontier service. He was familiar with trailing and led us at a good speed along the track of the stolen animals.

During the forenoon, we crossed the Arkansas River about thirty miles east of Pueblo, and, after riding rapidly all afternoon, camped for the night at some water holes on a branch of Apishapa Creek. Again our camp was a most uncomfortable one. This time, we were without food, having eaten all that we had brought with us; the water in the ponds was so dirty and full of tadpoles that we could hardly drink it; and swarms of ravenous mosquitoes added to our discomfort. The indications were that the thieves had camped there only a few hours before and now were proceeding more leisurely, evidently thinking themselves out of danger. Daylight found us ready to take up the pursuit again. About noon we reached the wagon road known as the Santa Fé Trail, over which was hauled from the Missouri River towns most of the merchandise and other supplies destined for Santa Fé and other points in New Mexico and Arizona. Following this road, we soon came to a wagon train in camp, where the men in charge, upon hearing of our hungry condition, provided us with a very satisfying meal.

From this point, the trail of the stolen animals followed the wagon road to Trinidad. Before reaching the latter place we met several people who had seen the party. One of the mules had cropped ears, which made it particularly noticeable and easily identified. The animals, as we now learned, were in charge of two Mexicans, which confirmed our suspicions as to the thieves.

At Trinidad, we had supper at a Mexican hotel, the food being plain but well cooked. Trinidad at that time was a typical Mexican town, and as few of our party had ever been in such a settlement before, many things were new and strange to us. The most interesting feature connected with our meal was the waitress, a Mexican girl about eighteen years old, who was dressed in a Mother Hubbard sort of garment and went pattering around in her bare feet.

After supper we again took up the pursuit, traveling along the wagon road over the Raton Mountains, hoping to overtake the thieves in the night; but, failing to do so, we camped again after midnight on the open prairie. Our party now was reduced to eight men, seven whose horses had about given out having turned back at Trinidad. We were up at daybreak the following morning, at which time it was decided that it was useless to follow the thieves longer unless we could get fresh horses. The only place where there was any hope of securing them was at the Maxwell

Ranch, about twenty-five miles distant. Upon reaching this decision, the party at once headed in that direction, and, by as hard riding as the wearied condition of our horses would permit, we reached the ranch soon after noon. We were kindly received by Mr. Maxwell, who, without hesitation, gave us the three fresh horses asked for, it having been decided that only the leader, Dan Gessinger, and two others should continue the pursuit. From information received at Trinidad, we knew that the thieves were heading for Mora, a village forty or fifty miles south of Maxwell's. The other five of the party, including myself, remained at the ranch as Maxwell's guests for the next week. Our stay there proved to be unexpectedly interesting.

The story of Lucien B. Maxwell's life reads like a romance. Born in Illinois, he entered the employ of the American Fur Company in early manhood and, while in its service, became familiar with much of the Rocky Mountain region. He accompanied Frémont's first expedition as a hunter for the party, and traveled with the second expedition from the Missouri River to the Rocky Mountains. Later, he married the daughter of Charles Beaubien, an early French trader of the Rocky Mountain region, and by the inheritance of his wife and through purchase afterwards, he acquired the whole of the Beaubien and Miranda Land Grant in New Mexico and southern Colorado, a tract of vast extent. It covered an area about fifty miles square lying between the Culebra Range and the Raton Mountains, and was

watered by numerous branches of the Red and
Cimarron Rivers. At the time of our visit, a considerable part of the valleys along these streams was
being cultivated by tenants or peons belonging to
Maxwell. It was said that he had more than a
thousand of the latter class under his control,—the
peonage system still being in existence in New
Mexico.

In traversing the Grant, we had seen his great
herds of cattle and flocks of sheep, and from the
home ranch, we could see his wide fields of grain extending in every direction. The home ranch was in
reality a good sized, bustling village. Besides his
residence, there was a large store building completely stocked with all sorts of merchandise, and a
grist mill of large capacity, at which the thousands of
bushels of wheat raised on his Grant were turned into
flour. In addition, there was a blacksmith shop and
very extensive barns for his many fine blooded horses,
several of which were noted race animals. Near by
was a well kept track where horse races were frequently held, attended by people from all over New
Mexico. The heads of the various departments
were Americans, all other employees being Mexicans.
The residence, palatial for that region, was a large
two-story building, constructed of sun-dried adobe
brick, the walls being plastered inside and out, and on
the outside marked in blocks to imitate stone. The
rooms were large, having high ceilings finished with
moulding, but in most cases were without furniture.
The room we slept in was carpeted, but had not even

a chair. However, in one corner, there was a pile of wool mattresses and bedding from which the servants made beds for us on the floor at night. So far as we saw, there was only one room in the house that had a bedstead and that was the one occupied by Maxwell and his wife. There were two dining rooms, one for the women of the household, and another for the men, the latter detached from the main house. The men's dining room was a large one with a table at which at least twenty persons could be seated, and it was none too big to accommodate the host's heads of departments and his many guests. Maxwell was noted far and wide for his generous hospitality.

The female servants of the house were Navajo squaws, of whom there were at least a dozen. We were told that Mr. Maxwell had purchased these squaws from Apache Indian warriors, who had captured them in various raids in the country of the Navajos, with whom they were at war. The squaws were dressed in Mexican style and seemed happy and contented. I imagine that they had little to do, as at that time Mexican housekeeping was rather primitive.

The policing of the Grant was given over to a band of about five hundred Apache Indians who were maintained at Maxwell's expense in a camp near the home ranch. It was claimed that they were faithful and trustworthy, and had reduced stealing from his herds and flocks to a minimum.

The surroundings and the whole atmosphere of the

place reminded me of descriptions that I had read of baronial estates in Europe in the Middle Ages. It was difficult to realize that here, away in the heart of the Rocky Mountains, was an estate of over a million acres, a considerable area of which was under cultivation, with great herds of cattle and sheep scattered over the surrounding country, all owned by one man, whose word was law, and who maintained hundreds of retainers to care for his varied interests.

At the end of the week, the three of our party that had continued the pursuit of the horse thieves returned unsuccessful. They had followed the thieves and horses into the Mexican settlement of Mora, but after that could get no trace of either, which seemed to make further effort useless. Consequently, we immediately made preparations to return home. Maxwell refused to accept anything for our board or the use of his horses. This was fortunate for us as the combined cash of the party by this time had been reduced to less than eight dollars, and we were over two hundred miles from home, which could not be reached in less than four days hard riding. It was not a pleasant prospect, but there was nothing to do but to start at once and face the unfortunate predicament.

We left Maxwell's late in the afternoon, and, about nine o'clock that night, passed a cornfield from which we secured roasting-ears sufficient to stay our appetites for the time being. The corn was roasted before our camp fire and eaten with great relish. After this meager supper, we lay down on the ground, out in the open without blankets, and slept three or four hours and then resumed our journey, reaching Dick Wooten's place, on the summit of the Raton Mountains, about breakfast time. He gave us a very poor meal, but as he trusted us for it we held no grudge against him. Wooten was one of the famous old hunters and trappers who came to the Rocky Mountains before the Mexican War, and whom I have mentioned as having started to build a house at the Manitou springs in 1858. It was said of him that having courted, successfully as far as the girl was concerned, a Mexican señorita at Taos, he had failed to secure her parents' consent to their marriage; whereupon, he had ridden to her home, and, finding her out of doors, had picked her up, put her on the saddle in front of him, and galloped off to the priest where they were married. After wandering around for a number of years, he finally built a toll road across the Raton Mountains, on the line of the Santa Fé trail, and spent his later years collecting toll and feeding hungry travelers.

From Wooten's we traveled night and day; that is, we alternately rode three or four hours, rested and slept about the same time, and then on again. This was kept up steadily until we reached Colorado City. During the last two days we had but two full meals, the last being at Trinidad; consequently we arrived home in an almost famished condition, and thoroughly tired out.

For various reasons, our family resources had become very much depleted by the fall of 1867, and it seemed necessary that I take up some outside work to help recuperate our finances. The Union Pacific Railway at that time was under construction through the present state of Wyoming, the line being near the northern boundary of Colorado, and that locality seemed to offer the best opportunity for remunerative employment. With this in mind, late in the summer of that year, I started northward with our team in company with John Wolfe, a ranchman living on Cheyenne Creek, who also desired work for himself and team during the winter. Wolfe had been my comrade during the Sand Creek campaign and was congenial in every way. Upon reaching Denver, we made several trips to Central and Georgetown with loads of freight at profitable rates. This occupied our time for a month or two, then we each bought a wagon-load of potatoes and started with them for the town of Laramie where, judging from what had been told us, we expected to sell them at a big profit. Laramie then was an important center in the construction work of the Union Pacific Railway, which was under way both east and west from that town. By this time it was rather late in the fall and, as might have been expected, we experienced very cold weather while we were crossing the mountains east of the Laramie plains. For two or three nights we had great difficulty in keeping our potatoes from freezing, only preventing it by maintaining fires around our wagons all night long. Upon reaching Laramie, we sold our potatoes at a fairly good profit, and then were induced to take a job hauling ties from the mountains south of Laramie to points along the grade of the Union Pacific. Soon after we reached the tie camp, there was a heavy fall of snow which made it impossible for our teams to haul over half a load at a time. We soon found that this made the work unprofitable, and consequently, threw up the job and decided to go down the line of the railroad grade to Cheyenne, hoping to be more successful at that point.

The weather had now become very cold and raw; piercing winds blew almost continuously from the north and made traveling,—especially camping out on the hills at night,—most uncomfortable. About fifteen miles west of Cheyenne we came to a grading camp where there was an urgent need of teams. Through the persuasiveness of the contractor and the high wages he offered, we were induced to join his forces and forthwith unhitched the horses from our wagons and started to work on the grade with scrapers. The wind was blowing a gale from the northwest and we had hardly started before we found the gravel cutting our faces in such a disagreeable manner that within half an hour we gave up the job and drove on down to Cheyenne. At that time, this place was a typical, unattractive railroad town, with many saloons and tough characters. The end of the track had just reached a point about twenty miles east of Cheyenne, and high rates were being paid for hauling freight from that point to town, so we engaged in that work for the next month or two. Finally, concluding that the compensation did not pay for the exposure and hardships we had to endure, it being midwinter, we secured a load of freight for Denver and decided to quit the business. Even at the high freight rates paid us, the venture had not proved very profitable, as the cost of living and the expense of feed for the horses had eaten up much of our earnings. However, I had acquired a good deal of valuable experience during the two or three months, and, in addition, I had learned through observation something as to the method of railroad building, which possibly was of benefit to me in later years.

From Denver I returned home, and during the following winter attended an academy founded and conducted at Colorado City by Professor Wray Beattie, formerly a professor of mathematics in the Iowa Wesleyan University. Professor Beattie was among the first of those who came to Colorado for their health.

In January, 1868, Professor Beattie's school was incorporated under the name of Fountain College, with John Evans, Wray Beattie, George M. Chilcott, E. T. Stone, Robert Douglass, Robert Stubbs, William Howbert, John C. Brown, and T. H. Robbins, as Trustees. John Evans was a former Governor of Colorado; Robert Douglass had been a judge, a state senator, and afterwards was a member of the Convention which gave Colorado its present constitution; George M. Chilcott was a delegate to Congress from this Territory, and later a United States Senator for a short period. It was the intention of these founders to build up at Colorado City an institution of higher learning that would be superior to any school in this Rocky Mountain region. However, Professor Beattie's health failed soon after, and within a year or two he had to give up all work. This ended the project as he was its most active promoter.

About this time some of the public spirited citizens of Colorado City contributed sufficient funds to buy a small but well selected collection of books for a Public Library.

There had been no trouble with the Indians in this immediate section during the last two or three years, but occasional hostile raids along the lines of travel and upon the exposed settlements of western Kansas had occurred every year during that period.   Nevertheless, the people of this region took nothing for granted, but, by keeping a sharp lookout, they felt themselves fairly safe upon their ranches.

CHAPTER X

BEGINNING OF THE INDIAN WAR OF 1868

In the spring of 1867, agents of the Indian Bureau attempted to negotiate a new treaty with the Cheyennes and Arapahoes, and for that purpose visited them at their camp on Pawnee Fork, a branch of the Arkansas River, near Fort Larned, Kansas. But spring was not the time of year when these Indians wished to make treaties. Consequently, after making several appointments for councils, none of which was kept, the savages suddenly disappeared and next were heard of raiding frontier settlements in Kansas and Nebraska and along lines of travel between Colorado and the Missouri River. The raids were kept up continuously during the next five or six months; but, after killing frontier settlers, robbing trains, and destroying much property all summer long, these Cheyennes and Arapahoes again came in professing penitence. Thereupon, following the usual custom, a new treaty was made with them, by the terms of which they agreed to give up their lands in Colorado and settle upon a reservation elsewhere. In addition to this, they promised that "hereafter they would not molest any coach or wagon, or carry off any white woman or child, or kill or scalp any white man." On its side, the Government agreed to pay the two tribes twenty thousand dollars annually, give each Indian a suit of clothes, provide farming implements, employ teachers, physicians, etc., in order to help them acquire the habits of civilization.

While it was not expressly so stated in the treaty, it was understood that these tribes were to be supplied also with arms and ammunition. The treaty was entered into by representatives of the Indian Bureau with all outward semblance of good faith, although, if those in charge of the Bureau knew anything, they must have realized that the pledge of a large percentage of the Indians to remain peaceable was utterly worthless. It had proved to be so year after year ever since the first settlement of this country. This treaty not only turned out to be valueless, but that part giving the savages arms and ammunition was criminal, as was shown by the results.

The Indians remained quiet during that winter, but in the spring they demanded the arms and ammunition that had been promised them. The Indian Agent urged that the Department grant the request, making a plea that members of the tribes would starve unless given means to kill buffalo and other game on the plains. Evidently, those in charge of that branch of the Government hesitated to arm the savages, but finally, influenced by these statements, the issue was authorized. By this time,

Major Wynkoop had been taken into the service of the Indian Bureau and appointed an Agent for the Cheyennes and Arapahoes. He was one of those who had been urging that arms and ammunition be issued to the savages. On August 10, 1868, Wynkoop wrote to the Department:

"I yesterday made the whole issue of annuity, goods, arms and ammunition to the Cheyenne chiefs and people of their nation. They were delighted in receiving the goods, *particularly the arms and ammunition*, and never before have I known them to be better satisfied and express themselves as being so well contented, previous to the issue. They have now left for their hunting grounds and I am perfectly satisfied that there will be no trouble with them this season."

On the very day that Wynkoop sent this letter, two hundred and fifty Cheyenne and Arapahoe warriors were raiding settlements on the Saline River in Kansas, killing settlers, burning buildings, stealing and driving off great numbers of horses, besides committing many other outrages. Before the end of August, according to the report of General Phil Sheridan for that year, forty white men had been killed by these savages along the frontiers of Kansas and Colorado, many were wounded, and a large amount of property destroyed.

But to return to occurrences in the Pike's Peak region, about ten days after the Wynkoop letter was written, a party of seventy-five Cheyennes and Arapahoes, all well mounted, came in from the plains and marched through Colorado City. Most of them had Government guns and, of course, were supplied with Government ammunition. They bore letters from Indian Agents and Peace Commissioners which stated that they were peaceable and should not be feared or molested. However, the people of Colorado City, lacking confidence in that kind of testimony, telegraphed to the Governor at Denver telling him of the Indians being here and asking if they could be trusted. He replied that they were not hostile and must not be interfered with. Our people were not yet satisfied as to that point, owing to the fact that at the time of their visit to Colorado City, the Indians were noticeably sullen and appeared to be observing everything in a manner that aroused suspicion. However, the savages left this vicinity without anything untoward happening and leisurely went on up Ute Pass into the mountains to fight the Utes, which they claimed was their object in coming here.

A day or two later, the party surprised a small band of Utes who were camped a few miles south of Hartsell's ranch in the South Park, and in the fight that followed they claimed to have killed six of the Utes, including two or three squaws; and they were known to have captured and carried off a small boy belonging to that tribe. On the day of this occurrence, Sam Hartsell, owner of the ranch above referred to, happened to have gone over to the mountains that form the eastern border of the South Park looking for wild raspberries. While on one of the low mountains of that locality he saw a group of mounted men in the valley below, a mile or so away. Hartsell had not heard that the Cheyennes or Arapahoes were in that neighborhood and naturally concluded that the horsemen were Utes. Having been on friendly terms with this tribe for many years and well acquainted with a considerable number of its members, he decided to ride down the mountain to meet them. However, as he came near the group he noticed that they were not dressed as Utes usually were, nor did they look like the people of that tribe. It was too late to retreat, as almost immediately afterward he was discovered and surrounded by the savages. By that time Hartsell, due to his general knowledge of Indians, realized that his captors were Cheyenne and Arapahoe warriors belonging to tribes that had been hostile to the whites much of the time during the four previous years and still were, in so far as he knew. Although knowing that he was in a dangerous situation, the ranchman tried not to show his alarm. But the savages evidently were not ready to begin hostilities against the whites, as was proved by their efforts to reassure Hartsell by exhibiting their certificates of good character from the Indian Agent. Nevertheless, this did not prevent them from at once taking possession of his revolver, ammunition, and pocket knife. They told him of their victory over the Utes, showed him the scalps they had taken and the boy that had been captured.

Finally, after keeping Hartsell in suspense for more than three hours, the Indians allowed him to go without injury and themselves departed eastward in the direction of Ute Pass.

The people of Colorado City knew nothing of this occurrence in the South Park until some days afterward. However, notwithstanding the assurance of the Governor and the Indian agents, the settlers of the Pike's Peak region continued to be very much alarmed at the presence of these savages, knowing their treacherous nature, and for that reason, from the time of the Indians' first appearance, were continuously on the alert to prevent being attacked unawares.

About ten o'clock in the morning, a few days after the savages departed up Ute Pass, three Indians suddenly appeared at Teachout's ranch on Monument Creek, eight miles northeast of Colorado City. They claimed to be friendly Utes, but Teachout, who was familiar with the Indian tribes of this region, knew that they were not Utes. After staying around five or ten minutes, during which time they seemed to be intently observing the surroundings and particularly the corral where Teachout's large herd of horses was kept at night, they left, following the main road southward. Mr. Teachout and his brother, who lived on the Divide, owned a hundred and fifty or more horses, which were kept at this Monument Creek ranch. After the Indians disappeared, Teachout, who was much alarmed, rounded up his horses and drove them into the corral, where they were kept during the daytime thereafter, letting them out to graze only at night, thinking that the safest plan.   Apparently, the Indians now had obtained all the information that they desired concerning this herd of horses and the settlements on the Divide and around Colorado City, for they disappeared.   Soon after, they were heard of raiding settlements east of Bijou Basin and on the headwaters of Kiowa, Bijou, and Running Creeks, where, in the next few days, they killed several people, looted numerous ranch houses, and ran off much stock.

By this time, it was known that these hostile Indians were the same Cheyennes and Arapahoes that had passed through Colorado City on their way to the South Park a week previously.

On August 27, 1868, these Indians killed Mrs. Henrietta Dieterman and her five-year-old son, on Comanche Creek, about twenty-five miles northeast of Colorado City.   The Dieterman household consisted of Mr. and Mrs. Dieterman, a daughter about twelve years old, a son of five years, a sister of Mr. Dieterman's, and a hired man.   The sister was soon to marry the hired man, and he and Mr. Dieterman had gone to Denver to buy furniture for the new household, leaving a German farmhand temporarily in charge.

On the morning of that day something happened to alarm Mrs. Dieterman.   Evidently she believed the Indians were near for she hurriedly started with her sister-in-law and the two children to a neighbor's house some distance away. After having gone a few hundred yards, she suddenly remembered that a considerable sum of money had been left in the house and with her small son went back to get it. They reached the house, secured the money, and again started away, but had gone only a short distance when they were overtaken by the Indians, who at once shot and killed them both. The savages shot the boy repeatedly and finally broke his neck, while his mother was shot through the body, stabbed, and scalped. Those who afterwards saw the victims, said that the mutilated bodies made one of the most horrifying sights they had ever looked upon. In the meantime, Dieterman's sister and daughter ran to where the German was working in a field near by. He stood off the Indians by pointing the handle of his hoe in their direction, making them believe it was a gun, and, in that way, covered the retreat of himself and the others to a neighbor's house.

Mrs. Dieterman formerly had lived near the northern line of El Paso County, and was well known to many of the old settlers. The story of her tragic death created a great sensation, not only in this county but in Denver and throughout the Territory.

News of this tragedy and of the many outrages perpetrated in the region east of the Pinery, reached Colorado City late in the evening, a day or two afterward. As there was a possibility that the savages might appear hereabouts at any moment, messengers were at once sent throughout the county notifying the people of the great danger that confronted them.   At that time, I happened to be at home with father and the family on our Bear Creek ranch.   We were aroused from sleep about eleven o'clock at night by a messenger who told us of the dreadful occurrences and advised us to go to Colorado City immediately for protection.   We at once appreciated the danger of our situation, so hitched up our team quickly, put a few necessary articles of wearing apparel and some bedding in the wagon, and started for town, three miles distant.   It was a dark night, which made the trip a weird as well as an anxious one.   My sisters and younger brothers rode in the wagon, father and I marched along behind it, each with a rifle in hand, knowing that there was a possibility that the Indians had already come into this region by stealth, and that almost any bush or rock on the way might conceal a savage.   However, nothing happened, and we reached town in safety.   It was an incident that made one appreciate to the fullest extent the disagreeable and dangerous features of frontier life.

Father rented a house in Colorado City, our household effects were moved over from the ranch, and the family remained in town until after the Indian troubles were ended.

Early in the morning of September 1, Mr. Teachout accompanied by a hired man, went out to bring in his herd of horses as had been his custom since the visit of the Indians a few days before.   They went down the Monument to Cottonwood Creek, then up that stream, where they found the herd scattered along the valley for a mile or more above a point where the Santa Fé Railroad now crosses that creek.   This is about six miles north of the present site of Colorado Springs.   The two rode leisurely up the valley along the south side of the stream and had reached a point about a half a mile above the place mentioned, when a half dozen mounted Indians suddenly came over the hill to the north of them and dashed at full speed in the direction of the principal part of the herd.   Soon after, other Indians appeared until there were at least twenty-five in sight. In a very short time they had rounded up most of the horses and a part of the band was driving them up Cottonwood Creek at a furious speed.   Meanwhile, Teachout and his employee were a few hundred yards away on the other side of the creek, expecting every minute to be attacked.   Neither of the men had a gun, but as they did not run, evidently the Indians believed them to be armed and kept some distance away.   While rounding up the remainder of the herd one Indian, who could speak English, yelled to Teachout as he passed by: "Damn you, we are going to take your horses."

Just after this, Teachout saw that the Indians had missed a bunch of fifteen or twenty colts that were grazing off to one side, and with his companion started after them, thinking to save at least that part of the herd, but the Indians soon discovered what they were after and set out in pursuit, firing as they came.   When affairs took this turn, there was nothing left for Teachout and his man to do but ride for their lives and get back to the ranch as quickly as possible, which they did. After rounding up the colts, the savages soon disappeared eastward up Cottonwood Creek, driving the entire herd. Less than an hour afterward the Indians with Teachout's ponies passed a ranch near the head of the creek, moving rapidly. At this place they attempted to add to their herd, but failed as the horses they were after happened to be picketed close to the ranch house, and a few shots from two well armed ranch men entrenched behind the walls of a log cabin drove off the raiders.

Upon reaching home, Teachout immediately sent a messenger to his brother on the Divide, with an account of the raid, and a request that the latter enlist as large an armed force as could be gotten together quickly to follow the Indians and, if possible, recover the horses. The brother acted promptly and that evening a party consisting of Dow and Bale Simpson, Jim Sims, "Wild Bill" and twenty-four others, started in pursuit of the savages. The party camped that night at a ranch about three miles southeast of C. R. Husted's saw mill, and at this point was joined by a Mr. Davis and Job Talbert, a brother-in-law of Mr. Husted's. These two men had expected to secure horses and arms at this ranch, but failing in this, the next morning they started back toward the mill. They had gone only a short distance when the Indians overtook them, killed and scalped both, leaving their mutilated bodies in the road, where they were found by friends a few hours later.

The Simpson party, as it afterwards was called, started out again early that morning and soon found the trail of the captured herd, which had been driven along the south side of the Pinery—now known as the Black Forest. They rapidly followed this trail eastward to Squirrel Creek, then across the country to the head of the Big Sandy and down that stream to the mouth of Brackett Creek, a branch that comes in from the north. The size of the herd made the trail plain and easy to follow. So far, no Indians had been seen and the indications were that the savages with the stolen horses were so far ahead that further pursuit would be useless. Instead of returning home directly, the pursuers decided to follow up Brackett Creek and scout the country east of Bijou Basin. A few miles up the creek they came to Mr. Brackett's ranch which they found deserted. The house was open and had been looted, but the owner was nowhere in sight. However, after considerable search, his dead body was found some distance away. He had been killed and scalped by the Indians and, as in every other case, the body had been horribly mutilated; and all the Brackett stock had been driven off.

After burying Brackett's body, the Simpson party continued in a northerly direction until the old Smoky Hill wagon road was reached. Here they met a company of eighteen men from the country to the north of Bijou Basin, and it was decided to combine the two forces. A short distance away from where they made camp together that night, they found and buried the bodies of two men who had been killed by the Indians a day or two before. During all this time no Indians had been seen and it appeared probable that they had returned to their villages on the plains. Believing this to be true, the combined parties turned back toward Bijou Basin the next morning. Early in the afternoon the group of eighteen, having decided that there was nothing further to be accomplished, left the others and started off northeasterly in the direction of their homes. Simpson's party continued on, marching rather carelessly, strung out over the prairie for a considerable distance. The eighteen were hardly out of sight when two of Simpson's men, who were some distance ahead of the main party, saw a few Indians on a hill not far away. Word was at once sent back to the stragglers and the ranks were closed up in double quick time.

Meanwhile, other Indians appeared until, in a short time, they greatly outnumbered the white men. This made it imperative that a place for defense be found as quickly as possible, and, apparently, the most favorable position was the extreme point of a short and somewhat isolated ridge near by, at which place the ground dropped off rather abruptly on three sides. The men rushed to this point, formed a circle and began to throw up temporary entrenchments, using butcher knives and such other implements as they had at hand. By this time the Indians, under cover of a ridge to the south, had opened a sharp fire. Bullets began whizzing around in a lively fashion and soon several of the horses had been wounded. But an encouraging feature of the situation was that many of the shots fired by the Indians fell short and struck the ground some yards away.

Simpson's men returned this fire at every opportunity and had reason to believe that in some instances their shots had been effective, although the Indians kept under cover as much as possible. Before darkness came on, a number of the Simpson party had been wounded and some of the horses killed. By this time, notwithstanding the strong defense that was being made, it became more and more a question whether or not the party could withstand a vigorous charge by the red men, who outnumbered them three or four to one.

Night coming on, the Indian firing let up somewhat and the besieged men were enabled to give some consideration to their situation. It was realized that neither the location, which was without water, nor their resources, which were limited, were favorable for a long siege, and for that reason help must be obtained as soon as possible. Among the party was a dare-devil sort of fellow, known locally by the name of "Wild Bill," who volunteered to take the fastest horse and in the darkness endeavor to break through the Indian line, which now completely surrounded the hill. Then, if successful, he was to hurry on to the settlements at Bijou Basin, fifteen miles away, and bring back reinforcements as quickly as possible. This suggestion met with the approval of every one and arrangements were immediately made to carry it into effect. About nine o'clock, Wild Bill, mounted on a race horse belonging to Dow Simpson, leader of the party, stole out from the entrenchments and quietly rode away. The night was moderately dark and Wild Bill had gone some distance before he was discovered by the Indians. He then put spurs to his horse and dashed away at top speed, the Indians following in a frantic endeavor to cut him off, shooting at him as they ran. Fortunately, neither Wild Bill nor the horse was hit, and in a short time he had left his pursuers far behind. After that, he was not long in reaching Bijou Basin, where arrangements were at once made to dispatch couriers to Colorado City and elsewhere, asking that reinforcements be sent speedily to the beleaguered men.

Meanwhile, those surrounded on the hill were most anxious for the safety of their messenger. They had heard the shots and knew that he had been discovered and that the Indians were in pursuit, but had no means of telling whether or not he had escaped. The only reassuring circumstance was that soon after this the firing slackened and finally stopped altogether. When daylight came, there were no Indians in sight. The besieged men realized that this might be a ruse and that possibly the Indians were lurking near, ready to take advantage of them after they had left their entrenchments. However, on account of their critical position—being entirely without water for themselves or their horses—the party decided to

make a dash and take chances on reaching the nearest settlement in safety.   They started at once, and
reached Holden's ranch in Bijou Basin about noon,
no Indians having been encountered or seen on the
way.

In the engagement none of their party had been
killed and no one was seriously wounded, probably
due to the poor ammunition that had been issued to
the Indians by the Government.   I suppose the white
people of this region should have been duly thankful
for that, at least.

CHAPTER XI

MORE DETAILS OF THE INDIAN WAR OF 1868

WHILE the engagement near Bijou Basin had been going on, stirring events were happening close to Colorado City, and elsewhere in the county. Within two days after the killing of Mrs. Dieterman and the stealing of Teachout's horses, most of the ranchmen living down Fountain Valley had brought their families to Colorado City for protection. The people of the Divide gathered for defense at McShane's ranch near the town of Monument, at John Irion's on Cherry Creek, and at the Husted Mill in the Pinery. The air was full of rumors of Indians having been seen at various places on the Divide and east of Colorado City, and, as a result, the people were in an extremely anxious state of mind. However, it was harvest time and imperative that crops be gathered, therefore chances had to be taken. For that reason it happened that when the crisis came many men from Colorado City were out in the fields away from town, I being among the number.

About noon on September 3, 1868, a band of about fifty mounted Indians came dashing down the valley of Monument Creek, taking possession of all loose horses in their path. The first white man they encountered was Robert Love of Colorado City, who was riding down the creek not far from the present town of Roswell. As soon as Love saw the Indians, instead of trying to get away, which he knew would be useless, he dismounted and stood with his pony between himself and the savages. And, by keeping his revolver pointed in their direction, he showed them that he was not defenseless. After maneuvering around Love for a short time, the Indians passed on, evidently convinced that some of them would get hurt if they attacked him. Apparently, it was not their policy to take many chances, as was shown throughout the entire time they remained in this vicinity. They seldom troubled people who seemed able to offer any great resistance, usually seeking as victims defenseless men, women, and children. Shortly after leaving Love, a few of the Indians crossed Monument Creek to the house of David Spielman, which was on the west side of that stream, about a half mile above the present Mesa Road bridge. Spielman had just returned from moving his family and household effects to Colorado City for safety, and, being tired, had lain down behind the front door, which was open, and had gone to sleep. The Indians looked in at the open door, but fortunately did not see him. They then went to his corral and took from it a horse that Spielman had purchased only the day before. After that, they recrossed the creek and joined the main body, and all rode rapidly southward along the east side, crossing the present athletic field of Colorado College on the way, and coming out on higher ground a few hundred yards south, near what is now the intersection of Mesa Road and Cascade Avenue in Colorado Springs.

A short time before this, Charley Everhart, a young man about eighteen years of age, had started from his home west of Monument Creek, near the present railway bridge above the Denver & Rio Grande Railroad Station, to look after his father's cattle, which were grazing on the present site of Colorado Springs. After crossing Monument Creek, the boy followed a trail that led eastward along the south rim of the high bank north of what is now known as Boulder Crescent. Everhart knew that there were Indians in the country and no doubt was on the lookout for them. He was mounted on a small pony and probably had gone as far east as the present location of Tejon Street when he saw the Indians as they rode out into open view to the north of him. He then turned his pony toward home and urged it to its highest speed, making a desperate effort to escape from the savages, but the little animal was no match for those of the Indians and they soon overtook him. Everhart had reached a point near what is now the intersection of Platte and Cascade Avenues, when a shot from one of the savages caused him to fall from the pony. One of the Indians then came up, ran a spear through his body and scalped him, taking all the hair from his head except a small fringe around the back part. This tragic occurrence was witnessed from a distance by several persons. An hour later, when the Indians had gone and it was safe to do so, a party went out to where the boy's ghastly, mutilated body lay and brought it in to Colorado City.

After killing Everhart, the Indians evidently saw, half a mile or more down the plateau, a lone sheep herder generally known as "Judge" Baldwin, and a part of the band immediately started after him. Baldwin was mounted and tried his best to escape when he saw the Indians coming. Having neither spur nor whip, he took off one of his long-legged boots and used it to urge on the animal. This, however, was ineffectual as his mount was not the equal of those of the Indians, and they overtook and shot him before he had gone very far. The bullet struck him in the shoulder and, as he was leaning forward at the time, angled up through his neck and came out through the jaw. Baldwin fell from his horse near the site of the present Lincoln school building. Although badly wounded, he now used the boot to fight off the Indians. The latter evidently thought his wound mortal, so without wasting any more ammunition upon him, one of their number proceeded to take his scalp. The savage ran a knife around the back part of Baldwin's head, partly severing the scalp from the skull, and then discovered that the herder had been scalped at some previous time. For some reason, probably of a superstitious nature, the Indians then abandoned their purpose of again scalping the man, and the entire band rode off, leaving their victim on the prairie to die, as they doubtless thought. It is true that Baldwin had been scalped by Indians in South America some years before, a piece about the size of a silver dollar having been taken from the crown of his head.

This group of Indians now divided into two parties, one of which went in a northeasterly direction and crossed Shook's Run near the point where Platte Avenue intersects it, at which place they were joined by other Indians that had been in hiding near by. During all this time two or three Indians, who were stationed on the hill where the Deaf and Blind Institute now is located, apparently directed the movements of those doing the killing by wigwagging with flags in a manner similar to that in use by the army at that time. The signal men fell in with the others as these came along and all rode rapidly to the eastward and soon disappeared out on the plains.

Meanwhile, the other band continued on down the Fountain Valley, and at a point near the Rio Grande railroad bridge across Shook's Run they came upon two small boys, sons of Thomas H. Robbins, who lived on the south side of the Fountain not far away. These two boys, eight and eleven years of age, were looking after their father's sheep. Evidently they saw the Indians coming when still some distance away and were using every possible endeavor to escape, but they had not gone far when overtaken. It was said that one of the boys fell upon his knees and lifted his hands, seeming to be begging the Indians to spare his life, but the savages never heeded any such appeals.   Two Indians reached down from their horses, each grabbing a boy by the hair held him up with one hand, and with a revolver in the other, shot him through the head, and then flung the quivering lifeless body to the ground.

The savages then continued down the Fountain valley, following along the edge of the bluffs to the north of the creek, moving very fast.   When south of the present Evergreen Cemetery, they attempted to capture some horses at the Innis Ranch, located in the valley a short distance away, but the presence of a number of armed men there, who shot at them whenever they came near, caused them to desist after two or three futile efforts.   Half a mile below this point, the Indians met Solon Mason, a prominent ranchman from the lower end of the county, who was on his way to Colorado City, accompanied by two or three others.   All of these men were well armed and, after an exchange of shots, the Indians gave the party a wide berth.   However, at George Banning's ranch, a mile below, the Indians took two horses, and then started northward toward the Pinery, which was their rendezvous while in this region.

As I have said before, armed parties were going out from Colorado City every day to harvest the grain that was over-ripening.   That morning I had joined a group of men who had volunteered to assist Bert Myers, a merchant of Colorado City, in harvesting a field of wheat on land then owned by him, now a part of Broadmoor. About two o'clock in the afternoon, while I was binding wheat behind a reaper at a point not very far from the present Country Club buildings, I saw a horseman coming from the east, riding furiously in our direction. When he reached us we found the rider to be a Mr. Riggs who lived near the mouth of Cheyenne Creek. He excitedly told us that the Indians were raiding the entire region, killing people in every direction; that Everhart, Baldwin, the Robbins boys, and probably many others, had been killed, and that the savages had driven off a large number of horses.

My first thought was that the Indians had come in during the previous night, concealed themselves in the underbrush along the creeks, and taken advantage of a time when most of the men were out in the harvest fields to attack our people. I knew such a thing was possible, as at that time there was not a person living along the route the savages naturally would take in coming from the Indian country to our settlement who might give us notice of their approach. I then recalled that my three small brothers, Edgar, Frank, and Charles were looking after our cattle near the mouth of Bear Creek and certainly were in great danger, if they had not already been killed. In order to ascertain their fate, I secured permission to take one of the horses from the reaper. Quickly stripping off all harness except the blind bridle, I mounted it bare-back, and dashed away in the direction of Bear Creek. I had a revolver with me which I had taken to the harvest field that morning as a matter of precaution. Few went far away just then without being armed.   After a ride at top speed, I met the boys about three quarters of a mile south of Bear Creek.   They told me that while eating their luncheon in the milk house near our dwelling, they were alarmed by the excited barking of their dog.   Running out to see what was the matter, and looking across the Fountain to the present site of Colorado Springs, they saw the savages and witnessed most of the occurrences that I have related.   Then becoming alarmed for their own safety, they started to run to some of the neighbors on Cheyenne Creek and were on their way when I met them.

As soon as I had heard their story, which assured me that the Indians had ridden away and that the boys were in no immediate danger, I rode back to the harvest field.   There was no more work that day and soon we hitched up the team and all came to town.

In the meantime, the Robbins family, whose two boys had been killed, had come by our Bear Creek ranch on their way to Colorado City and taken my brothers to town with them.   By the time others of the harvesting party and myself reached Colorado City, the bodies of Everhart and the Robbins boys had been brought there.   Baldwin had been found alive, but was expected to die.   It was thought that he could not live more than a day or two at most, but, to the surprise of every one, in a short time he began to recover, and in a few months apparently was almost as well as ever.

Of course the excitement in Colorado City and throughout El Paso County was intense. We realized that the Territorial authorites were unable to give us any help, and that the General Government had turned a deaf ear to our appeals for protection; that, consequently, the people must rely once more, as they had done in 1864, solely upon themselves. In this emergency, we repaired the old stockade around the Anway Hotel, organized our forces in the best manner possible under existing conditions, and awaited developments.

Only a few hours after the raid, a messenger from Bijou Basin arrived bringing news that the Simpson party was surrounded by Indians near there (an account of which I have already given) and asking that men be sent to its relief. Taking into consideration the strength of our forces, it was decided that a few men could be spared for that purpose. Accordingly that night ten, including myself, volunteered to go to the assistance of the besieged. For this expedition a Mr. Hall, who then lived on what has since been known as the Pope Ranch, loaned me an excellent horse and a Colt's rifle, a kind of gun that I had not seen before nor, for that matter, have I seen one like it since. It was a gun built exactly on the principle of a Colt's revolver. The trouble with it was that one never knew just how many shots might go off at once.

Early the next morning the party started out, following up the Monument to the mouth of Cottonwood Creek, thence along that creek over the ground where Teachout's herd of horses had been captured. We stopped a few minutes at the Neff Ranch, which we found deserted, and then went east along the identical route taken by the Indians when running off the Teachout herd. Less than an hour after leaving Neff's, while we were marching along within a short distance of the Pinery, upon looking to our right we saw a band of about twenty-five mounted Indians half a mile away on the east bank of the ravine through which runs Cottonwood Creek. We were so wrought up by the murders of the previous day that, without a moment's hesitation, our party wheeled about and rode toward the savages as fast as the horses could go. Realizing that we might be running into an ambuscade, I urged our men not to cross the ravine at the place where we had first seen the savages but to go to one side or the other. However, the men were in such a state of frenzy at sight of the savages that they would listen to nothing; so we dashed directly to the edge of the ravine, the banks of which were so steep that we had to dismount and lead our horses down and up the other side. Fortunately for us, there were no Indians at the point where we were crossing, but we had not gone a quarter of a mile when, looking back, we saw a mounted Indian on the bank at that identical spot, and probably there were others hidden nearby.

As soon as the main body of the Indians saw us coming, they started on the run in a southeasterly direction, and, when some distance away, gradually turned eastward. By this time, our party began to realize the desirability of keeping a way of retreat open in case of defeat in the expected encounter. For that reason, we veered a little to the right and kept on until we were directly between them and Colorado City. Meanwhile the Indians had dismounted on a large, open flat about three quarters of a mile distant from us, formed a circle, with their ponies in the center, and seemed to be awaiting our attack. We could see their bright Government guns flashing in the sunshine, and while we were surprised at this movement, being so contrary to the usual custom of Indians, we did not hesitate a moment, but started toward them as fast as our horses could go. Seeing this, the savages evidently changed their minds, mounted again, and started rapidly in the direction of the Pinery about a mile away. We could not head them off, as their horses were much better and fleeter on an average than ours. When they entered the timber we knew that it would only be inviting disaster to follow them further.

We then resumed our march in the direction of Bijou Basin, having no thought of allowing ourselves to be swerved from the purpose for which we had set out. An hour or two later, we passed the extreme southeastern edge of the Pinery at the point where the old Government road crossed Squirrel Creek. Here, judging from the great number of pony tracks visible, a large number of Indians must have passed only a short time before. After a slight rest at that point, we steadily pushed on and arrived at Bijou Basin before dark that evening.

At the Basin we learned that the besieged party had come in the day before and that all the men except the wounded ones had returned to their homes. These wounded were being well cared for at D. M. Holden's ranch. As seemingly there was nothing for us to do in that locality, we started back home early the following morning. On our way we found many fresh pony tracks at points along the eastern and southern edge of the Pinery, showing that the Indians still were around in considerable numbers, but we saw none during the day.

After leaving the Pinery, our party followed the wagon road that passes through what is now known as Templeton's Gap. As we came down a hill a mile or two northeast of the Gap, we noticed a number of horsemen congregated near that point. From their actions we knew that they were not Indians but white men who evidently were much excited, thinking us a band of savages. They gathered around some tall rocks that stand a little way to the eastward of the gateway and were preparing for defense. We tried by signaling and otherwise to make ourselves known, but were unsuccessful until almost within gun-shot. They were a scouting party from Colorado City and were greatly relieved when they ascertained who we were. We then joined them and all returned to Colorado City without anything further happening.

Incidents similar in character to the one just described were of almost daily occurrence as long as the Indians remained in this region. Every animal on a distant hill became an Indian horseman to the excited mind of ranchman or cowboy, and without further investigation, he would rush off to Colorado City and give the alarm. No lone man on horseback allowed another horseman to approach him without preparing himself for defense, and every object at a distance that was not clearly distinguishable was viewed with alarm. Throughout the ten or twelve days following the raid over the present townsite of Colorado Springs, the Indians had virtual possession of the northern and eastern portions of El Paso County. During this time, they raided Gill's ranch, east of Jimmy's Camp, and drove off his herd of horses, taking them out of the corral near his house in the night, although the animals were being guarded by armed men. It appears that the Indians stole up to the corral on the opposite side from where the guards were posted, made an opening in it, let out the horses, had possession of them and were away before the guards realized what was going on. The first notice they had of the raid was that the corral was empty.

During this period, the Indians killed a demented man named Jonathan Lincoln at the Lincoln Ranch in Spring Valley on Cherry Creek, just north of the El Paso County line. Lincoln and a Mexican were out in the harvest field binding oats when they saw the Indians approaching. The Mexican saved himself by flight, but Lincoln folded his arms and calmly awaited the coming of the savages. Without hesitation they killed him, took his scalp and departed again into the recesses of the Pinery. They also killed John Choteau on East Cherry Creek, John Grief and Jonathan Tallman on East Bijou, and raided the John Russell Ranch on the head of East Cherry Creek, from which place sixteen head of horses were stolen.

A few days previously, a small band of Indians, while prowling around in the neighborhood of Monument, threatened the house of David McShane, located half a mile away from town, at a time when all the men were absent. Mrs. McShane and some neighboring women and children were the only ones there. Having the true pioneer spirit, the women under the leadership of Mrs. McShane, put up such a strong show of defense with the guns at hand that the savages abandoned their attack in short order, apparently glad to get away unharmed. The same party burned Henry Walker's house, which stood about a mile east of the present Husted station on the Denver & Rio Grande Railroad.

Undoubtedly, the Indians had established a camp at some secluded place in the timber of the Divide from which small parties went forth in every direction, killing and robbing when opportunity offered. Every day during the ten or twelve following the raid over the plateau that later became the townsite of Colorado Springs, Indians were seen at various places on the Divide and in the eastern part of the county. However, by this time, practically all the ranchmen had taken their families out of danger and were so constantly on the alert that the Indians had few chances to surprise unprepared people; but the deserted ranches suffered from their looting.

As soon as the people of El Paso County had recovered somewhat from the first shock of this outbreak, steps were taken to form a military company to be regularly employed against the Indians, its members serving without pay. It was the intention to keep the company in the field until the savages were driven out of this region. On or about September 15, 1868, I joined a company composed of about eighty mounted and well armed men who had enlisted for this purpose. We assembled at Husted's Saw Mill on the Divide, ready for service, and perfected a military organization by the election of the usual company officers. A. J. Templeton, a veteran of the Mexican War and an officer of the Third Colorado Cavalry at the battle of Sand Creek, was elected its captain.

Evidently our officers received word here that the savages were leaving the country, as the Company immediately took up its line of march directly to Bijou Basin instead of being distributed in groups through the Pinery, as we had expected. We remained at Bijou Basin that night and, the next morning, moved on in an easterly direction, taking in the hill where Simpson's party had withstood an attack by the savages about two weeks before. After examining with much interest the scene of this fight, our command marched to Big Sandy where we struck the trail of the Indians apparently leaving the country. We followed this trail down the valley of that stream to Lake Station on the Smoky Hill wagon road about ten miles east of the present town of Limon. Not an Indian had been seen in our entire march, and judging from the trail and other indications, they were at least a day ahead of us. As we moved down the valley of the Big Sandy, we saw many dead cattle, both above and below the present towns of Ramah and Calhan, most of them cows that had been killed by the Indians only a short time before. That these cattle had been wantonly killed was shown by the fact that no part of them had been taken for food. In almost every instance, they had been shot with arrows, many of which were sticking in the dead animals. Besides the dead cattle, we saw scattered over the hills and down the valleys as far as we went hundreds of live ones that the Indians had driven off from the ranches of El Paso and adjoining counties.

At a point about ten miles down the Big Sandy from the present town of Limon, the trail of the Indians left the valley and turned northeastward to the head waters of the Arickaree, a fork of the Republican River. At this place,—as we learned afterwards,—we were only about seventy-five miles away from the Beecher Island battle ground where Major Forsyth and his fifty men were, at that very time, making their heroic defense against an overwhelming number of Cheyenne and Arapahoe warriors under command of the notorious chief, Roman Nose. Whether the band of warriors we were following had been called in by Roman Nose or were leaving the country through fear of Captain Templeton's Company, probably never will be known. However, the lack of haste shown in their retreat leads me to believe that they had not yet heard of the great disaster suffered by their own people.

Upon discovering the course taken by the Indians, Captain Templeton, on account of his small forces, deemed it imprudent to pursue them further. An additional reason for facing about was that our food supplies were about exhausted. When we enlisted it was understood that our service should be confined to El Paso County and that our subsistence would be provided at the ranches; hence, no commissary arrangements had been made aside from a small amount of food that each one brought from his home. Had we gone on, we should have had to subsist on the wild game of the region, which would have been a risky thing to attempt. As it was, on, our way homeward we had nothing to eat other than the meat of cattle that we killed. Not having a camp outfit, we broiled the meat on forked sticks before camp fires and then ate it without salt. To me this fare was the nearest to a starvation diet of any that I ever was compelled to subsist upon.

The Company reached Colorado City in due time without having seen an Indian during the whole campaign. It was evident that the Indians were gone and, that, on account of approaching winter, we had little to fear from them during the remainder of the year, as their raids always came in summer when the ponies were fat. There apparently being no further use for its services, our Company disbanded.

The period following the first appearance of the Indians about the 20th of August until it was definitely known that they had returned to their villages on the plains, was an anxious one for the settlers. At least a dozen persons had been killed in El Paso County and adjoining territory on the Divide. Many houses had been destroyed and crops needed for winter use lost through inability to harvest them, and probably five hundred horses and at least one thousand head of cattle had been driven off by the savages. Altogether, it made a loss in life and property that was extremely heavy for a sparsely populated county such as El Paso was at that time. The contest had been an unequal one from the start. The settlers possessed only a miscellaneous lot of guns, most of which were muzzle-loading rifles, while the Indians were armed with breech-loading Government guns, using metal cartridges. Fortunately, the ammunition issued to the Indians by the Government agents was of poor quality, as was shown in the fight east of Bijou Basin and elsewhere; and judging by the careful manner in which it was used, it is probable that the supply was not large. This undoubtedly saved the lives of many people, as it was noticed from the first that the Indians never wasted their ammunition, seldom attacking an armed person.

During all the time the savages were going up and down the county on their raids, the General Government did not make the slightest effort to give our people protection, although attention was repeatedly called to the desperate conditions existing in this locality. The only assistance we received was from the Territorial authorities at Denver who supplied our county with a limited number of old Belgian muskets, together with the necessary ammunition. These guns were so much inferior to those in the hands of the Indians that they added little to our security. With this exception, the early settlers of El Paso County were dependent for protection upon their own resources from the beginning of the Indian troubles in 1864 until the end, which came with the building of the Union Pacific Railroad along the northern border of the Territory in 1868, and the completion of the Kansas Pacific a year or two later.

In September, 1866, General William T. Sherman, Commander-in-Chief of the United States Army, on his way north from an inspection of the forts in New Mexico, accompanied by a large number of staff officers and a strong escort, stopped over night in Colorado City. Having been in constant danger from the Indians since the beginning of the trouble in 1864, our people thought it an opportune time to lay the matter before him and ask that protection be provided. My father, Reverend William Howbert, was appointed spokesman of the committee that waited upon the General. In his talk, father explained our exposed and defenseless condition and suggested that a force of Government troops be permanently stationed at some point on our eastern frontier, so as to intercept any Indians that might be attempting raids upon our people. General Sherman received the appeal with utter indifference, and replied that he thought we were unnecessarily alarmed, since there were no hostile Indians in this region. He then sarcastically remarked that it probably would be a very profitable arrangement for this community could it have a force of Government troops located near here, to whom the farmers might sell their grain and other products at a high price. With this remark he dismissed the committee, the members of which left the room quite indignant at the manner in which their appeal had been received.

Later in the year, General Sherman evidently concluded that there were hostile Indians in this western country and that they needed severe punishment, for, after the massacre of Lieutenant-Colonel Fetterman and his entire command near Fort Phil Kearney, Wyoming, he telegraphed General Grant saying: "We must act with vindictive earnestness against the Sioux, even to their extermination, men, women and children; nothing else will reach the root of the case."

Two years later, in 1868, the General came to Denver along the line of the Kansas Pacific Railway, then under construction, the terminus at that time being in western Kansas, and was glad to have a strong escort to guard him through the region of the hostile Indians. Following this trip, he made a strenuous effort to punish the savages elsewhere, but made no attempt to protect the settlers along the eastern borders of Colorado.

It was always a question of the influence that could be brought to bear upon Government officials at Washington. After the Indian outbreak in Minnesota in 1862, the Government took prompt measures and not only punished the Indians unmercifully, but removed them from the state. However, this was undoubtedly due to the fact that Minnesota then had two senators and several members of Congress, who were able to bring the necessary influence to bear; while, during the entire period of our Indian troubles, Colorado was still a Territory with only a delegate in Congress, who had no vote and consequently, very little influence. As a result, no attention was paid to our pleas for protection and we were left to defend ourselves as best we could.

The entire eastern frontier of El Paso County faced upon territory occupied by the Cheyennes and Arapahoes, than whom there were no more crafty and blood-thirsty savages upon the American Continent. There were at all times bands of these Indians roaming around on the headwaters of the Republican and Smoky Hill Rivers, not more than a hundred and twenty-five miles away from Colorado City, and it would have been easy for them to reach this region without being observed. Considering these facts, it now seems a wonder that the settlements of El Paso County were not wiped off the face of the earth. Probably the principal reason why we were not exterminated by the savages from the plains lay in the fact of our contiguity to the country of their hereditary enemies, the Utes, for whose remarkable fighting ability they had a wholesome respect. They knew that they ran the risk of having to fight the Utes as well as the whites, if they came here. In 1858 a large band of Cheyennes and Arapahoes had an all day fight with the Utes in and around Monument Park, now the site of the Modern Woodmen of America Sanatorium, six or eight miles north of Colorado Springs. During the winter of 1865–66, a large body of Ute Indians camped for several months on the south side of the Fountain opposite Colorado City. Again, in the winter of 1866–67, a thousand or more of the same tribe camped for several months below the Boiling Springs—now Manitou—between the Balanced Rock and the Fountain.

After the battle of the Washita in November, 1868, heretofore referred to, the larger part of the Cheyennes and Arapahoes was put upon a reservation and compelled to stay there. This ended their raids in this locality, and, thereafter, the people of El Paso County were unmolested by savages, although spasmodic outbreaks occurred at various places elsewhere in the west for several years.

During the Indian troubles of the 1868 period, as in 1864, a few settlers left the county and sought places of safety elsewhere. A great majority of our people, however, pluckily stood their ground, and, as soon as it was definitely known that the Indians had left the county, most of the ranchmen moved their families back to their homes.

CHAPTER XII

ELECTED COUNTY CLERK—FOUNDING OF COLORADO SPRINGS

AT the general election held in October, 1869, I was elected County Clerk of El Paso County, without opposition, having been nominated by the Republicans and endorsed by the Democrats. The nomination had come to me as somewhat of a surprise for the reason that my connection with politics up to that time had been slight, and I had made no effort to secure the office. However, my election undoubtedly was the turning point in my life, because of the varied experience and wide acquaintance it gave me.

Previous to the time I took charge of the office, late in October, 1869, the duties of the County Clerk had not been of an onerous character. The entire assessed valuation of El Paso County at that time amounted to about two hundred and twenty-five thousand dollars, and the total number of voters in the county was in the neighborhood of three hundred. My predecessor had established his office in a frame house on the north side of Colorado Avenue at about the center of Colorado City, the county-seat, no county building having as yet been erected. This structure was the one in which the Territorial Senate held two or three sessions at the time the Legislature convened in Colorado City in 1862. The County Clerk's office occupied the rear part of the building, and the large front room was set apart for court purposes. The Clerk's office was not plastered, and, notwithstanding the fact that there was a big stove in the center, it was most uncomfortable. Ink froze in the bottles almost every night during the time I occupied the room. Some months later, this condition having become almost unbearable, I persuaded the County Commissioners to rent an adjacent log cabin and moved my office into it. Although less pretentious, it was much warmer and more comfortable in every way than the room I vacated.

By many this log building is erroneously supposed to be one of the original Capitol buildings of the Territory. Built in the early days of the town, it was occupied in 1862, at the time the Territorial Legislature met in Colorado City, by Dr. Garvin and M. S. Beach, the latter a member of the House of Representatives. It is no doubt true that much of the preliminary business preceding the convening of the Legislature was discussed by Mr. Beach and other members of the House in this log cabin, but that is as near as it ever came to being a Capitol building. During recent years it has been used as a Chinese laundry.

When I moved into this log house, I was able to

carry over to it all the records of the county in less than half an hour; and in its two rooms was transacted all the business of El Paso County for the next two or three years. It was the office of the County Commissioners, the County Treasurer, the County Assessor, as well as that of the County Clerk. A majority of the County Commissioners lived on ranches some distance away from town, and regular meetings of the Board were held only five or six times a year. The County Treasurer, Benjamin F. Crowell, had a sheep ranch which required a great deal of attention. Consequently, because of the absence of these officers much of the time, it became necessary for me to attend to most of their duties, and generally supervise the business of the county, besides looking after the work of my own office.

By the summer of 1870, new-comers began to arrive in considerable numbers, most of them intending to locate permanently in this region. Little of the lands of the county had been taken up, leaving a large acreage subject to preëmption, homestead, and private entry. Since there was as yet no one in the county making a business of attending to the details necessary in the location and entry of public lands, I soon found myself compelled to take up this task in addition to my regular duties. On this account the work of the Clerk's office grew by leaps and bounds, and entering of land and preparing papers for final proof in homestead and preëmption cases became a very considerable part of my business. To be fitted for this work, I had to familiarize myself with the United States land laws; and in the same connection, I found it necessary to make a sectional map of the county, no other being in existence at the time, as far as I know. Besides all this, I had to attend to the entire pension business of the region. That I might be able to help soldier friends in securing pensions, I applied for and received permission to practice before the Pensions Bureau at Washington.

Two or three years previously, a telegraph line had been constructed from Denver to Pueblo, and, I think, on to Santa Fé. It was a cheaply built affair, but answered fairly well for the limited amount of use required of it. Although this line ran through El Paso County, no telegraph office had been established within its boundaries up to the time I was elected Clerk. However, soon after I moved into the log building, the manager of the line installed a set of instruments in my office and taught me sufficient telegraphy to enable me to answer calls and test the line. He also installed a mechanical arrangement for receiving telegrams, consisting of a series of cog wheels with weights, which, after it was wound up and set in motion, recorded on a slip of soft paper the dots and dashes that made the message. Knowing the Morse alphabet, I was in that way able to receive and interpret messages, but with all his teaching, I never became proficient enough to send them. After Matt France, an experienced operator, moved to the county in 1870, he was appointed the Telegraph

Company's regular agent, but, as he was engaged in the cattle business and came into town only Saturdays, opportunities for sending telegrams were decidedly limited. General Palmer, on his visits here before Colorado Springs was laid out, usually brought an operator with him to send his messages.

Soon after I became County Clerk and while my office was in the log cabin, it became known that I was interested in the geology of this Pike's Peak region, and especially in the petrifactions found along Monument Creek and the eastern base of the mountains. As a result, people began to bring in to me many specimens ranging from numerous baculites, to the body of a large turtle on which the markings of the shell were complete, and my case soon became too small to hold the accumulation. Later, it took up so much of my time answering questions about the collection that, when opportunity offered, I gave it to a college in Ohio, an act that I afterwards regretted very much, realizing that the proper home for it was in Colorado College.

In the spring of 1870, General William J. Palmer, accompanied by a number of people, among whom were William P. Mellen, his daughter,—who afterwards became General Palmer's wife—and Colonel Greenwood, later Chief Engineer of the Denver and Rio Grande Railroad, came to Colorado City from the line of the Kansas-Pacific. This railroad then was under construction through eastern Colorado, with General Palmer in charge. At Colonel Greenwood's request, I accompanied the party on horse-

back to the Soda Springs,—now Manitou—to the
Garden of the Gods, and other places of interest in
the Pike's Peak region. It appears that General
Palmer on a previous visit had become convinced
that there was need of a railroad running southward
from Denver along the eastern base of the mountains to southern Colorado and New Mexico, and
was much impressed with the advantages, as a
townsite, of the plateau east of Monument Creek
facing Pike's Peak.

Not long after this visit, General Palmer's agent,
A. C. Hunt, a former governor of the Territory of
Colorado, called on me as he passed through Colorado
City, looking over the proposed route for the railroad, and gave me an inkling of what General Palmer
had in mind. Upon his return to Denver, Governor
Hunt organized a railroad company under a name
which I do not remember, that ostensibly had for
its purpose the building of a railroad covering substantially the same route as now occupied by the
Denver and Rio Grande. Governor Hunt, F. Z.
Saloman and myself were the incorporators, but we
understood that this company was organized merely
to hold the field until General Palmer had his plan
perfected. Later, I rode with Governor Hunt in a
buggy from Denver to Colorado City, much of the
way along the line of the proposed railway. Still
later, Governor Hunt came to me and disclosed the
fact that General Palmer and his associates wished
to acquire a large tract of land to the east of Monument Creek with the intention of laying out a town

on that site, and ultimately bringing a colony of eastern people thereto. I at once realized that such a movement, in connection with the building of a railway into this section, would be of incalculable benefit to the entire Pike's Peak region; consequently, when requested to aid in securing the land, I took up the work with much enthusiasm. Most of the area that General Palmer desired, belonged to the Government, and was what was called "offered land," that is, land subject to private entry. The Government regulations then were, that any surveyed land which had been open to preëmption and homestead for five years and had not been taken, could be purchased in unlimited quantities at $1.25 per acre. A large part of the land on which Colorado Springs is located was of that character, although along Shook's Run and Monument Creek a number of people had taken up preëmption and homestead claims, and it was my part of the work to secure their relinquishments. This I succeeded in doing without much trouble and at a smaller expense than I had anticipated. In my land work a few months before, I had found vacant and taken up as a homestead a one hundred and sixty acre tract, covering land now occupied by the yards and depots of the Denver and Rio Grande Railroad, Antlers Park, and extending over to the vicinity of what is now Tejon Street. For this claim Governor Hunt gave me $250.00. He offered to let me retain the best forty acres of it, which, as I now remember, lay directly north of and adjacent to the present site

222 The Pike's Peak Region

of the Antlers Hotel. I knew that this tract would be valuable as soon as the town was fairly started, but having induced the other claimants to relinquish their holdings for a nominal consideration, I felt it would be unfair for me to retain any portion of mine.

After having secured a cancellation of all previous claims, Governor Hunt used Agricultural College scrip in the purchase from the Government of these tracts and an additional ten thousand acres adjoining acquired at the same time. A few years prior to this time, Congress had made a large grant of public lands to the various states for the purpose of encouraging the establishment of agricultural colleges. To the states having no public lands, scrip was issued, which entitled the holder to use it in place of cash in the purchase from the Government of vacant public lands in any part of the United States. The result of this provision was that the supply of scrip greatly exceeded the demand, and many states sold theirs at a very low price. I was told that Governor Hunt paid eighty cents per acre for the Agricultural College scrip used in acquiring the land on which the town of Colorado Springs was laid out.

The Denver and Rio Grande Railroad Company was organized in the autumn of 1870 and construction work began at Denver in January, 1871. The Colorado Springs Company was formed May 20, of the same year. Its directors held their first meeting at Denver, June 21, 1871, at which time, officers were elected and the principal features of the proposed town of Colorado Springs were decided upon, including the organization of the Fountain Colony through which settlers were to be obtained. At the same meeting, the construction of roads, bridges, and a hotel on the proposed town site was authorized. On the 31st day of July, several officers and directors accompanied by Colonel Greenwood, Chief Engineer of the Denver and Rio Grande Railroad, left Denver to inspect the proposed town site and start the work of laying out the new town, to appraise the lots, and begin operations generally. The first stake was driven the following day, at what is now the southeast corner of Cascade and Pike's Peak Avenues. The work of subdividing the townsite into lots and blocks was done under the direction of E. S. Nettleton, the engineer who had laid out the town of Greeley.

Colorado. Springs was planned along unusual lines and its broad streets, avenues and parks were given uncommon names. During the period preceding the coming of the Americans into this western region, the Spanish influence had been dominant to the south of this locality, and that of the French trapper element to the north. Apparently recognizing this historical fact, Spanish names were given to many cross-streets south of Pike's Peak Avenue, such as Huerfano, Cucharas, Vermijo, Moreno; and to many of those north of Pike's Peak Avenue, French names were given, such as Bijou, Platte, St. Vrain, Cache la Poudre. The principal north and south avenues, Cascade, Nevada and Wahsatch, were named after mountain ranges. Instead of designating the two small parks in the heart of the town as "North" and "South," the distinctive names of "Acacia" and "Alamo" were given them.

At the time the Colorado Springs Company was formed, General R. A. Cameron was appointed General Manager and William E. Pabor, Secretary of the Company. Both of these men had been connected with the Greeley Colony since the time of its inception, and were thoroughly familiar with the method of advertising and the mode of procedure that had brought excellent results to that town. Soon after his appointment, General Cameron sent out a circular describing the proposed colony and setting forth the requirements and conditions to be complied with in order to become a member of it, among which were the following:

"Any person may become a member of the colony who is possessed of a good moral character and is of strict temperate habits, by the payment to the Treasurer or the Assistant Treasurer of one hundred dollars, which will be credited to him on the selection of such lots and lands as he may desire.

"Titles will be given to members whenever their improvements are made according to the conditions heretofore mentioned, said titles to contain a clause forever prohibiting the manufacture, giving or selling of intoxicating liquors in any public resort as a beverage."

Copies of this circular, together with other interesting matter concerning the proposed town and its surroundings, were widely distributed throughout this country and Great Britain during the next few months. This advertising soon began to bear fruit, and within a few months thereafter, colonists began arriving in considerable numbers. In fact, for awhile they came so rapidly as to make it difficult to take care of them. To meet this condition, one hundred and fifty portable houses were ordered from Chicago and set up around the town. These houses undoubtedly prevented much suffering during the first winter of the town's existence, and were in use to a considerable extent for several years thereafter.

Early in August, 1871, James P. True began construction of the first house in Colorado Springs. Alva Adams, afterwards Governor of Colorado for two terms, erected a building at about the same time, which he used as a hardware store. Among other early structures was a two-story hotel of considerable size, which was built on the southeast corner of Cascade and Pike's Peak Avenues. This building, known as The Colorado Springs Hotel, was opened on the 1st day of January, 1872, and was a familiar landmark for a number of years.

From the start, General Palmer and his associates did everything which forethought could devise to make the town a success. Among the most important things was the purchase of some of the oldest, as well as largest, water-rights on the Fountain, and the construction of a large irrigation canal taken out from that stream at a point above Colorado City and continuing to the northern limits of Colorado Springs. This canal was completed late in December, 1871; and, now, fifty-four years later, is still in use.

Early the following spring, a water supply for irrigation being assured, the Colorado Springs Company arranged for the delivery of a large number of small round leafed cottonwood trees from the valley of the Arkansas River, to be set out along the principal residence streets. Up to that time, the tract on which the town was located was a dreary plain with a few cheap, wooden houses scattered over it, the only trees in sight being an occasional one along Monument Creek. In a few years, however, the trees set out by the Company made a remarkable transformation in the appearance of Colorado Springs. What General Palmer did in this connection set the pace that has resulted in the forest of trees which now covers every part of the city and adds so much to its beauty. Colorado Springs was most fortunate in having such a far-sighted and broad-minded man as General Palmer for its founder.

In a report issued by Secretary Pabor, dated January 18, 1872, five months after driving the first stake, he says:

"The number of houses that had been erected up to January, 1872, was one hundred and fifty-nine.

Contracts for fifteen others were then in the hands
of builders; the total population was seven hundred
and ninety-five; an excellent newspaper had been
founded and many business houses and two churches
had been built. A free reading room had been
opened, and a contract for a fine public school
building given; nineteen miles of canal, two and a
half feet deep and six feet wide, had been excavated;
which, with the seven miles additional then in
progress, would place all the colony lands under
irrigation. Something over thirteen miles of lateral
canals had been put through the town; seven miles
of shade trees had been planted; two public parks
laid out; and the educational interests of the future
provided for by liberal reservations for free schools,
academies and colleges."

Among those who ably assisted General Palmer
in building the Rio Grande Railroad and founding
Colorado Springs, was Dr. W. A. Bell of England,
who was with Palmer during the time he was making
surveys to the Pacific coast for the Kansas Pacific
Railroad Company. As a result of the intimate
friendship which grew up between them at that time,
Dr. Bell became associated with General Palmer in
all his principal ventures, this association continuing
for many years thereafter. It was through Dr. Bell
that their enterprises were extensively advertised
in England, which resulted in a considerable number
of young Englishmen coming to Colorado Springs
during its first years. Notable among them was

Maurice Kingsley, a son of the well known writer, Canon Kingsley. Maurice Kingsley was Assistant Secretary of the Colorado Springs Company during the early years of its existence. His sister, Miss Rose Kingsley, came to Colorado Springs late in the fall of the first year and spent most of the following winter here. She gives a very entertaining account of that first winter in her book *South by West*, published after returning to England. Miss Kingsley is said to have been the first woman to make an ascent of Mt. Rosa, which was named in her honor. Owing to the fact that there were so many English residents in the town, Colorado Springs, somewhat later, was dubbed "Little London" by the people of Denver and other localities in the State.

There were few women among the inhabitants of Colorado Springs during the first year, for the reason that many of the colonists were waiting to ascertain whether or not this region was all that had been claimed for it, before bringing their families here. The first winter was an unusually cold one, and the new inhabitants suffered considerable discomfort owing to the flimsy nature of the houses that had been hurriedly put up the previous summer.

While this epoch-making development was taking shape, another enterprise of great importance to El Paso County was under way. Up to this time there was no wagon road through Ute Pass into the mountains over which heavily loaded teams could be taken, the road then in use having been made during the early days of the Pike's Peak region. As before stated, the first three or four miles west of the Soda Springs, or Manitou Springs, as they are now called, ran over the hills a quarter to a half a mile south of the Fountain, and had excessively heavy grades. The question of building a good wagon road up through the Pass along the Fountain was considered at various times during the six or eight years prior to the founding of Colorado Springs, but on account of the great expense involved, no definite action was taken in the matter. Finally, after much discussion, the question of issuing county bonds to the extent of $15,000.00 to build the road was submitted to the people at an election held on the 20th of June, 1871. Many of the old settlers thought it most extravagant to bond the county for such an amount and predicted that it would be bankrupted thereby. Nevertheless, it turned out that the progressive, wide-awake citizens of El Paso County were in the majority. The bonds were voted and the road was constructed as it now exists, excepting that it was narrow in places. Later it was widened from time to time, making it the splendid highway that it now is.

After the Rio Grande Railroad was completed to Colorado Springs and before the building of the South Park line from Denver, the new Ute Pass road was used by many large freighting concerns; and for a time, it was one of the most important thoroughfares of southern Colorado. The traffic over it between Colorado Springs and Leadville was immense. It was estimated that at one time there were twelve thousand horses and mules used in transporting freight over the Ute Pass road to the mining towns of South Park, Leadville and elsewhere throughout western Colorado. This traffic continued until the completion of the South Park Railroad from Denver to Leadville, after which freighting over the Ute Pass road virtually ceased. However, the extensive use of this road during the period mentioned doubtless brought the country between Colorado Springs and the South Park into public notice much sooner than otherwise would have been the case, thus materially expediting the settlement of that region.

The Denver and Rio Grande Railroad was completed to Colorado Springs, October 21, 1871, and regular train service between Denver and that town was established a day or two later. Since this road was one of the first narrow guage lines of any great length built in the United States, it attracted much attention and considerable criticism. It answered the purpose for the time being, however, and, as the country developed and traffic grew in volume, larger ties and heavier rails were laid, and the size of the cars, both passenger and freight, was increased. Eventually, the main line was broadened to a standard gauge.

In the latter part of the summer of 1871, I again received the nomination for County Clerk from the Republican party without opposition, and was elected by a good majority, although the Democrats nominated a candidate for the place who made a rather strenuous campaign against me. This was the only time during ten years that I held the office of County Clerk that I had any organized opposition whatsoever.

The growth of the new town of Colorado Springs added greatly to the business of the County Clerk's office, as well as to that of the other County offices, and a larger building for the transaction of County business soon became necessary. But no action could be taken in the matter because, early in 1872, the people of Colorado Springs began making a determined effort to take the county-seat away from Colorado City, and for the next two years the movement kept this section in a continual turmoil. Wherever people met it was the principal topic of conversation. Just before election, the county was canvassed from end to end by representatives of the two towns. The people of Colorado City promised, in the event that the county-seat was not removed, to erect and give to the County a suitable building for the accommodation of the courts and the various County offices. When the question came before the people for a vote, the contest resulted in favor of Colorado City by a fair majority. The agreement concerning a county court house was promptly carried out and the large brick building still standing near the center of Colorado City—at one time used as a school house— was erected and turned over to the County. But this did not stop the agitation. Colorado Springs was growing at a rapid rate and the election was no sooner over than its people began to plan another county-seat campaign. On the other hand, Colorado City under the leadership of Anthony Bott and others of its prominent citizens, was alert to thwart the schemes of its rival and many interesting incidents occurred in connection with the contest.

Among the ardent supporters of Colorado City in its efforts to retain the county-seat was "Judge" Baldwin, as he was called, the sheep-herder who had been scalped and left for dead by the Indians of South America, and afterwards shot and partially scalped by savages on the present townsite of Colorado Springs. Baldwin had now fully recovered physically, although his mind was slightly affected as a result of wounds and an inordinate appetite for whiskey. By this time he had acquired a few sheep of his own which he kept on his ranch near Austins Bluffs. His chief object in life seemed to be securing money with which to visit Colorado City and indulge in a "big drunk." Baldwin was of Irish descent and spoke with a strong brogue. In addition, the shot fired by the Indians which passed through his shoulder and up through his jaw had interfered somewhat with his articulation. When the county-seat contest came on Baldwin espoused the cause of the "Old Town," as Colorado City was commonly called, and during the campaign previous to the election he never failed to mount a box wherever he could get an audience, in Colorado City, Colorado Springs, or elsewhere, to harangue the people about the rights of the "Auld Town," as he pronounced it. His saying that the "Auld Town has got it and is goin' to kape it" became familiar all over the county.

Poor Baldwin. He was his own worst enemy. A year or two later, after a rather worse drunken bout than usual, he left Colorado Springs for his ranch one evening about eight o'clock. The next morning his body was found in a well inside a slaughter house just east of town. His horse was hitched to the fence near by, and it was supposed that having become sleepy when this point was reached, he had gone into the building and in his drunken, helpless condition had stumbled into the open well and been drowned. It was common report that Baldwin was a member of a prominent family of Chicago.

At the general election held in the fall of 1873, Colorado Springs succeeded in its efforts to secure the county-seat, winning by a good majority. Soon after the votes were counted and the result declared, the County offices were moved to Colorado Springs and of course I changed my residence to the latter place.

Immediately after Colorado Springs came into existence the Colorado Springs Company built a long one-story frame structure on the northwest corner of Tejon and Kiowa Streets which was known as the "Colony Building." When the county-seat was changed to Colorado Springs, this building was vacated by the officers of the Colorado Springs

Company and turned over to the County for the use
of its officials. My office occupied the corner rooms,
and in these much of the largely increasing business
of El Paso County was transacted for the next two
or three years.

By the beginning of 1875, the population of
Colorado Springs and El Paso County had materially
increased, and the business of my office had grown
accordingly. This made it necessary to enlarge
my office force from time to time. As I always
made it a practice to employ at least one member
of the opposite party, usually my Chief Clerk was a
Democrat, and it so happened a number of times
that he was Chairman of the Democratic County
Central Committee at the same time that I occupied
a similar position in the Republican party. I never
was a very strong partisan, which perhaps accounts
for the little opposition that I had from the Democrats during my political life.

From the beginning there was a disposition on
the part of a few of the residents of Colorado Springs
to ignore the clause in the Company deeds prohibiting the sale of intoxicating liquors. And in
the summer of 1873, this culminated in establishing
what was virtually a saloon in a building at the
southeast corner of Pike's Peak Avenue and Tejon
Street. A high partition cut off a part of the room,
and in this partition there was a revolving wheel
divided into four compartments. Any one wanting
a drink of liquor put the price in one of these compartments, mentioning what he desired loud enough

for the man inside to hear, and then revolved the wheel. In a few moments another revolution brought forth the drink. This wheel was generally known about town as the "Katy King Spiritual Wheel," so named after a noted spiritualist of Boston of that period.

Later, the Colorado Springs Company brought suit against the owners of the property on which this illegal procedure was being carried on. At the hearing, the Company produced conclusive evidence that the clause in the deeds prohibiting the sale of liquor had been violated, and asked for a decree of the court declaring the property forfeited to the Company under the forfeiture clause. The petition was granted and a decree to that effect was entered by the Court, June 18, 1874. An appeal was taken to the higher courts, and finally reached the Supreme Court of the United States, which body, on January 30, 1880, affirmed the decisions of the lower courts. Thus the Colorado Springs Company again became owner of the property. This decision effectually settled the question as to the validity of the forfeiture clause in the deeds.

While Colorado Springs was making rapid strides in wealth and population, Colorado City also was growing fast, evidently profiting by the extensive advertising that had been given the new town. Among the new-comers who chose to settle in Colorado City, were many of the floating class, and others who did not approve of the liquor restrictions in the Colorado Springs deeds. As a result, the number of saloons in Colorado City increased rapidly, and it soon became a town in which drunken brawls were of common occurrence. The history of Colorado City was one of ups and downs, high hopes and bitter disappointments rapidly succeeding each other from the beginning up to the time when, by a vote of its people, the town became a part of Colorado Springs.

Late in 1871, General Palmer and his associates purchased all the land surrounding the Boiling Springs and proceeded to lay out a town. The ground was surveyed by E. S. Nettleton who had made the original plat of Colorado Springs. Under instructions from General Palmer, Mr. Nettleton made his survey conform to the unusual contour of the site, the result being an irregular and unconventional arrangement of streets, blocks and lots. The town was first named La Font, but, a little later, this was changed to Manitou, a name derived from Ruxton's legend of the mineral springs.

Even before the plat of the Manitou townsite was completed, the Colorado Springs Company began the erection of the Manitou House. This proved to be a very popular hotel and was filled with guests soon after completion. A short time later, this became overcrowded and the Mansions was built, which, in turn, was followed by the Cliff House and other hotels erected by various individuals. The Manitou House was completely destroyed by fire a few years afterwards; and still later, a part of the Mansions was burned.

For a time Manitou grew rapidly, then there was a comparative lull for a number of years. Later the town took on new life and its growth, although not rapid, has been continuous since that time. Now its hotels are filled to capacity every summer, the place having become a famous resort, and the water from the springs is being bottled and shipped to all parts of the country.

CHAPTER XIII

EARLY VENTURES IN BANKING AND MINING

AT the time of my first election as County Clerk of El Paso County in 1869, Benjamin F. Crowell was chosen County Treasurer, and we held our respective offices continuously for the next ten years. Being thus thrown together constantly during this long period, a warm and intimate friendship grew up between us which continued unbroken as long as he lived. Undoubtedly he was the man who exercised the greatest influence in El Paso County affairs from the time that he arrived in Colorado City in 1860 to the end of his life.

Benjamin F. Crowell was born January 8, 1835, at Manchester-by-the-Sea, Massachusetts. He was the son of Captain Samuel F. Crowell, who followed the sea the larger part of his life. Young Crowell went to Boston when thirteen years of age and took a position in a book store. Later, he secured employment in a book-binding establishment, where he remained until he came west. He had, in the meantime, by sheer ability, risen through the various grades of the establishment until, at the time he left, he was virtual head of all its operations. Meanwhile, his health had become somewhat impaired by the close confinement of these years and a change of climate seemed desirable.

About this time, the newspapers were full of accounts of gold discoveries in the Pike's Peak region, and young Crowell soon caught the fever. It happened that he was distantly related to the Tappan Brothers who, in 1859, had founded mercantile establishments in Denver and Colorado City. From a member of this firm, Crowell received such favorable reports about the Pike's Peak gold diggings that he decided to visit them. Early in 1860, he arranged to make the trip to the Rocky Mountains with a wagonload of freight, which Tappan Brothers were sending out from Lawrence, Kansas. Crowell went directly from Boston to Lawrence, where he met A. Z. Sheldon, a Mr. Spencer, and James Tappan, a cousin of the Tappan Brothers. These men were to share with him in the responsibility of driving the team with its load of freight through to Colorado City. For this service they were to have their blankets and provisions sufficient for the trip hauled free of charge.

The team consisted of two yoke of oxen and a wagon. When the party was ready to start, it developed that no one of the four was familiar with the handling of ox teams, or in fact with any other kind of team. Nor did any of them know how to yoke or unyoke the cattle; so they hired a man to yoke the oxen and hitch them to the wagon. It then occurred to Crowell and the others that they would not know on which side each particular ox belonged unless they had some definite way of distinguishing one animal from another. To avoid making a mistake, they painted a horn of the near ox of each yoke red. And, as they were much more familiar with the sea than the land, they called one the larboard and the other the starboard ox.

After everything was ready, the party started with Crowell on one side of the team and Tappan on the other, each with a large stick to be used in keeping the oxen in the road. The only serious trouble occurred in the afternoon of the first day. They had been traveling steadily along, and, the weather being hot, the cattle evidently had become very thirsty. As they were approaching a stream where there was a ford near the bridge, the oxen, seeing the water, made a break for it in spite of all the drivers could do. Before they could be halted, the animals were down in the stream; but Crowell and Tappan managed to stop the wagon on the brink. By unloading it, they succeeded in gettng it out of its precarious position and back on the road. With the wagon reloaded the party started on again and had little trouble thereafter, as they soon became accustomed to managing the oxen.

Their route was across the prairies of Kansas in a southwesterly direction until they reached the Arkansas River—a road not much used that year on account of border troubles preceding the Civil War and the threatening attitude of the Comanche Indians—then westerly up that river towards the mountains. By the time they reached the river they were well into the Indian country, but the savages did not molest them.

The greatest danger that threatened was from the large herds of buffalo that often covered the plains as far as the eye could reach. Other parties traveling that route about the same time had found the buffalo in such compact masses and moving so fast across the road, that the only way these people could keep from being overwhelmed and trampled upon was by killing considerable numbers of the advancing herd, thus forming a barrier which compelled the buffalo to divide and go around.

Finally, after about thirty-five days of continuous travel, Colorado City was reached and the team and freight safely delivered to Tappan Brothers.

Soon after, Crowell visited the various gold diggings in and around the South Park, and at every place found many more gold seekers than the extent of the placers warranted. After spending a month or so in this way, he concluded that there was little probability of success in that direction, and returned to Colorado City with a view of getting employment, having now spent the larger part of his available funds. About this time many people had begun to realize that the land in the valleys of the streams along the eastern base of the mountains might be of value agriculturally. As a result, ranches were being located in the valley of the Fountain below Colorado City and along the different creeks tributary to it.

In line with this movement, Mr. Crowell located a ranch on what was known as the Big Flat—afterwards called Bachelors' Flat—about a mile southeast of the mouth of Cheyenne Creek. He was unable to do anything more at that time than file upon the land, build a cabin, and have a ditch surveyed from Cheyenne Creek, since his funds now had entirely given out and he was forced to go to work. He hired a team and most of the time during the remainder of that summer and the following winter was employed in hauling freight between Denver and Colorado City. In that way, by the spring of 1861, he had accumulated enough money to secure seed for the crop that he proposed to plant. Meanwhile, he and others living in that locality had constructed a ditch to bring water from Cheyenne Creek to irrigate their lands. It was only by the strictest economy that he was able to get through the summer, in fact at times, had it not been for the wild game he killed, he would have suffered for food. Fortunately, he raised an excellent crop and sold it at a very remunerative price, and this in a measure relieved his financial necessities. His success in this new venture was remarkable considering that he knew nothing whatever about farming or irrigation except what he had learned since coming to the Rocky Mountains. His whole after life showed that he was a resourceful man, of rare ability and extraordinary common sense. He could readily adapt himself to any condition, however strange or unusual it might be.

At the first general election for Territorial and County officers in 1862, Mr. Crowell was elected a member of the Board of County Commissioners of El Paso County, and later was made chairman. He took a leading part in organizing the County government. Since the population of El Paso County at that time was small and the assessable property very limited, it required great care and economy on the part of the County Commissioners to keep the expenses of the County within its income; but this Mr. Crowell insisted be done.

Mr. Crowell's duties as County Commissioner left him much time for his own affairs, and during this period he brought his ranch to a good state of cultivation and found a ready market for his crops. Later he engaged in sheep raising, being one of the pioneers in that industry in this Pike's Peak region. In that, as in all other ventures, he was unusually successful and soon had one of the best flocks in the county.

In 1869, as I have said, Mr. Crowell was elected County Treasurer, a position which he held for the next ten years, excepting during 1871–72, when he was a member of the House of Representatives of the Territorial Legislature. While in that body he took an active part in all legislative matters and became one of its prominent leaders.

Although Mr. Crowell and I had every reason to believe that we could hold our respective offices indefinitely, by the time we had been in office four or five years we began to tire of political life because of its many unpleasant features, and were ready to take up some congenial business whenever oppor- tunity offered. Having this in mind, but without any definite object in view at the time, we joined others in organizing the First National Bank of Colorado Springs in 1874, and were elected members of its Board of Directors. However, a few months later, not being entirely satisfied with the bank management, we retired from the Board, but re- tained our stock holdings.

Early in January, 1878, Mr. James Knox, cashier of the First National Bank, died suddenly, leaving no one in line of succession fitted for the office. To my surprise, on the 22nd of that month, without having been consulted, I was elected his successor by the unanimous vote of the Board of Directors. I was without banking training, my chief qualifica- tion for the work being that, through my long service as County Clerk, I probably had a larger acquain- tance and was better posted as to land values, than any man in the county. As the position offered me was in line with my ambition, I accepted it without hesitancy, and, in order to give my undivided atten- tion to the bank, I turned over to A. S. Welch, my Chief Deputy, the administration of the County Clerk's office, to which, for the fifth time, I had been elected three months previously.

I had no sooner become in a measure familiar with the affairs of the bank than I found that con- ditions were not as they should be. And I realized that I had a serious problem on my hands which I should have to solve with little inside aid, as Charles B. Greenough, the president of the bank, was at that time in Rio de Janeiro, Brazil.   On account of my inexperience in banking and the reluctance of the employees to give me information, it was some time before I arrived at an understanding of the true state of affairs; but when I fully realized the condition of the bank I was appalled, and I knew that I must speedily get aid from somewhere if the institution was to be kept alive.   In this emergency, I sent a cablegram to President Greenough in Rio de Janeiro at the cost of almost three hundred dollars informing him of the situation.   I knew that he was a very wealthy man and that, if he could be reached, he doubtless would, at the earliest possible moment, provide the funds necessary to save the institution. Mr. Greenough had come to Colorado Springs from Rio de Janeiro the year before as a health seeker, and, at the request of his friend James Knox, the cashier, had bought some of the bank stock and accepted the presidency.   However, he had acquired very little knowledge of the internal affairs of the institution before leaving again for South America two or three months later, and consequently was greatly surprised by the news I sent him.   As soon as he was able to arrange his affairs he returned to the United States and came directly to Colorado Springs.

Meanwhile, Mr. Crowell had been elected a director, and with his help and that of some banking friends in other parts of the State I managed to keep the bank going, although there was much difficulty in prevailing upon the Comptroller of the Currency not to close it. When Mr. Greenough arrived, he advanced the money necessary to tide over the institution for the time being. Later, we induced the stockholders to submit to a voluntary assessment of twenty-five per cent. and with this money and that which I had collected by suit or otherwise from former officers and others indebted to the institution, and by the sale of property taken over, we restored the capital and put the bank in a sound and stable condition. All this was accomplished within the first year after Mr. Crowell and I took charge. I speak of Mr. Crowell and myself as having, in large measure, accomplished these things for the reason that Mr. Greenough, being an invalid and a comparative stranger in this locality, was not able to give us much assistance except in a financial way. Since that time, the First National Bank of Colorado Springs has had an uninterrupted period of growth and prosperity.

Early in 1878, some rather remarkable discoveries of high grade silver ore were made at Leadville, near the old placer mining camp of California Gulch. And later in that year, there were other finds of an unusual character in the same locality. The ore was of remarkable richness and lay in blanket form, in many instances within fifty to one hundred feet of the surface; consequently it was cheaply mined and taken out. By reason of the great size of the ore bodies, the richness of the mineral, and the relatively small cost of mining, the owners of several of the larger properties in the district accumulated fortunes in a marvelously short time.

In December, 1878, a resident of Colorado Springs whom I knew but slightly as a small depositor in the bank, asked me to join him in the purchase of a mining claim in the Leadville district known as the Robert E. Lee, on which he had recently secured the promise of a bond and lease. Because of the excitement then existing over the Leadville discoveries, his proposition interested me. Upon questioning him I found that the claim was situated about one thousand feet away from the Little Pittsburgh Mine, which at the time was the great producer of the Leadville district. The price asked for the property was seven thousand five hundred dollars, of which two thousand five hundred was to be paid at the time of the execution of the bond and lease, and the remaining five thousand at the end of ninety days. He said that there was a shaft on the property about one hundred feet deep, and over it a small hoisting plant. The promoter was positive that, by sinking the shaft only a few feet further, good bodies of ore would be opened up, and that within ninety days, the life of the bond, we should be able to realize from ore sales sufficient money to make the final payment.

It occurred to me that seven thousand five hundred dollars was a very small price for a property so near the big bonanzas of the district, and that there must be some drawback of which I had not been informed, but the promoter assured me that everything was all right and that the only reason for the low price was that the claim was in an undeveloped locality, which was true. Although not entirely reassured, I concluded to take the chance and agreed to loan the two thousand five hundred dollars for the first payment and become the owner of two thirds of the bond and lease, the promoter to retain the other third as his commission. It was decided to proceed with further development work as rapidly as possible, each of us—the promoter included—to pay his proportion of the expense. Meanwhile, realizing that I was not financially able to carry all of my part of the load, I divided my interest with my associates, B. F. Crowell, the vice-president, and J. F. Humphrey, assistant-cashier, of the First National Bank.

We then employed as superintendent a Mr. Loomis, an assayer located in Leadville, who formerly had been a resident of Colorado Springs, and instructed him to proceed at once with such development as he thought necessary to demonstrate whether or not the property had any value. A week or two later, Mr. Loomis reported that an examination had proved that the shaft had been sunk in apparently barren ground, and that on account of the flow of water it would be impossible to sink it deeper without pumps. After doing a little further prospecting without any result, Mr. Loomis wrote suggesting that I come to Leadville and look over the situation. As I had not yet seen the property, I decided to comply with his request. This being before the day of railroads into the district, I made the trip from Colorado Springs by team and was three days on the way. Upon reaching Leadville, friends familiar with the district twitted me with being a "Tender-foot" and an "Easy-mark" as I had bought what they called a water hole, in a region entirely outside of the mineral belt. After I had looked over the property, I felt that possibly I had been buncoed; but, after consideration, I decided to have some further development work done before surrendering the option. Instructing Mr. Loomis to run a drift in whatever direction he thought best, I returned to Colorado Springs and awaited results. Loomis at once started drifting eastward from the bottom of the shaft and pushed the work as rapidly as possible, but at the end of a month had discovered nothing of value. Finally, two or three weeks before the end of the ninety days named in our option, I wrote him to change the direction of the drift and drive it at right angles to his former course; then, if good ore was not soon discovered, we would abandon further effort and forfeit the bond. He did as I directed, and had driven only about twelve feet when he struck a small seam of chloride ore, rich in horn silver, the ore being entirely different from any other that had been found in the Leadville district up to that time.

Upon receiving notice of this, I at once went to Leadville, this time by railway to Cañon City, and by buckboard from that place to my destination.

On my arrival, finding that the seam had widened a little, I instructed Loomis to push the development and take out the ore just as rapidly as possible, in order to provide funds for final payment of the bond, the date of its expiration being near at hand. As the development work progressed the vein continued to increase in width until it soon formed a body of considerable size. Apparently, our original drift had been run almost parallel to this seam of ore and only a few feet away from it. Later developments showed us that, had we, at the beginning, drifted south instead of east, we should have struck ore worth a thousand dollars a ton within eighteen inches of the shaft. Our development further showed that, while we were outside the original carbonate belt of the district, we had discovered an entirely new mineral zone, chloride in character.

Naturally the discovery of this chloride belt caused a great sensation, not only in Leadville, but throughout the State. Owing to the extraordinary richness of the ore on our claim, it seemed to us that almost everybody in the Leadville district that ever had walked over this ground, commenced a suit against us in the next few months. For several years thereafter we were involved in a perfect maze of litigation, and for a considerable time, it became necessary for us to hold possession of the property by armed guards. We erected a small house around the shaft and in the center of it, with sacks of ore, we made a circular barricade which commanded the only entrance. This barricade was occupied by one or more of our group of partners almost every night during the spring and summer of 1879, with arms and plenty of ammunition close at hand.

Leadville then had the reputation of being one of the toughest mining camps in America; murders and robberies were of nightly occurrence. Reports of proposed attempts to take our property away from us by force were constantly brought to us, and, knowing that it would be an easy matter for any one so disposed to hire ruffians for the purpose, we were continually on the alert. Meanwhile, we were pushing development work vigorously, which after a time resulted in opening up some large and marvelously rich ore bodies. With such a showing, we finally concluded that it would be wise to make a settlement with the various litigants, if any terms within reason could be obtained. After extended negotiations, we ultimately settled the principal suit by the payment of a large sum and ceding a one-fifth interest in the property to the men who brought about the agreement.

After all litigation had been disposed of, we put additional machinery on the mine and pushed its development with great vigor. The further south we went the richer and larger the ore bodies were. Frequently, ore shipments of several hundred tons each were sent to the smelter, for which we received in the neighborhood of a thousand dollars a ton. Consequently, our profits each month were large, and we soon paid off the indebtedness incurred in settling the litigation. The output of the mine during the first three months of systematic mining had a gross value of almost half a million dollars. But, unfortunately for Mr. Crowell, Mr. Humphrey, and myself, in settling with the various litigants, we had been compelled to give up the larger part of our original holdings.

In October, 1879, we took out $125,000 in ten days, and of this, $100,000 came from lots of ore that ran from $700 to $10,000 per ton, silver then being worth $1.10 an ounce. On the 13th of January, 1880, ninety-five tons were mined and shipped within twenty-four hours, the total gross value of which was $118,500. Of course this extremely rich ore had been discovered some time before and had been blocked out and made easily accessible, with the object in view of taking it all out at one time when it could be protected by those most interested. When the time came, all of the owners, with one exception, were present. One wagonload of this ore contained silver to the value of a little over $40,000. The owners, all well armed, accompanied this load to the Eddy and James Sampler and stayed with it until the ore had been sampled and its value ascertained. We never again found such rich ore in any considerable quantities, although small pockets were opened at times for a year or two afterwards. However, the mine continued to produce in a moderate way for a number of years. Less than a year after that remarkable shipment of ore, my Colorado Springs associates and I sold our interests in the property to our New York partners and withdrew from the Leadville district.

Owing to the continued ill health of Mr. Greenough, the president of the First National Bank, the management of the institution largely rested upon me as cashier almost from the beginning. As soon as the bank had been placed in a sound financial condition, Mr. Greenough went back to Brazil to look after his interests there. He and his associates in New York had constructed and owned the street railway system of Rio de Janeiro, from which they received large profits. Early the following year he returned to Colorado Springs, but remained only two or three months, and then went abroad, where he died in the latter part of 1879. On the 19th of January, 1880, I was elected president of the bank as his successor. From that time on my hands were more than full, as I had the responsibility of the bank resting upon me while, at the same time, as I have already related, I was largely directing the operations of the Robert E. Lee Mine at Leadville.

During the first ten years of its existence, Colorado Springs was without a theatre building, and only such plays and musical attractions came to town as could be given in a hall. At that time the only room of any size was in the second story of a building on Huerfano Street—now Colorado Avenue. This hall had a seating capacity of about five hundred, and a makeshift sort of stage. At one time a traveling theatrical company tried to give a play there in which a horse had to be used. They succeeded in getting the animal up the stairs and onto the stage, but when in the play the actor mounted and tried to flourish his sword, the result was a dismal failure, as the sword would strike the ceiling every time he raised it.

After our fortunate venture in Leadville, B. F. Crowell, J. F. Humphrey, and myself decided to remedy this deficiency by building a modern, up-to-date Opera House, on lots that we owned on the west side of Tejon Street, just north of the First National Bank corner. The building was completed early in 1881 and the decorations finished in time for an opening on April 18. Aside from the Tabor Opera House in Denver, our theatre was the most completely equipped of any in Colorado.

The opening play was Camille, presented by Maude Granger, a prominent New York actress of that day, supported by a good company. The house was crowded and everything went off satisfactorily. However, Camille seemed a bit unfortunate as an opening play in a health resort such as Colorado Springs. But, as I remember, we had little choice in the matter of the play, as at that time virtually the only theatrical companies that played in Colorado were those on their way to California. Usually they were booked by the Tabor Opera House in Denver for one week in that city and another on the circuit composed of Colorado Springs, Pueblo, Leadville, and Grand Junction. Our house had to take what was allotted to it.

Two of our employees of those early days later became prominent in connection with the profession: Ray Henderson, our ticket seller, afterwards was manager for Forbes-Robertson and other successful actors; and Lon Chaney, one of our stage hands, became famous as Quasimodo in the moving picture of The Hunchback of Notre Dame.

The Opera House filled its purpose fairly well for twenty-five years, during which period most of the prominent actors of the United States appeared on its stage. Later, it was superseded by The Burns, a modern and up-to-date theatre, after which the old building was remodeled for offices.

From 1890 on for a number of years, I was chairman of the committee of citizens that secured for Colorado Springs the water rights on Beaver Creek and the large tract of land on the south side of Pike's Peak on which the city's principal reservoirs were built. I went before Congress on several occasions, and, with the assistance of our senators, each time secured the passage of an act granting lands to the city. The aggregate of these grants and of purchases made on the advice of our committee was more than five thousand acres. Later, our committee was instrumental in having a pipeline laid down Ruxton Creek along the line of the Cog Railway, in order to prevent polution of the water. In securing the right of way for this pipeline we had great difficulty in reserving the power rights; the owners of the Cog Road insisted on retaining the right to develop and use power from the pipeline as compensation for the right of way, while we contended that the city must hold the power for use in generating electricity to be used in lighting the streets, if found desirable. Finally, they conceded the force of our argument and granted the city the right of way without burdensome conditions. It may be imagined how disappointed some of us were later when the right to use this power was given to a corporation for a long period without proper remuneration.

CHAPTER XIV

SETTLEMENT OF EASTERN COLORADO—EXPERIENCES
IN POLITICS—CRIPPLE CREEK—WAITE CAMPAIGN

AFTER the crushing defeat of the Southern
Cheyennes and Arapahoes by General Custer in the
battle of Washita in 1869, these savages and all
other bands of the two tribes wandering on the great
plains, were rounded up and placed upon a reservation in the Indian Territory. This left unoccupied
and subject to preëmption and homestead all of the
country between the Platte and Arkansas Rivers,
from the western border of the settlements of Kansas
and Nebraska to the eastern limit of those of Colorado, a distance of about four hundred miles.

For a number of years, this unoccupied "No
Man's Land" between Kansas and Colorado was
used as a broad highway over which great herds of
cattle were driven from Texas to western Nebraska,
Wyoming, and Montana.

As soon after the expulsion of the Indians from
this region as the people were assured that there
would be no more temporizing with the savages, the
settlements of the three states began slowly to
approach each other, those of Kansas and Nebraska,

however, extending westward much more rapidly than those of Colorado eastward. Owing to the skepticism that existed in the latter state as to the value of the lands of that section for agricultural purposes, most of its new settlers were cattle and sheep raisers, a class that always was in search of wider ranges. Finally, the settlements from the east overflowed into Colorado and, in their advance toward the mountains, soon came in contact with the stock raisers of El Paso and other counties. These new settlers immediately began to take up ranches in every direction, thus greatly reducing the ranges of the stockmen. The latter up to that time had succeeded in holding the large tracts of Government land which they needed for their herds, but they soon realized that the day of the open range in this region was nearing an end, and within the next six or eight years most of the flocks and herds of El Paso County were moved elsewhere.

Many of the new-comers in eastern El Paso County had little means and soon were in financial straights. In order to prevent suffering and to enable these people to plant and raise their first crops, a number of Colorado Springs men, myself included, formed an organization to make temporary loans at reasonable rates to those needing financial aid. Any kind of security that they could give was taken, but the loans were limited to as small amounts as would meet the immediate requirements of the borrowers. In that way, the twelve thousand dollar fund, that had been raised for the purpose, took care of most of those needing help. Fortunately, the crops were good that first summer and the two succeeding ones, and by the end of that period all the loans, excepting a small one of less than a hundred dollars, had been paid. For several years afterwards, with others of the loan organization, I visited the region referred to late in the summer, and every time returned more and more pleased with the evidences of increasing prosperity in that section.

Undoubtedly the marvelous change in this arid region is due, in great part, to the increased rainfall, which in turn is the natural result of the plowing and cultivation of so much of the surface. Most of the land in that section originally was covered with a thick mat of short gramma, or buffalo grass as it was called, through which the rain did not penetrate to any extent, but, instead, ran off rapidly. Now, a considerable part of the rainfall is absorbed by the deeply plowed fields, the evaporation therefrom going back into the atmosphere to a much greater extent than formally.

The fact that the arid plains east of the Rocky Mountains could be turned into a productive farming country without irrigation was a revelation to the old settlers. What was true of El Paso County was equally true of all the other counties in Colorado east of the mountains. Everywhere farms soon were in evidence, proving that Colonel Zebulon Pike, who was in command of the first American exploring expedition across the great plains to the Rocky

Mountains in 1806, was a false prophet when in his report he said:

"In that vast country of which I speak, we find the soil generally dry and sandy . . . here a barren soil, parched and dried for eight months in the year, presents neither moisture nor nutrition sufficient to nourish timber. These vast plains of the western hemisphere may become in time as celebrated as the sandy deserts of Africa; for I saw in my route, in various places, tracts of many leagues where the wind had thrown up the sand in all the fanciful forms of the ocean's rolling waves, and on which not a speck of vegetable matter existed.

"But from these immense prairies may arise one great advantage to the United States, viz.: The restriction of our population to some certain limits, and thereby a continuation of the Union. Our citizens being so prone to rambling and extending themselves on the frontiers will, through necessity, be constrained to limit their extent on the west to the borders of the Missouri and Mississippi, while they leave the prairies incapable of cultivation to the wandering and uncivilized aborigines of the country."

The remarkable increase in the population of eastern Colorado doubtless was much expedited by the railroads that were built across the plains to the mountains during this period, beginning with the Union Pacific which was constructed along the northern boundary of Colorado in 1867, and the Kansas Pacific which reached a point near the western border of Kansas in 1868 and was completed to Denver two years later. These railroads were followed by the Burlington, the Santa Fé, the Rock Island, and the Missouri Pacific, in fairly rapid succession.

By the beginning of the year 1889, the population of eastern Colorado had increased to such an extent that the Legislature of that year deemed it necessary to form nine new counties along the eastern border of the State.

At the general election held in November, 1882, I was elected State Senator from El Paso County. During my term of office I took an active part in the legislative proceedings and the election of two United States Senators.

Prior to this election, it was virtually conceded that Governor Pitkin would be chosen United States Senator at the coming session of the Legislature, and almost every Republican member was elected with either the direct or tacit understanding that he would vote for him. Honorable F. W. Pitkin, then Governor of the State for the second time, was a man of education and high character, and a lawyer of great ability. His opponents were Judge Thomas M. Bowen and H. A. W. Tabor, neither of whom was in any way comparable with Governor Pitkin in ability or fitness for the position. Because of my confidence that, if elected senator, Governor Pitkin would be a credit to the State, I supported his candidacy with all the energy that I possessed. When the Legislature convened, the Republicans had a good working majority in both Houses, but a canvass of the situation made soon after showed that many senators and representatives supposed to be favorable to Governor Pitkin were lukewarm in his support. His friends worked earnestly in his behalf, using every honorable means to secure his election, but instead of growing stronger, apparently he lost ground all the time. Finally, he asked that his name be withdrawn, whereupon Judge Thomas M. Bowen was elected. We who knew the high character and ability of Governor Pitkin were greatly disappointed at the result.

Two years later, at the legislative session of 1885, I again took an active part in the senatorial fight. This time the contest was between Honorable H. M. Teller and Senator N. P. Hill whose term was about to expire. Mr. Teller, in 1882, had resigned his place in the United States Senate to accept the position of Secretary of the Interior in President Arthur's cabinet, which responsible position he held until the expiration of the President's term in March, 1885. There had been a political feud in Colorado between Mr. Teller and Mr. Hill for many years, which now was accentuated by Senator Teller's aspiration to succeed Senator Hill. The fight was a bitter one. I had been a warm friend and adherent of Senator Teller's for many years, and of course arrayed myself with those working in his behalf. After many successive nights of caucusing, Mr.

Teller won the Republican nomination by a small majority and his election to the United States Senate followed a day or two later.

Among the various legislative enactments that I was responsible for during my four years term as State Senator was a law authorizing cities and towns to purchase lands for park purposes outside the corporate limits. This was sought to allow Colorado Springs to buy a tract extending from the junction of North and South Cheyenne Creeks up the former for three-quarters of a mile or more. This was the beginning of the City's wonderful park system. I also secured the passage of a law entirely remodeling the Colorado School for the Deaf and Blind, and another establishing a Forestry System within the State. The latter bill encountered much opposition, as at that time the people of the State did not appreciate the desirability of protecting our forests. At my suggestion, Edgar T. Ensign of Colorado Springs was placed in charge of the new department. Mr. Ensign had made a study of forestry and was a capable officer. He made a vigorous effort to carry out the provisions of this law, and, notwithstanding the fact that he received little support from any source, he accomplished a great deal in the way of protecting the forests. However, it soon became evident that this measure was ahead of its time, and in a few years the law was repealed in its entirety. Years later, the people of the United States awakened to the necessity of doing that which some of us in Colorado tried to do a quarter of a century earlier, and a National Forestry Law was enacted. At the end of my term of office I refused reëlection as I had neither the time to spare from my business nor inclination for further political life.

From the earliest days, the people of the Pike's Peak region looked forward to the time when a railroad would be built up through Ute Pass into the stock-raising and mining sections of central and western Colorado, but realization of that dream seemed far in the future. The first definite move in that direction was made in 1885 by people who were operating a saw mill in what is now known as Manitou Park, and had built six or eight miles of narrow gauge railroad in that locality to bring logs to the mill. H. D. Fisher, manager of the enterprise, conceived the idea of building a broad guage railroad through Ute Pass and on westward, with the intention of making the Manitou Park narrow gauge road a branch of it. Interested with Mr. Fisher in the contemplated project were Henry T. Rogers, a Denver lawyer, and Thomas Wigglesworth, who previously had been a locating engineer in the employ of the Denver & Rio Grande Railroad. Mr. Wigglesworth had made a preliminary survey through Ute Pass and was satisfied as to the feasibility of constructing a broad gauge railroad through it with no prohibitive grades. These three men soon afterward organized the Colorado Midland Railway Company. Later, at their request I became a member of the Board of Directors; and about the same time J. B. Wheeler—then one of the firm of R. H. Macy & Co. in New York, but afterwards a resident of Colorado—and Orlando Metcalf of Colorado Springs, both men of considerable means, also became interested in the project. With this start, it was decided to have preliminary surveys made of the entire line, and each director contributed his quota towards the expense.

Not long afterward, Mr. Fisher succeeded in interesting J. J. Hagerman who had recently come to Colorado Springs from Milwaukee, Wisconsin, for his health. Mr. Hagerman, during the next few months, corresponded with capitalists in New York concerning the matter, but without success. However, by this time he had become too much interested in the project to give it up without further effort and he now sought other avenues for raising the money. In this he succeeded much sooner than any of us anticipated, by inducing an English firm to take the entire bond issue.

Up to that time I had been a director in the Railway Company, but I now resigned to become treasurer of the Construction Company. The Railway Company soon found itself with a large construction fund on hand but only a small part of the proposed line definitely located, most of the surveys up to this time having been merely preliminary ones. However, hasty locations were now made and contracts let for grading the first fifty miles of road west of Colorado Springs. As a result of this haste, the road in many places was badly located, cost more to construct, and afterwards was expensive to operate.

Before the line was completed the cost of construction had far exceeded the estimates. Although little of the initial financing of the road had fallen to me, I was the one who had to stand between creditors and the Railway Company during the many months while additional funds were being raised. As soon as the road was finished to Glenwood Springs and Aspen, in the spring of 1888, I tendered my resignation as treasurer. This was in accordance with an understanding when I accepted the position, that I should serve only during the construction period. At the time I severed my connection with the road, its earnings were almost sufficient to pay all operating expenses and fixed charges.

Some time before completion of the Colorado Midland Railroad to Glenwood Springs, it virtually had been decided to extend the line from New Castle, by way of the White River and Strawberry Valley, on to Salt Lake City. Surveys were made through this region and an excellent line, both as to cost and grades, was found. Had the road been continued as then planned, I have not the least doubt that the Midland would have proved a most profitable investment instead of a losing one.

In the spring of 1888, Mr. Crowell and I disposed of a controlling interest in the First National Bank of Colorado Springs to J. A. Hayes and his associates, prominent capitalists of this city. I had decided, some time before, that the indoor confinement connected with banking was too wearing upon me and that I must have more outdoor life. I then had no thought of reëntering the banking business; however, a year or two later, I was induced by Mr. Hayes again to become officially connected with the institution. By this time, a more intimate acquaintance with Mr. Hayes had shown me that he was an unusually able banker and a gentleman with whom it was a pleasure to be associated. And the many later years of our close business relations only tended to increase this high opinion.

At the State Convention of the Republican party held at Pueblo in the spring of 1888, I was elected a delegate to the National Republican Convention to be held in Chicago the following June. My colleagues were Senator Teller, ex-Governor Elbert, and three other prominent men of the State. I attended the Convention on my way abroad, and found its sessions most interesting because of the many notable men there assembled. There were half a dozen candidates for the presidency and an intense rivalry existed between the more active ones. Notable among the candidates were Senator Allison of Iowa, Honorable Chauncey Depew of New York, Judge Gresham of Illinois, Senator Harrison of Indiana, and Governor Alger of Michigan. The leader of our delegation, Senator Teller, strongly favored Judge Gresham who had been his associate in President Arthur's cabinet. Naturally, we sided with Senator Teller and did everything possible to secure Gresham's nomination.

However, our efforts in that direction were unavailing. After balloting had continued for a day or more, Benjamin Harrison of Indiana was nominated by a good majority. Before the final vote was taken our delegation concluded that Gresham had no chance of winning, and was among the first that changed to Harrison, which helped turn the tide in his favor.

Early in the year 1891, there began to be much talk in Colorado Springs concerning the discovery of gold on the west side of Pike's Peak, but those who were familiar with mining had little faith in the reports. One reason for this was that a few years previously there had been much excitement over reported gold discoveries near Mt. Pisgah, in that locality, which was quickly over since the reports proved to have little basis. Late in 1889, a mining engineer of experience told me that gold actually had been found by an old miner near the headwaters of Four Mile Creek on the west side of Pike's Peak, and advised me to investigate the matter. But, knowing the miner to be an erratic sort of fellow, I gave the report little further attention, believing that if there had been anything of value in that region, it would have been found long before. Consequently, when rumors of gold discoveries in the same locality were repeated in 1891, I gave them slight notice. But by the spring of 1892, stories were current in Colorado Springs that mines a few miles southwest of the summit of Pike's Peak were making carload shipments of a good grade of ore. Even then I was skeptical, thinking that possibly a little surface ore had been found which was not likely to develop into anything of permanent value. I was particularly incredulous because I knew that for ten years Major Demary, an experienced mining man of Park County, had been keeping his cattle on the lands where the gold discoveries were said to have been made, and I reasoned that, if gold in paying quantities existed there, Major Demary surely would have detected it. Later developments showed how badly mistaken I was. Demary's ranch was located in what became the Cripple Creek Mining District, and his house was directly over the very rich and extensive ore bodies of the future Vindicator Mine. Although Major Demary was in the mining business in Park County, he usually spent three or four months on his cattle ranch each year; yet all this time he remained oblivious of the fact that he was living over bodies of ore infinitely richer than any that had ever been discovered in Park County.

Early in the summer of 1892, the president of the Atchison, Topeka, and Santa Fé Railroad Company, which at that time controlled the Colorado Midland, asked J. J. Hagerman to make an examination of the Cripple Creek mining district and report whether or not the mineral development there would warrant construction of a branch of the Midland into that camp. Owing to the fact that Mr. Hagerman's health would not permit him to do this work personally, he requested me to make the examination and report in his stead, which I consented to do.

The only comfortable way of making the trip to the new mining camp at that time was by the Midland Railway to Florissant and then by coach to Cripple Creek. While waiting at Florissant for the coach to start, I saw a number of wagon loads of ore being loaded into a car, and, on examining the ore closely, I found a good many specimens showing free gold. This made me realize that perhaps I had been mistaken in my opinion of the camp. I reached Cripple Creek that night and stopped at Wolf's Hotel, the best in town. It was built of rough boards and the partitions were so open that I could hear the snoring of sleeping men in different parts of the building. The following morning I started out on horseback and during the next day or two made a fairly thorough investigation as to the development and production of the better known mines. The workings of none of them extended down more than a hundred feet. By the time I had finished, I had become convinced that the possibilities of the Cripple Creek District were much greater than I had anticipated. In my report, on returning to Colorado Springs, I referred to the mining outlook in the camp as promising, and advised that preparations be made to begin construction of a branch railroad from either Florissant or Divide at the end of six months, provided the mineral development continued favorable. Notwithstanding that the gold camp grew rapidly, the Santa Fé Railroad took no further action in reference to the proposed line.

In 1892 occurred the first big labor strike at
Cripple Creek, and while it lasted, the striking
miners had virtual possession of the camp. They
refused to recognize the legally constituted authorities, and by their actions brought about a condition
of anarchy that continued for a number of months.
The miners were led by able and unscrupulous men,
a number of whom were ex-convicts. In spite of
every effort to enforce the law by the authorities
of El Paso County, of which the Cripple Creek
District was then a part, the strikers ran things
with a high hand. Finally, after all of his deputies
had been driven out, the sheriff of El Paso County,
by direction of the County Commissioners, enlisted
a force of several hundred men to be used in re-
establishing law and order in the District. These
deputies not only were armed with guns but also
had artillery, which was thought necessary owing to
the fact that the strikers had erected a fortification
on Bull Hill, in the eastern part of the camp.

When completely equipped, the deputies, under
command of Sheriff Bowers and County Commissioner Boynton, took up their line of march towards
Cripple Creek by way of Divide station on the
Midland Railroad and Gillette, a small town on the
outskirts of the District. Near the latter place
they had a slight skirmish with the strikers. When
the strike leaders found that the deputies were
coming, they became panic stricken and implored
Governor Waite for protection. He complied with
this request by promptly sending several hundred

militia to the scene of action and having them placed between the strikers and the deputies.

Prior to the beginning of this strike, Davis H. Waite, of Pitkin County, had been nominated and elected Governor of Colorado by the Populist party, which was made up of the discontented elements of the State. His sympathies, as openly expressed, were on the side of the strikers and he needed only a slight excuse to intervene in their favor. This forced a settlement which made it a partial victory for the strikers. However, the law came out victorious in the end as a number of the leaders were arrested, tried and sentenced to the penitentiary, and most of the others fled from the State to avoid punishment for the crimes they had committed. With the ending of the strike, the mines of the Cripple Creek District entered upon an era of great prosperity which continued for many years thereafter.

Governor Waite was a most erratic person, thoroughly imbued with socialistic and other fantastic ideas as to matters of government, and had unlimited confidence in his own opinions. During his term the State was in continuous turmoil of one kind or another, and there was an ever present uncertainty as to what capricious thing he would do next. At one time he called out the State Militia to oust from Denver's City Hall certain Police Commissioners whom he had removed but who refused to recognize his authority to do so, and a conflict between the State troops and the Denver police was narrowly averted.

By the spring of 1894, the conservative people of Colorado, regardless of party, had become convinced that Governor Waite's actions and utterances were doing the State great harm and that he must be defeated at the coming election. It was generally conceded that this could be accomplished only through the Republican party, but to insure success party politics must be eliminated from the campaign as far as possible. At the request of many of my business and political friends throughout the State, as well as of the party managers, I consented to take the position of Chairman of the State Republican Central Committee. I received my appointment some time prior to the State Convention, since, on account of the disorganized condition of the party, it was thought advisable to begin preliminary work thus early. I accepted the position with the distinct understanding that I should be permitted to run the campaign on business rather than political lines, and I adhered closely to this plan during the whole of the succeeding contest. My plea to the voters was for the reëstablishment of conservative government and enforcement of law. This platform brought many Democrats to my support. In making up my organization, I eliminated the old politicians as far as possible and surrounded myself with an Executive Committee of representative men and women from various parts of the State.

At the Populist State Convention held in Pueblo, September 4, Governor Waite was renominated,

although not without a good deal of opposition
from the more conservative element of his own party.
Almost immediately afterwards, he began an active
speaking campaign throughout the State. Waite
had a manner that appealed to the discontented
and those infected with socialism. On account of
his strength in this direction and the fact that he
had won at the previous election by a majority of
more than five thousand over Judge J. C. Helm,
the Republican candidate, and now had behind him
the State Government with its numerous officials
and appointees, many feared that he could not be
defeated.

The Republican State Convention met in Denver
September 11, and after a good deal of preliminary
canvassing and balloting, Judge A. W. McIntyre of
the southern part of the State was nominated for
governor. The campaign that followed was con-
tested more earnestly than any in the previous
history of Colorado. A unique feature of it was
the active part taken by the women. This was the
first election after the adoption of the amendment
to the State Constitution granting them the right
of suffrage. Actuated by the belief that, if women
were to vote, they should also participate in party
management, I appointed Mrs. Peavey of Denver,
Vice-Chairman, and Mrs. Frank Hall, Assistant
Secretary, of the State Central Committee. Also,
I named a woman Vice-Chairman of the County
Central Committee in every county of the State.
Following out this policy, I urged the various county

committees to appoint women upon precinct committees, and so far succeeded that in the one hundred and one precincts in Denver alone there was at least one woman on each precinct committee. A large majority of the women were on the side of good government and signalized their entrance upon the field of politics by an intelligent earnestness and activity that was irresistible. In fact the extraordinary victory achieved was, in my judgment, largely due to the women voters.

So far as possible, a canvass of the voters was made in every county; consequently a week before election I was able to predict the result very closely. The committee on public speakers planned a speech making campaign that took in every city and town and began simultaneously in all parts of the State. Many of the speakers were prominent Democrats who could not have been induced to take the stump for a Republican candidate excepting in an emergency such as Governor Waite had forced upon the people.

Judge McIntyre was elected over Governor Waite by a plurality of 19,604, and the other Republican candidates won by majorities almost as large. Naturally, there was great rejoicing among business men and property owners over the result of the election, as it gave assurance of sane, conservative government for two years at least.

Meanwhile, the silver question was coming rapidly to the front; in fact I had much difficulty in keeping that issue from assuming a prominent place in the campaign of 1894, and only succeeded in doing so by overshadowing it with pleas for restoration of good government.

Up to the time of the discovery of gold in Cripple Creek, Colorado was essentially a silver state, the average value of the "white" metal produced yearly being three times that of gold. Consequently, the drop in the price of silver that occurred during the period between 1890 and 1894, brought widespread disaster, not only to the mining camps, but also indirectly to the entire state of Colorado. There was a general feeling that the demonetization of silver was unnecessary, and that the drop in price of that metal could have been in a measure prevented had an effort been made by the General Government in its behalf. As the Republicans were in control, that party was held responsible by a majority of the people of the State, including not only Democrats and Populists, but many Republicans as well.

I soon became convinced that it would be utterly useless to attempt to keep any considerable part of the Republican voters in line for a presidential candidate nominated upon a gold platform such as was almost sure to be adopted by the Republican National Convention. Having reached this con-clusion, I bent my energies toward holding the party together, at least as far as the State government was concerned.

At the Republican State Convention which met in Pueblo on May 13, 1896, for the purpose of electing delegates to the Republican National Convention, the silver forces largely predominated. After a lively and acrimonious debate, the delegates were instructed to withdraw from the National Convention unless resolutions favorable to the restoration of silver were adopted. During the National Convention, which met in St. Louis soon after, the Colorado delegation, led by Senator Teller, made a strenuous fight for the white metal, but was beaten by an overwhelming vote; whereupon, the members withdrew as they had been instructed to do. As a result of this action, the Republican party again was rent asunder throughout the State, the silver faction having a large majority.

My only object in accepting the position of Chairman of the State Central Committee in the first place had been to aid in redeeming the State from the radical Populistic government then in control. After that had been accomplished I did what I could to keep the party from throwing away the results of its victory, but the conditions were against me and I failed. As the party appeared bent on destruction, a result which apparently I could do nothing to avert, I concluded to retire from the Chairmanship, although my term of office would not have expired until some months later. My resignation was presented and accepted at a meeting of the State Central Committee held in Denver in July, 1896, pursuant to call issued by me. Fortunately for the State, the Democrats that fall nominated and elected as Governor Honorable Alva Adams, a safe and conservative man, which insured the continuance of stable conditions so far as the enforcement of law was concerned.

While abroad in 1897, I received word that my old friend and associate, Benjamin F. Crowell, was hopelessly ill in Colorado Springs. Upon hearing this sad news, I decided to leave my family in Paris and return home at once. Sailing for New York on the next steamer out of Cherbourg I fortunately reached Colorado Springs two or three weeks before Mr. Crowell's death. I was thankful indeed that I had been permitted to see him alive again, and my return seemed to give him great pleasure. We had been the warmest of friends and intimate business associates for many years, and his death was a sorrowful event to me. He was one of the truest friends that any man ever had.

Early in the history of Colorado Mr. Crowell became a leader in the Republican party. For more than thirty years he was a delegate to most of the Territorial and State Republican Conventions; and he repeatedly refused the nomination for governor, when such nomination was equivalent to election. He represented Colorado in the Republican National Convention in 1884 which nominated James J. Blaine for President, and was one of the three hundred and six who stood out to the end for the nomination of General Grant.

When it was decided to erect the State Capitol Building in Denver, Mr. Crowell was appointed one of the Capitol Commissioners to have charge of its planning and erection; and from the inception to the completion of the structure, Mr. Crowell took an active personal interest in the work.   Before the construction began, he traveled extensively throughout the country at his own expense, investigating capitol buildings in many different states, afterwards utilizing the best points in each.   The history of the structure is exceptional in that never a breath of scandal was heard in connection with any detail of its building.

During the later years of his life, Mr. Crowell and his sisters usually spent the summers at their old home town of Manchester-by-the-Sea, Massachusetts, and the remainder of the year in Colorado Springs.   He passed away at the latter place June 5, 1897, and was buried by the side of his father and mother in Manchester.   There his sister, Miss Susan E. Crowell, later erected a beautiful chapel as a monument to his memory.

CHAPTER XV

BUILDING THE CRIPPLE CREEK SHORT LINE.
COLORADO COLLEGE PARK SYSTEM

By the latter part of 1896, Cripple Creek had developed into a wonderful mining district in which gold was being produced in large quantities. Fortunately for Colorado Springs, its residents owned most of the important mines, having secured them at the beginning when people of other localities were skeptical as to their permanency. At the time the first gold discoveries in the Cripple Creek District were made, business was extremely dull in Colorado Springs and there was little building under way, leaving many mechanics and others out of employment. The new mining camp being so near, these men naturally were attracted to it. Having little money, many went on foot directly across the mountains, packing their blankets and a small supply of provisions. Few of them knew anything whatever of mining and consequently located claims that an experienced mining man never would have considered, but some of these most unpromising prospects afterwards developed into such great bonanzas as the Independence, the

Portland, the Gold Coin, the Pharmacist, the Elkton, and the El Paso, besides others of lesser note. In this way Colorado Springs early secured a predominant interest in the new mining district, and, through the increased income of its citizens— derived from the production of their mining properties and the sale of mining stocks—in a few years the city became exceedingly prosperous.

The intimate business relations between Colorado Springs and Cripple Creek, thus early established, made it very desirable that the railways between the two localities be operated in a way that would promote the interest of both. At that time, Colorado Springs was being discriminated against in favor of Denver and Pueblo, since both the Midland and the Midland Terminal Railroads were controlled by people having no interest in this locality. The sole idea of the management of these roads apparently was to charge, for both freight and passenger traffic, the utmost that it would bear. The result was that a line of four horse stages ran daily over the Cheyenne Mountain wagon road, carrying many passengers to the District; and there were numerous other public and private conveyances on that highway at all times. The wholesale merchants of Colorado Springs found it necessary to ship their freight by team in order to do any business with the merchants of Cripple Creek in competition with Denver and Pueblo wholesalers. Our people protested against the high rates, but to no effect. Finally, the demand for independent railroad communication with the District became so great that the City Council of Colorado Springs made an appropriation to pay for surveys to ascertain whether or not a direct line to the District was feasible, and appointed a committee consisting of J. J. Hagerman, W. S. Jackson and myself to supervise the work. The committee soon afterwards employed H. I. Reid, an experienced engineer, thoroughly familiar with the country through which the proposed road must run, to make the examination. Some months later Mr. Reid reported that he had found a comparatively short and direct line by way of Bear Creek and Seven Lakes, but that it would have heavy grades and require a cog road for a considerable distance. This line was rejected by the committee as not meeting the requirements.

By this time, the question of a cheaper method of treatment of low grade ores of the Cripple Creek District also had become a vital one to many of the mines. Due to this, several of the big Cripple Creek mining companies were contemplating the construction of reduction works, preferable at Colorado Springs in order that such mills might be operated under the personal supervision of their officers, most of whom lived there. With this in mind, strenuous efforts again were made to secure from the existing railways freight rates on ores to this point that would enable such plants to compete with mills at Florence and Pueblo.

Meanwhile, those in control of the Florence and Cripple Creek Railroad were bringing all the pressure possible to force the location of all reduction works at Florence, on the Arkansas River. This move being in defiance of the expressed wishes of a large majority of the mine owners, it now was decided that Colorado Springs must have a railway to the District that would give the town and its mine owners fair treatment, whatever the cost. In view of this, engineers were at once put in the field to make the necessary preliminary surveys.

As a step in this movement, in March, 1899, E. W. Giddings and myself, as trustees representing a syndicate of Colorado Springs men, purchased the Cripple Creek District Railway, an electric road which at that time was being operated between the towns of Cripple Creek and Victor. The intention was to use it as the Cripple Creek District terminal of the proposed line from Colorado Springs.

Following the purchase of the Cripple Creek District Railway, I was made president of the company. Later the name of the organization was changed to the Colorado Springs and Cripple Creek District Railway Company, its capital stock increased to $2,000,000, and a bond issue for the same amount authorized.

I went to Washington soon after, and secured the passage of an act by Congress giving the Colorado Springs and Cripple Creek District Railway Company a right of way over the Pike's Peak Forest Reserve between Cripple Creek and Colorado Springs.

A few months later, the engineer reported that he

had found a fairly good line from Colorado Springs to Cripple Creek using the pass south of Mt. Rosa, over which the Colorado Springs and Cripple Creek wagon road ran, and that such line would have a little lighter grades than the Colorado Midland.

Early in September, steps were taken to connect up all surveys, make permanent locations, and raise money for the construction of the line. Subscription lists were circulated, and in a short time the mine owners of the Cripple Creek District, bankers of Colorado Springs, and others, had subscribed a million and a half dollars toward financing the enterprise. This was deemed a sufficient sum to warrant proceeding with the construction; consequently, late in December, 1899, contracts were let for grading the road bed from Colorado Springs to the edge of the Cripple Creek District. Within sixty days, grading parties were scattered along the entire line, and fifteen months later the Short Line— the name by which it was generally known—was completed, and began operating both passenger and freight trains.

Although the Short Line was one of the costliest pieces of construction per mile of any railroad undertaken in Colorado up to that time, it was carried through to completion without serious financial difficulty. At the beginning of the enterprise we had no conception of its possibilities as a scenic road, and it was not until construction was well under way that it dawned upon us that we had one of the grandest lines of that kind in the world.

Thirty days from the opening of the road it was doing a profitable business, and within six months, the net earnings were largely in excess of operating expenses and fixed charges.

By that time our competitors had lost much of their traffic and their earnings had shrunken correspondingly. In an endeavor to stop this encroachment upon their business, they now instituted a rate war. This continued for the next eight months and resulted in bankruptcy for their company; while the earnings of our road during the warfare were only about twelve thousand dollars short of operating expenses and fixed charges.

The building of the railway resulted just as we had anticipated, for it had not been in operation any great length of time until the construction of additional reduction works in the vicinity of Colorado Springs was under way, and the mill previously established in Colorado City took on new life. Within three or four years from the time the new road began operations, a large part of all Cripple Creek ores was being treated in reduction works adjacent to Colorado Springs.

From the beginning, it was understood that sooner or later we must dispose of the road, as under the best of conditions a short line among numerous larger systems is in a most difficult position. From time to time we had various offers for the road, and late in 1904 sold it to the Colorado and Southern Railway Company for a consideration that gave all of the original stockholders a handsome return on their investment, besides making a market for the bonds at prices that gave good profit to such of the bondholders as desired to dispose of their holdings.

Some years afterwards, the Burlington Railroad—through the acquisition of the Colorado and Southern Railroad—became owner of the Short Line, but later abandoned it, which resulted in the road being sold recently under a foreclosure of the first mortgage. The purchaser promptly took up the rails and ties, smoothed off the road bed, floored the bridges, and broadened some of the fills, thus turning the road into a first class automobile highway. This promises to become as popular as was the original railway.

The increased prosperity of Colorado Springs due to the building of the Short Line and the great production of gold in the Cripple Creek District was reflected to some extent in Colorado College, both in the size of the student body and in the contributions to the building and endowment funds.

In the very early days of this region, the wide vision for which General Palmer was noted led him to the conclusion that here at the foot of Pike's Peak was an ideal location for an institution of higher learning, and he never wavered until such an institution had been founded and its future assured. In the plat of Colorado Springs made at the time the town was laid out, a tract of twenty acres on the west side of Cascade Avenue—then and for some years afterwards, in the outskirts of the town— was reserved for college purposes. And later, an additional twenty acres on the east side of the avenue, opposite the original tract, were set aside for the same use.

As the first step in carrying out General Palmer's educational plan, Colorado College was incorporated in the spring of 1874. On May 4th of that year, a preparatory department was opened with a small number of students, in the Wanless Block, on the corner of Tejon Street and Pike's Peak Avenue, where the First National Bank Building now stands, with Reverend Jonathan Edwards as Principal. In 1875, the latter was succeeded by Reverend James G. Dougherty, as President; and he, in turn, the following year, by Reverend E. P. Tenney. The school continued in a small way, for the first few months, as I have said, in the quarters on Tejon Street, and then for several years in a temporary building of three rooms erected for the purpose on Tejon Street, west of Acacia Park.

In 1880, through the generosity of Henry Cutler of Wilbraham, Massachusetts, an Academy Building was erected on the tract west of Cascade Avenue originally set apart for college purposes. This structure was of stone and was considered rather pretentious for the time. It had just been completed when I became a member of the Board of Trustees. This new building gave the institution an air of permanency that previously had been lacking, but it did not stimulate its growth to the extent that was expected. Doubtless this was due to the fact that the school still was without adequate financial support. Few donations were offered and apparently no one connected with the institution had the ability to raise the needed funds. However, the Trustees managed to keep the school alive and, in a limited way, doing good work, but the outlook for the future was not at all encouraging.

President Tenney resigned in 1885, after nine years of faithful but fruitless effort to raise sufficient money to support and at the same time develop the College; and the institution was without a president for the next three years. Finally, this vacancy was filled in the summer of 1888 by the election of Reverend William F. Slocum of Massachusetts. Dr. Slocum possessed remarkable executive ability, and the real life of the College dates from the time he assumed direction of its affairs.

Prior to the election of Dr. William F. Slocum to the presidency, Colorado College lacked adequate buildings, teachers, equipment, and endowment, and was in fact little more than an academy. Being familiar with the affairs of the College at the time, I admired the new president's courage in facing an undertaking that appeared to be so unpromising. However, after he took up the work, not once did he falter, but carried it on courageously. He was fortunate in having the backing of General Palmer, who constantly had the interest of the College at heart. The institution was without other income than the small tuition paid by the few students, and, as a result, for the first two or three years, the funds for the professors' salaries and other expenses of running the school had to be raised by constant solicitation. At times even this method failed and General Palmer had to come to the rescue and advance the needed funds, often to the extent of several thousand dollars.

Meanwhile, President Slocum was using every endeavor to secure funds, not only in Colorado but in the East, to pay the current expenses, build up an endowment fund, and erect additional buildings, in order that the educational work of the school might be expanded to that of a real college. In this work he was eminently successful.

The first building secured was Hagerman Hall which was erected and equipped by J. J. Hagerman and other members of the Board of Trustees. Then a president's house was purchased and remodeled with funds donated for that purpose by J. M. Bemis and others. The previously mentioned buildings were followed by twelve others, either purchased or constructed with funds contributed by friends of the college at the solicitation of Dr. Slocum.

In the meantime, President Slocum had, in four different drives, built up an endowment fund of over a million and a half dollars. As a result of his efforts, the number of students in attendance at the college increased from sixty-six in 1888, when he came to the institution, to seven hundred and seventy-eight in 1917, the year he retired from the presidency, that number being all that could be accommodated at the time. These students were from twenty-five or more different states.

President Slocum retired from the presidency of

Colorado College in 1917 after twenty-nine years of arduous service. When he came, as I have said, the college was one in name only; he left it an institution having an equal standing with the best of its class in the United States. This was recognized by Harvard University in the annual exchange of professors, an arrangement that still is in effect.

At the annual meeting of the Board of Trustees in June, 1922, I refused reëlection, having served as a member for forty-two years and feeling that a younger man should take my place. The first eight years of my connection with the Board were ones of anxiety and discouragement, but the growth and development of the college that followed under the administration of President Slocum made service on it a great pleasure.

At the time General Palmer gave to Colorado Springs the larger part of the unique and varied park system that it now owns, I was appointed, at the donor's request, a member of the Park Commission, a position that I held a number of years.

The following extracts from the first report of the commission, covering the period from the time of its organization in July, 1907, to January, 1909, will give a better idea of the extent and varied character of the parks of Colorado Springs than anything I could write:

"Fortunately for the people of Colorado Springs—both for its present and future residents and its visitors—the City possessed a generous citizen,

who, realizing the danger of further delay in securing for the people public grounds for public use,
solved the problem for us by securing and donating
to the City extended areas for a splendid park system.

"General Palmer's plan for a park system was
bold, far sighted and comprehensive. He sought
to make practical and effective use of every advantage which the position of the City gave it; open air
and sunshine, mountains and plains; to surround
the City with near-by parks, mountain driveways,
woodland paths and trails; to furnish places for
healthful out-door exercise, and quiet, restful enjoyment; thus capitalizing for us these natural resources,
otherwise practically unavailable to our people
except to the most limited extent.

"He aimed to secure public recreation grounds
within the limits of the City, and purchased the
unsightly two mile stretch along the valley of the
Monument between the right of way of the Denver
and Rio Grande Railroad and the low bluff to the
west of Cascade Avenue; he transformed this un-
inviting tract into a beautiful and serviceable park,
filled with shaded walks, trees, shrubs, lakes and
malls, and children's playgrounds, where the people
could have enjoyment, rest and recreation, without
the intrusion of vehicles of any kind—a park for the
people, a park almost in the center of the City and
easily accessible to the people.

"He sought to secure some vantage spot from
which one could overlook the mesa upon which the
City is built, to the range lying to the north and

south of Pike's Peak; and securing the tract to the northeast of the City known as Austin's Bluffs, he opened its six hundred acres throughout with roads, trails and paths, for our out-door life and happiness, yet leaving it almost as nature fashioned it; and made access easy by constructing the Boulevard and the Paseo from the City limits to the Park.

"This Park, which the Trustees insisted should be hereafter known as Palmer Park, with its shrubs and small pines, its attractive picnic grounds, its miniature cañons and bluffs rising abruptly from the plains, affords a most magnificent view over the City, of the Front Range, of Pike's Peak, of Mt. Baldy, of Mt. Rosa and of Cheyenne Mountain to the west and southwest; of the Spanish Peaks to the south; of the plains to the east; and rivals in its varied beauty and effectiveness, in its view ever changing with sunshine and shadow, the scenery from any point near the City.

"Loving nature, always keenly enjoying his outings through the mountains on foot or horseback, General Palmer sought to give others the means of enjoying healthful outings which the Front Range and the near-by mountains offered, so he planned and carried to completion The High Drive from the limits of Colorado Springs up over the hills, up through Bear Creek Cañon, over the high intervening ridge, and into North Cheyenne Cañon, a sixteen mile drive, for seven miles winding over the mountains through the pines, overlooking and through the cañons, with the ever changing scenery of mountains and plains. Then, as an accompaniment to The High Drive, he built the Cutler Mountain and Crystal Park trails, which wind up along the steep sides of the mountains, affording views of the strange rock sentinels, of tall pines, of streams, falls, cañons, recesses amid the forest trees, and the great plains far off to the east."

"This generous present from General Palmer to the people of Colorado Springs opens up a wonderful future for the City. Colorado Springs has received through gift that which has cost other cities many hundreds of thousands of dollars."

In addition to these munificent gifts of General Palmer's, the city had previously acquired three hundred and twenty acres along North Cheyenne Creek, a stream that runs through a beautiful cañon with high walls. This cañon, filled as it is with shrubs, pines, blue spruce, and other kinds of trees, of all shades of green, is almost as lovely in winter as summer.

Perhaps the best known part of our park system is the Garden of the Gods, which was given to Colorado Springs by the heirs of Charles E. Perkins, of Burlington, Iowa, in accordance with a request in his will. It includes a tract of four hundred acres in which are many tall, massive red rocks, unusually picturesque and impressive both in formation and coloring.

After the building of the new wagon road along the Fountain, through Ute Pass, the old one over the hills adjacent to the historic Ute Indian trail was abandoned. Fearing that the location of this noted trail, used for many centuries by the native races of this region, would be lost, it was decided, in the summer of 1912, to perpetuate it by placing stone markers at intervals along the part extending from Manitou to Cascade.

It happened not long after this decision was reached that Buckskin Charley, one of the head chiefs of the Ute Indians, with about a hundred of his tribe, was in Colorado Springs to take part in a pageant of the early days of the Pike's Peak region. This old chief remembered going over the Ute Pass trail with war parties many times during his youthful days; and at our request he consented to lead his band over it and verify the location for us, to insure the proper placing of the markers. The Indians were taken to the western end of the Pass, near the town of Cascade, where they were provided with horses. They came decked out in all their Indian finery of beaded jackets, moccasins, feathers, and blankets, and presented a very picturesque appearance. The party assembled at the place on the Fountain, a short distance below the town of Cascade, where the Ute Pass trail left the creek and crossed the hills three miles or more to the "Boiling Springs." Led by Buckskin Charley, the Indians started over the trail and soon were strung out single file for quarter of a mile or more. By the time they had reached the top of the first hill, they seemed to enter into the spirit of the occasion and began chanting their monotonous songs and letting out war whoops at intervals, which continued until they arrived at the springs in Manitou. Here Buckskin Charley and the principal men of the band formed a circle around the spring on the north side of the creek and went through their old Indian ceremonies, making offerings to the "Great Spirit," and ending with a short address in the Ute language by Buckskin Charley. The whole proceeding was participated in most seriously and made an unusually picturesque and impressive occasion. The Indians seemed gratified to have been given an opportunity to assist in marking their old highway and thus perpetuating the memory of the days when they roamed through this region.

This occurrence brought back memories of the early days and gave me a more vivid realization of the wonderful transformation that has taken place in every part of this Pike's Peak region during my lifetime. The contrast between the past and the present is strikingly apparent in every direction. For example, the country in the eastern part of El Paso County over which wild horses roamed in great numbers in the early days is now covered by farms, and in traveling over it one goes through lanes miles in length, with farm houses in sight on all sides. The trail along the Big Sandy over which the hostile Cheyennes and Arapahoes came in from the plains in 1868, and which Captain Templeton's company followed in pursuing them out of this region—an account of which I have given heretofore—at this date is closely paralleled for many miles by the Rock Island Railroad.   And in the Pinery—or Black Forest, as it is now called—the hiding place of the Indians during the time of the raid just referred to, virtually all the open parks or valleys are occupied by farmers, stockraisers, and dairymen.

On the plain east of Monument Creek, where the Indians killed Charley Everhart and the two Robbins boys, and wounded Baldwin, is Colorado Springs, a city which, including its surrounding suburbs, has a population of about forty thousand people.   If one were to follow the route taken by the savages over the present town site, it would lead through the best residential districts of the City, over Colorado College grounds, Washburn Athletic Field, and a mile or more along or adjacent to Cascade Avenue, one of the most important streets of the city.

The wheat field where I was working at the time of this raid is now a part of Broadmoor, and is dotted over with attractive houses in well kept grounds.

The old historic town of Colorado City, after many years of strenuous effort to maintain a separate existence, finally gave up the struggle a few years ago, and became a part of Colorado Springs.

The "Boiling Springs," which were in a state of nature when I first saw them in 1860 on my way from the placer mines to Colorado City, now are enclosed, and surrounded by the resort town of

Manitou having a population of approximately 2,500. The springs attract people from every part of the country, just as they did the native races of this Rocky Mountain and plains region from time immemorial before the white men first came here.

In making the ascent of Pike's Peak, instead of climbing over rocks and fallen timber as my companions and I did in 1863, one nowadays can walk or ride to the summit over a smooth trail, take a cog railway train, or drive by automobile over a well kept highway. And the ascent has even been made by aeroplane.

To go from Manitou into the mountainous region west of Pike's Peak, in place of traveling by horseback or wagon over steep and rough roads, one now can choose between riding in a railway train or driving in an automobile over good roads having easy grades. And this country north and west of the Peak, which Ruxton, the English traveler, described as a hunter's paradise and which was an uninhabited wilderness when I passed through it in 1860, has become a well populated region where dairy ranches abound and the lettuce raising industry is growing rapidly, it having been discovered that the climate and soil of that locality are especially adapted to the cultivation of that plant.

Although the gold seekers of 1858–59–60 came to the Rocky Mountains expecting to find gold in the neighborhood of Pike's Peak and prospected every part of the country adjacent to it, they failed of success, the nearest mines discovered at that time being fifty miles away. Yet thirty years later, gold mines richer than any before opened up in Colorado were found by chance at Cripple Creek, only seven miles southwest of the summit of Pike's Peak. From this mining district over four hundred million dollars in gold have been taken since that date.

However, in this land that has taken on a new aspect since the white men came, there is one prominent object that remains unchanged, except for a few scars along its side made by the building of the cog railroad and the automobile highway to its summit, and that is Pike's Peak. Standing on the border of the great plains, it was a beacon for the native races during the countless ages before the white men came; it guided the Spanish adventurer and explorer, the French trapper, the American hunter and trader, in their wanderings through this region; and the gold seeker of later years, eagerly scanned the western horizon for a glimpse of it while far out on the plains. This was the peak that in the early days gave its name to all this Rocky Mountain region and still remains its most interesting feature.

THE END

A Note About This Index

The first edition of this title did not have an index. We have added this one. It was prepared for us by Katherine McMahon of Albuquerque. It is not an especially complicated index, but it sure comes in handy as you read the book. The first edition was published in 1925. Author Irving Howbert was obviously one of the old timers, for like all the others, he has frequently used surnames without given names; all the old timers did it. Where it was possible, we have supplied the missing name; where it was not possible, we have left a blank space.

The Publishers

Adams, Gov. Alva--225, 277

Addleman, John--62, 79, 80

Anthony, Maj. Scott J.--147, 148, 149, 153, 154, 155

Antlers Hotel--222

Anway Hotel--110, 201

Apache Cañon, N. M.--137

Apache Indians--152, 154

Arapahoe Indians--15, 41, 56, 95-99, 111, 131, 139, 141, 145, 150, 152, 155, 177, 179-81, 183 208, 213, 214, 257, 295; history of, 97

Arkansas River--4, 5, 19, 44, 45, 84, 85, 89, 92, 111, 112, 121, 132, 166

Arthur, Chester A.--262

Aspen, Colo.--266

Auraria. *See* Denver, history of

Baird, William J.--102-03

Baldwin "Judge"--196-97, 200, 232, 233, 296

Banking--244, 245, 246, 266, 267

Baxter, Capt. O. H. P.--118, 157

Beach, M. S.--44, 67, 69, 75, 83, 91, 92, 216

Bear Creek--22, 185, 199, 200

Beattie, Prof. Wray--175, 176

Beaubien and Miranda land grant--168

Beaver Creek--111, 113

Beecher Island, battle of--208

Bell, Dr. W. A.--227
Bemis, J. M.--289
Bijou Basin--188, 190, 191, 192,
    193, 201, 203, 204, 207
Black Hawk mines--19, 22
Black Kettle, Cheyenne Chief--
    145, 153, 155
Bley, John--70
Blue River--19, 64
Boggs, Anthony--102
Boiling Springs--36, 38, 214,
    236, 294, 296. *See also*
    Manitou Springs
Boreas Pass--26
Bott, Anthony--5, 117, 232
Boulder--19, 22
Bowen, Thomas--261, 262
Bowlby, Mr.____--62
Brackett, Mr.____--188
Breckenridge--7, 19, 26, 31, 32
Brown, John C.--175
Buckskin Charley, Ute Chief--
    294, 295
Buckskin Joe mine--7, 26
Buffalo--12, 13, 36, 88, 89, 241
Bull Bear, Cheyenne Chief--
    145
Burlington Railroad--261, 286
Bute, George A.--5, 70
Cable, Rufus E.--44, 83
California--3, 7, 11, 17
California Gulch mines--7, 19,
    26, 31, 246
Cameron, Gen. R. A.--224
Camp Creek--43, 44, 82, 101,
    102, 116

Canby, Gen. E. R. S.--137
Cañon City--21, 78, 79, 81, 249
Carson, Kit--37
Cascade, Colo.--37, 294
Castle Rock, Colo.--77
Central City, Colo.--19, 22,
    173
Central Hotel--63, 73
Chaney, Lon--255
Cherokee Indians--4, 5
"Cherokee Party"--5
Cherry Creek, Colo.--4, 6, 17,
    18, 93, 111, 112, 145, 147
Cheyenne, Wyo.--174
Cheyenne Creek--50-51, 64, 66,
    77, 79, 82
Cheyenne Indians--15, 41,
    95-99, 111, 131, 139, 141-42,
    145, 150, 152, 154-56, 177,
    179-81, 183, 208, 213-14, 295;
    history of, 97
Chilcott, George M.--175
Chivington, Col. John M.--21,
    121, 132, 135, 136, 137, 138,
    140, 141, 147, 149, 155, 158,
    162; account of the Battle of
    Sand Creek, 150-54
Choteau, John--206
Civil War--59, 60, 61, 62, 63,
    79, 101, 109, 116, 135, 142;
    Colorado Volunteers in,
    136-38
Claim Club--45, 46, 70
Clark, Henry S.--69
Cliff House, Manitov, Colo.--
    236

Coby, Henry--117
Colfax, Schuyler--68
Colley, Maj. Samuel G.--153, 155
Colorado and Southern Railway Co.--285
Colorado City--21, 30, 35, 51, 52, 61, 67, 68, 76, 78, 82, 92, 106, 215, 296; as Territorial capital, 69, 70-74; description of, 43, 44, 49, 60, 216; El Paso County seat, 231; first telegraph, 218-19; Fountain College, 175-76; growth, 217, 235; hotels, 63, 73, 110, 201; incorporated with Colorado Springs, 256, and Indian raids, 102, 104, 108, 112, 180, 182, 184-85, 191, 193-95, 201, 205, 211; legislature in, 216; liquor problems, 234, 235, 236; mining mill, 282, 283, 284; Public Library, 176
Colorado City and Denver Express Line--63
Colorado City Journal, The-- 61
Colorado City Town Company --44, 74
Colorado College--50, 106, 195, 219, 286, 287, 288, 289, 290, 296
Colorado Enabling Act--69
Colorado Midland Railway Company--264, 265, 266, 269, 270, 271, 281, 284

Colorado School for Deaf and Blind--197, 263
Colorado Springs--44, 50, 87, 88, 195, 196, 219, 221, 223, 229, 295; Agricultural College scrip, 222; City Council, 233; El Paso County seat, 233; English colony, 227, 228; as health resort, 245, 254, 265; The High Drive, 292-93; hotels, 222, 225; Opera House, 254, 255; parks, 263, 290-93; townsite, 66, 85, 86, 106, 110, 220, 221, 223, 224; town plan, 223, 225, 226, 227, 286; water rights, 255
Colorado Springs and Cripple Creek District Railway-- 283
Colorado Springs Company-- 222, 224, 226, 228, 233, 234, 235
Colorado Springs Hotel--225
Colorado, Territory--alternate names for, 68; Capitol of, 69, 70, 71, 72, 73, 74, 75; formed, 68-69; history, 137; legislature, 69-74; problems of, 133, 134, 135, 141, 142, 213
Columbine, The--92
Comanche Indians--40, 41, 42, 43, 146, 147, 152, 154, 240
Committee on the Conduct of the War--113. See also Sand Creek, battle of, Congressional Investigation

Cone, A. T.--103
Copeland, John--117
Cottonwood Creek--185, 186,
    187, 201, 202
Council Bluffs, Iowa--11
Cramer, Lt.____--140
Cripple Creek--269, 270, 271,
    276, 280, 281, 282, 298; labor
    strike, 271, 272
Cripple Creek District Railway
    --283
Crocker, George--72, 73
Crowell, Benjamin F.--46, 61,
    67, 70, 217, 238, 239, 241, 242,
    243, 245, 246, 248, 252, 254,
    266, 278-79
Crowell, Susan E.--279
Curtis, Gen. S.R.--146, 154,
    155
Custer, Gen. George A.--161,
    162, 257
Cutler, Henry--287
Davis, Mr.____--187
"Dead Man's Cañon"--78, 79
Demary, Maj.____--269
Denver--12, 17, 19, 45, 56, 75,
    76, 77, 99, 112, 254; history,
    6, 17, 18, 46, 56, 93, 118
Denver and Rio Grande Rail-
    road--47, 77, 219, 220, 221,
    222, 223, 227, 229, 230, 291
Devlin, Pat--47, 48
Dieterman, Henrietta--183, 184,
    193
Dougherty, Rev. James G.--
    287

Douglass, Robert--175
Eastern plains country--260,
    261, 263
Edwards, Rev. Jonathan E.--
    287
Eggleston, Dr.____--102
Elbert, Samuel H.--267
El Paso County--66, 67, 69-70,
    82, 87, 92, 93, 95, 108, 112, 113,
    116, 117, 118, 119, 141, 205, 207,
    209, 210, 213, 228, 229, 234,
    259; County Clerk, 215, 217-
    18, 231, 234, 238; County
    officials, 217, 231, 243, 271
El Paso County Pioneer Society
    --71, 86
Espinosa brothers--78, 82
Evans, Gov. John--110, 112,
    113, 116, 117, 140, 141, 154,
    155, 175; testimony on Battle
    of Sand Creek, 142-46
Everhart, Charley--195, 196,
    296
Fairplay mine--7, 26, 31, 80
Farming--45, 49, 50, 51, 64, 65,
    66, 67, 84, 92, 242, 258-59
Fetterman, Lt. Col.--212
Finley, Robert--117
First National Bank of Colorado
    Springs--244, 248, 253, 254,
    266, 287
First Regiment of Colorado
    Cavalry--115, 116, 117, 121,
    136, 147, 153, Company A, 63
Fisher, H.D.--264, 265
Florence--282, 283

Florence and Cripple Creek
    Railroad--282
Florissant--35, 51, 79, 271
Fontain-qui-Bouille River--4,
    5, 17, 84, 111
Forsyth (Forsythe) Maj. George
    --208
Fort Garland--81
Fort Kearney (Kearny), Nebr.
    --11, 12, 15, 146
Fort Larned, Kans.--177
Fort Lupton--16, 112
Fort Lyons--121, 122, 141, 144,
    148, 150, 153, 158; Indian
    Agency, 140, 153
Fort Phil Kearney, (Kearny),
    Wyo.--212
Fort St. Vrain--16
Fort Sheridan, Nebr.--88
Fountain--17
Fountain College--175, 176
Fountain Colony--223
Fountain Creek--17, 35, 37, 44,
    51, 53, 66, 88, 92, 93, 100, 110,
    112, 116, 165, 225, 226, 229
Fountain valley--110, 111, 197,
    198, 241
France, Matt--218
Frémont, John C.--16
"Frémont's Orchard"--16
French, Colo.--19, 26
French trappers--84, 223, 298
Game animals--36, 51, 76, 88,
    209
Garden of the Gods--71, 82, 83,
    101, 102, 220, 293
Garvin, Dr.___--62, 216

Garvin, William--103
Georgia, Colo.--19, 26
Gerrish and Company--62
Gerry, Elbredge--111, 112
Gessinger, Dan--166, 168
Giddings, E.W.--283
Gilpin, Gov. William--69
Girten, Mr.___--35, 51
Glen Eyrie--82
Glenwood Springs--266
Gold, discovery of--3, 4, 7-8;
    in Colorado, 4, 5, 6, 7, 8, 18,
    24, 25, 26, 27, 31, 64, 268, 269.
    See also Mining
Golden--20
Graham, Lt. Joseph-118
Grand Junction--254
Granger, Maude--254
"Great American Desert"--14
Great Salt Lake Valley--109
Greeley, Horace--99
Greeley Colony--224
"Green Russell Party"--5, 6
Greenough, Charles B.--245,
    246, 253
Greenwood, Col.--219, 223
Gregory diggings--6
Grief, John--206
Hagerman, J.J.--265, 269, 282
Hall, Mr.___--201
Hall, Chief Justice--73
Hall, Gen. Frank--137
Hall, Mrs. Frank--274
Hamilton, Colo.--19, 22, 23, 26,
    31, 33, 34, 35, 51, 52, 53, 54, 56;
    history, 27, 29, 30, 32, 59
Harper's Weekly --63

Hartsell, Sam--180, 181, 182
Hayes, J. A.--266
Henderson, Ray-255
Hill, Sen. N.P.--262
Howbert family--7, 54-55, 62,
    102, 185, 199-200
Howbert, Rev. William--62,
    175, 211
Humphrey, J.F.--248, 252, 254
Hungate family--100, 101, 145
Hunt, Gov. A.C.--220, 222
Idaho Springs--6, 22
Indians--17, 18, 36, 38, 55, 56,
    160; and guns, 100, 178, 179,
    203, 210, 211; hostile, 45, 86,
    95-96, 98, 99, 100-17, 130-31,
    135, 141-43, 152, 164, 177, 179,
    182-91; lands, 96, 98, 100,
    109, 213; and military, 147,
    148, 153, 155, 161, 212;
    protectors, 121, 139, 140;
    raids in Colorado, 193-203,
    205-08, 210; and retaliation
    by white settlers, 187-92,
    198, 201-04, 207, 209; super-
    vision of, 141-44, 153, 155,
    178, 180, 181; treaties, 98,
    177. *See also* U.S. Bureau
    of Indian Affairs; Tribes by
    individual name.
Jackson, W.S.--282
James, Dr. Edwin--37, 92
"Jimmy's Camp"--17, 88, 115,
    146, 205
Johnson, Rev.___--46
Joint Special Committee of

Congress. *See* Sand Creek,
    battle of, Congressional
    Investigation
Julesburg--61
Justice, early--20, 45, 46-49
Kansas, state--19, 45, 132
Kansas City, Mo.--4
"Kansas City Party"--5, 6
Kansas Pacific Railway--88,
    211, 212, 219, 227, 261
"Katy King Spiritual Wheel"--
    235
Kelly, Scott--70
Kenosha Hill--22
Kingsley, Maurice--228
Kingsley, Rose--228
Kiowa Indians--97, 98, 146, 147,
    152, 154
Knox, James--244, 245
Laramie, Wyo.--173
Laughlin, Jim--47, 48
Lawrence, Kans.--5
"Lawrence Party"--5, 6
Leadville--7, 229, 246, 248, 249,
    250, 251, 254
Left Hand, Arapahoe Chief--
    147, 156
Little Fountain Creek--79
"Little London"--228
Little Pittsburgh mine--247
Lincoln, Abraham--141
Lincoln, Jonathan--205
Long's Expedition--37, 92
Long's Peak--16
Loomis, Mr.___--248, 249, 250
Love, Robert--194

Lumber--28, 29, 56, 57, 58, 66

McIntyre, Judge A. W.--274, 275

McShane, Mrs. David--206

Maggard, Mrs.___. *See* Central Hotel

Manitou House--236

Manitou Springs--37, 38-39, 91, 214, 220, 229, 295, 296-97; hotels, 236; legend, 38-43; townsite, 236, 237, 264

Mansions, The--236

Mason, Solon--198

Maxwell, Lucien--16, 168, 169, 170

Maxwell Ranch, N. M.--167-68; described, 168-71

Mellen, William P.--219

Methodists--8, 21, 24, 27, 31, 32, 64, 136; Des Moines, Iowa, Conference, 8, 22; Kansas-Nebraska Conference, 136; Missions in Colo., 136

Metcalf, Orlando--265

Mexicans, conflicts with--46, 47, 80, 81, 84, 164, 165, 167. *See also* Espinosa brothers

Mexico and the Rocky Mountains --88

Midland Terminal Railway--281

Miller, Henry--118

Mining--246, 247, 248, 250, 251, 252, 254, 280; placer methods described, 24, 25, 26. *See also* Gold, discovery of

Missouri Pacific Railroad--261

Missouri River--8, 9, 12, 16

Modern Woodmen of America Sanatorium site--214

Monument Creek--44, 50, 53, 93, 102, 103, 106, 110, 112, 113, 116, 182, 185, 194, 220, 221, 226, 296

Mora, N. M.--168, 171

Mount Baldy--292

Mount Rosa--228, 284, 292

Murray, Samuel--117, 118

Myers--Bert--198

Nettleton, E. S.--223, 236

Neva, Arapahoe Chief--145, 146

New Mexico--33, 89, 164, 165, 166, 167, 211; Civil War battle, 136-39

Orahood, Capt. Harper--157

Pabor, William E.--224, 226

Palmer, Gen. William J.--87, 29, 220, 221, 225, 226, 227, 236, 286, 287, 288, 289, 290, 291, 292, 293

Palmer Park--292

Parry, Charles, C.--91

Pawnee Fork--177

Pawnee Indians--15, 41

"People's Counts"--20, 70. *See also* Justice, early

Peavey, Mrs.___--274

Perkins, Charles E.--293

Petit, Judge___--62

Pigeon's Ranch, N. M.--138

Pike, Col. Zebulon--259
Pike's Peak--5, 71, 90-92, 292,
    297; auto road to, 286, 298;
    Cog Railroad, 255; Half-
    Way House, 90
Pike' Peak Forest Reserve--
    283
"Pike's Peak or Bust"--15
Pitkin, Gov. F. W.--261, 262
Platte River, 6, 12, 17, 18, 22,
    45, 53, 56, 111, 112; valley, 9,
    10, 11
Plattsmouth, Nebr.--9, 10, 11,
    54
Point of Rocks--111, 113
Politics--267, 272, 273, 274,
    275, 276, 277
Pueblo, Colo.--21, 46, 254
Pueblo County--118
Quincy, Iowa--8, 55
Railroads--47, 63, 77, 88, 211,
    212, 219-23, 227, 229-30,
    260-61, 264-66, 269-71, 281,
    282, 283, 284-86, 296. *See
    also* individual railroads by
    name
Ranching--62, 82, 83, 258
Raven, Arapahoe Chief--147,
    156
Reid, H. E.--282
Riggs, Mr.____--199
Rio Almagre--84
Rio Nepesta--84
Robbins boys--197, 198, 296
Robbins, T. H.--175
Robert E. Lee mine--247, 253

Rock Island Railroad--261, 296
Rogers, Henry T.--264
Roman Nose, Cheyenne Chief--
    145, 208
Roswell, N. M.--50, 102
Rouse, Van E.--86
Ruxton, George F.--36, 38, 236
    297
Ruxton Creek--90, 255
Saint Joseph, Mo.--11, 75
Salida, Colo.--77
Saloman, F. Z.--220
Sand Creek, battle of--121-23;
    Col. Chivington's testimony
    on, 150-54; Congressional
    Investigation of, 134-47; Gov
    Evan's testimony on, 142-46
    military attitude toward, 147
    148, 153, 155, 161
Santa Fe Railroad--261, 269, 27
Santa Fe Trail--166
Sayre, Maj. Hal--157
Scrip, Agricultural College--
    222
Sheldon, A. Z.--239
Sheridan, Gen. Philip H.--161
    179
Short Line (Railway)--284, 285
    286
Shoshone Indians--40, 41, 42, 4
Sherman, Gen. William T.--
    211, 212
Shooks Run--86, 197, 221
Shoup, Col. Geo. L.--117, 14
    146, 150, 157
Silver "issue"--275, 277

Simpson Party--187, 188, 189,
190, 201, 204, 207
Sims, Jim--187
Sioux Indians--15, 96, 97, 152,
154
Slocum, Rev. William F.--288,
289, 290
Slough, Col. John P.--137
Smith, Rensselaer--103
Smoky Hill River--124, 127, 131,
148, 149, 155, 213
Smoky Hill wagon road--188
Snow--60, 64, 89, 118, 119, 163,
174
Soda Springs--38, 43, 95, 220,
229. *See also* Manitou
Springs
Soule, Capt.___--140
South By West--228
South Park Railroad--229, 230
South Platte River--5, 11, 22
Spanish explorers--84, 85, 86,
223, 298
Spanish Peaks--17, 292
Spencer, Mr.___--239
Spielman, David--194
Sprague, A.D.--69, 70
Steck, Amos--73
Stone, E.T.--175
Stone, Wilbur F.--71
Stubbs, Robert--175
Sumner, Col. E.V.--99
Tabor, H.A.W.--261
Talbert, Job--187
Tallman, Jonathan--206
Tarjos, N.M.--16, 17

Tappan, James--239, 240
Tappan, Lt. Col. Samuel F.--
137, 138, 139, 141
Tappan and Company--63, 239,
241
Tarryall mines--7, 24, 25, 27,
35
Teachout, Mr.___--182, 185,
187, 193
Teller, Sen. H.M.--157, 262,
263, 267
Templeton, Lt. A.J.--118,
207, 209, 295
Templeton's Gap--66, 101, 204
Tenney, Rev. E.P.--287, 288
Third Regiment Colorado
Volunteer Cavalry--117, 119,
120, 121, 135, 140, 143, 150,
156, 157; Company G., 118
Tobin, Tom--81, 82
Transportation: freighters, 75,
76, 173, 174, 175, 229, 230,
242, 281; stage coaches, 54-
55, 281; wagon trains, 9, 10,
11, 12, 14, 15, 22, 55, 239,
240. *See also* Railroads
Trinidad--167, 168, 172
True, James P.--225
Union Pacific Railway--173,
211, 260
U.S. Bureau of Indian Affairs
--139, 144, 159, 177, 178, 179.
See also Indians, supervision
of
Ute Indians--36, 37, 96-97, 99,
107, 109, 180-81, 213-14,

294, 295; description of, 97
Ute Pass--36, 38, 91, 96, 180,
  182, 294
Ute Pass, wagon road--37, 45,
  228, 229, 294
Vindicator mine--269
Waite, Gov. Davis H.--271,
  272, 273, 274, 275
Wan-kan-aga--42, 43
War of the Rebellion. *See*
  Civil War
Washita, battle of--214, 257
Weather--60, 61, 62, 92, 93, 94,
  132-33, 174
Welch, A.S.--244
Wheeler, J.B.--265, 266

White Antelope, Cheyenne
  Chief--145, 146
Whitley, Agent--145
Whitsitt, Dick--73
Wigglesworth, Thomas--264
"Wild Bill"--187, 190, 191
Wild horses--87, 88, 295
Willis, Bob--74
Witter, Daniel--74
Wolf (Wolfe), John--118, 173
Wolf's Hotel--270
Woodbury, J.C.--67
Wootten, Dick--37, 172
Wynkoop, Maj. E.W.--139,
  140, 147, 148, 179

A portfolio of photographs both old and new, showing scenes in Colorado Springs years ago, and today.

r view of Colorado
rings c. 1970. Picture
ken by Stewarts Com-
ercial Photographers,
c., and supplied by
amber of Commerce.

Colorado Springs circa 1913 (t

ca 1970 (bottom).   By Stewarts/C. of C.

The First Nation
Bank of Colorad
Springs in about
1875.
Stewarts/C. of C.

1890

The First Natio
Bank of Colorad
Springs in about
1890.
Stewarts/C. of C

The First National Bank of Colorado Springs in about 1970. Stewarts/C. of C.

First, second and third Antlers Hotel. First one, top left, was
built by Gen. William Palmer in 1882. It was destroyed by fire in
1898. The second one, bottom left, was built in 1901, and torn down
in 1964 to make way for the present building (right). C. of C.

Covered wagons on Ute Pass, c. about 1878. Same place about
1890--note horse and buggy turning around. Ute Pass now, in 1970.
Getting places in Colorado now is easy as pie; a century ago, it was
hope and a prayer. The roads were bad, and so were the Indians,
and traveling was easier said than done. C. of C.

Top: Old Pike's Peak cog train resting half way to the summit; below: A Pike's Peak cog car today. No matter what one's connections, here he starts at the bottom. C. of C.

Top: Just imagine, charging money to travel on a road like that!
Below: This is better. C. of C.

Top: Pike's Peak summit house about 1875 or thereabouts. At this
time it is still an Army Signal Corps lookout and message station.
The modern structure is the present summit house, and a most comfortable change. C. of C.

This is a party of Pike's Peak climbers in 1891. We could find no indication as to the identity of any of the climbers, but a quarter to a doughnut says they left a slew of kids who about now would be about the same age as the climbers in 1891. Anyone recognize themselves? C. of C.

Two views of the Broadmoor Hotel; at top, a good view of the lake and
Cheyenne Mountain. Below, the Broadmoor complex and Pike's Peak.
In the late 1800's, you hadn't lived unless you had stayed a night at
the Broadmoor. Photos: Broadmoor Hotel.

A downtown scene of the handsome new buildings; looking west down Pike's Peak Avenue.   Photo: Stewarts/C. of C.

Above: Penrose Public Library.

Below: First United Methodist Church on North
Nevada Avenue. Photos: Robert McCoy.

Streetscenes: Top, Tejon Street north from Pike's
Peak Ave.

Middle: Tejon Street south from Platte Ave.

Bottom: Tejon Street north from Kiowa St. Photos:
Robert McCoy

Western
Americana

F
776
H84
1970

Howbert, Irving, 1846-1934.
    Memories of a lifetime in the
Pike's Peak region. Glorieta, N.M.,
Rio Grande Press [1970, c1925]
    298 p. illus., map, group port. 24
cm.
    SBN 87380-044-3

    1. Colorado--History. 2. Indians
of North America--Colorado.
3. Sand Creek, Battle of, 1864.
I. Title.

F776.H84 1970   970.488/56
                             73-115107

SUPAT   B/NA A B8-197678   03/28/79